TEACHING RE
COLLECT

D0617526

APPROACHES TO EDUCATIONAL
LEADERSHIP AND PRACTICE

William Smale
&
Kelly Young

DETSELIG
ENTERPRISES LTD

Approaches to Educational Leadership and Practice

Library and Archives Canada Cataloguing in Publication

Approaches to education leadership and practice / William Smale, Kelly Young, editors.

Includes bibliographical references.
ISBN 978-1-55059-346-4

1. Educational leadership. 2. School management and organization.
I. Smale, William, 1961- II. Young, Kelly, 1969-
LB2806.A598   2007   371.2   C2007-904630-4

Detselig Enterprises Ltd.
210, 1220 Kensington Road
NW Calgary, Alberta
T2N 3P5

DETSELIG
ENTERPRISES LTD

www.temerondetselig.com
temeron@telusplanet.net
Phone: (403) 283-0900
Fax: (403) 283-6947

We acknowledge the support of the Government of Canada through the Book Publishing Industry Development Program (BPIDP) for our publishing program.

We also acknowledge the support of the Alberta Foundation for the Arts for our publishing program.

Alberta Foundation for the Arts   Alberta
                                         COMMUNITY DEVELOPMENT
COMMITTED TO THE DEVELOPMENT OF CULTURE AND THE ARTS

SAN 113-0234
ISBN 978-1-55059-346-4
Cover Design by Alvin Choong

CONTENTS

ADULT AND HIGHER EDUCATION

ECOLOGICAL AND SOCIO-CULTURAL APPROACHES

PREFACE

The study of educational leadership has its beginnings in the establishment of educational administration as an area of graduate study in education and was developed around the attributes and functions of the titular head of school. Soon this focus expanded to include studying other supervisory roles in the school system, such as superintendent of curriculum and director of education, and their various work contexts. The focus was almost exclusively on schools and schooling, with graduate students being extant and aspiring supervisory officers. Administration at other educational sites, such as colleges and universities, was not usually part of the syllabus of educational administration studies.

The view of administration of schools as a process of controlling and manipulating capricious variables towards the goal of improved school outcomes shifted gradually to a management model, while still holding on to the former and continuing to operate within the frame of scientific management as adopted from business and industry. When improved student learning and achievement were projected as the primary outcomes of schooling, the business model of management seemed inadequate and there was a shift from the manager who supervises operations and administers policies, often generated elsewhere, to the curriculum and instructional leader. Curriculum and pedagogy were now seen as having higher value in schooling than supervising the building and managing the people therein. Nonetheless, these latter functions remain very important, for they help to create a supportive environment for leadership action.

To give effective leadership in developing and delivering the curricular program requires an expansion of the context of learning beyond the school building, so the vision of educational leadership has become broader and broader to include the school community in particular, and more generally, a variety of geopolitical and cultural communities. Thus, the construct of educational leadership gets more complex and its practice more challenging as it becomes more inclusive of a variety of contexts. One response of the traditional top-down, hierarchical decision making structure of earlier administrations to the complexity of contexts lies in collaboration, exchanging one person rule for distributive leadership; in other words, decentring the titular leader and practice leadership that is participatory.

Educational leadership has moved a long way from the manager administering policies and operations to addressing, as well, how a multiplicity of forces in a diverse context combine and interact to influence what happens in schools. Among the many forces that must now be considered are globalization, diversity in many senses (gender, culture, religion, and class), equity and justice issues, environmental concerns, increased differentiation in organizations.

The first section of this book recognizes the centrality of administration to the theory and practice of educational leadership and locates that leadership in a legislative framework. Doing so is a reminder of how legislation works with education to effect change towards the goals of equity and fair treatment of everyone, especially given the diversity that exists in many social and cultural contexts. It is also a reminder to the practitioner that there are prescribed boundaries that provide some protection at the same time as they indicate the landscape for creative action. This book places leadership in other educational sites besides schools, hence the contributions in Section Two focus on people and their stories of organizational issues and impact at the postsecondary level. The third section of the book contemporizes the context of leadership, be it at the school or the postsecondary level by bringing to the fore, current concerns of social justice and environmental care, promotion of inside-out strategies that challenge the reader to problematize leadership issues as paradoxes, and an invitation to deconstruct stereotypical notions of person (whom do I see when I see you?), place (are you where I expect you to be?) and privilege (what is it like when your plus becomes a minus?).

A common observation in texts on educational leadership is the stated inability or reluctance of the authors to define the construct because it is so broad, so cultural, so contextual, so differentiated and so complex; hence is best explored from multiple perspectives. That is what the editors and the contributors in this volume have done. In doing so, they are provoking the reader to frame and reframe their view of educational leadership in a variety of contexts beyond that of schools and schooling: to put the person rather than the organization at the heart of their professional practice; to replace the title cult of leadership with distributive leadership; and, in theorizing about leadership, to play with the paradoxes presented by an array of disparate workplace realities.

Sybil Wilson, PhD

EDUCATIONAL ADMINISTRATION

ONE

INTRODUCTION:
MULTIPLE APPROACHES TO EDUCATIONAL
LEADERSHIP AND PRACTICE

Kelly Young & William Smale

The impetus for this collection comes from our conversations exploring schooling and educational leadership and practice. We divide our book into three sections that address approaches to educational leadership and practice in educational administration, adult and higher education, and ecological and socio-cultural approaches to education. The articles in this collection are connected to the field of education and eco-social justice perspectives. We frame our book around themes that present education as a matter of responding to the larger contexts of the educational community and the school as an organization.

This book came together by drawing upon a group of experienced educational researchers and practitioners, all of whom currently work primarily in educational settings across Canada. Exploring the issues of educational administration, the authors approach them from multiple theoretical paradigms. Our intention is to offer a framework grounded in personal reflections, research, and classroom experiences that may help others respond to the complexities of human learning.

Several previously published books consider leadership from an educational perspective, but failed to engage the reader in a wider conversation about educational practice. This book is unique in that it offers a variety of perspectives, inviting the reader to engage in a conversation about the multiple dimensions of the relationship between educational leadership and practice in relation to three broadly defined areas. The most important implication of such an edited collection involves bringing together the socio-cultural and ecological perspectives and research in educational administration and adult and higher education.

In the first section, we have included a collection of chapters addressing the topic of educational administration. André P. Grace focuses on school administrators and their ethical and professional responsibility toward students across sexual-minority differences. Grace discusses the educational policy changes prompted by Supreme Court judgments to reflect the Charter of Rights and Freedoms' guarantees. He offers suggestions to help school administrators to develop better transactional and transformational leadership skills. In this regard, Grace provides a list of steps to assist school administrators with self-directed learning and resource building that will enable them to become caring leaders who focus on inclusive education for sexual minorities. Grace concludes with an assessment of sexual-minority issues in Canada and makes suggestions for future educational and cultural work.

Yvette Daniel, who has spent considerable time in schools and has worked closely with school and board administrators, explores the role of school administrators as public intellectuals. Her chapter provides a framework for a discussion about the extent to which school leaders take on the role of public intellectuals within the constraints and demands of running a complex institution that leave little time for praxis. Although school leaders alone cannot take on the task of transformation all on their own, most are well-intentioned professionals who would benefit from learning appropriate skills and strategies through redesigned leadership preparation programs. Daniel also examines the initiatives that have been taken in some parts of the United States toward leadership preparation fostering the development of transformative intellectuals. Daniel ends by outlining the implications of her work within the context of Ontario school administration.

Ken Brien, who previously worked as a high school teacher and administrator, explores the role of a school vice-principal. He reviews the legal responsibilities and tensions faced by school administrators with respect to student discipline. Using legal, pedagogical, ethical, and practical perspectives, Brien discusses the reasons for, and drawbacks of, suspending students from school. His chapter further examines the extent to which laws and policies support the use of disciplinary alternatives to suspensions. Brien also writes about the barriers and obstacles to using creative alternatives to suspensions.

William Smale explores the issue of early school leaving from a young offender perspective. The first section of his chapter provides a historical overview of the juvenile justice system in Canada in order to provide a basis for understanding the *Youth Criminal Justice Act* (YCJA). Smale's work is framed by the following research question: What demographic and crime-related factors, if any, contributed to the participants dropping out of high school? His findings are discussed in relation to a variety of theoretical and empirical research literature and perspectives.

In the second section of the book, we have included chapters that address adult and higher education. Through contrasting two texts, the 1946 Yearbook of the Association for Supervision and Curriculum Development and Allan Glatthorn's 2000 formulation of the principal as a curriculum leader, William Pinar explores the differences between the situation our predecessors faced and that confronting us today.

Darren Stanley's chapter draws upon ideas from the emerging field of complexity science to suggest that healthy learning organizations resemble other healthy life forms and, as such, must function through distributed processes and forms of leadership. Stanley aims to make several key principles of living systems comprehensible for the purpose of explaining the crisis of perception and the growing disease in current educational practices. Stanley notes that the complexity science perspective may be useful for understanding the unhealthy nature of education at present.

Luigi Iannacci addresses an important topic in education, that of English as a Second Language (ESL). Iannacci examines how teachers from cultural and linguistic minority backgrounds can negate their funds of knowledge as they acquire a teacher identity. A response analysis to a case study examined in a professional development course demonstrates how teachers reproduced assimilative notions through their understandings about and responses to students learning English as a Second Language (ESL). Critical autobiographical work is discussed in relation to its potential to help teachers reclaim cultural and linguistic resources that can foster liberating rather than oppressive pedagogies.

Carmen Pickering explores freedom of association in the context of the casual workforce in the teaching profession. Her research illustrates the extent to which legislation and employer policies have treated casual teachers as a marginalized group within the teaching profession. Pickering's chapter provides an overview of the principle of Freedom of Association and serves as the foundation for further exploration of the merits of having all teachers represented collectively and speaking with a single unified voice.

Tatiana Gounko discusses higher education reforms in Russia since the 1990s. Gounko's research is informed by her ten years as a lecturer in the Faculty of Foreign Languages at Yakutsk State University in Russia. Discussing the transformation of higher education principles, roles, administration, and financing, Gounko notes that between the 1990s and 2000s, the Russian government changed its position of *provider* for higher education to one of *facilitator* of reform. Gounko emphasizes that the policy shift has been away from welfare towards a neoliberal state policy perspective. Specifically, she takes up the issue of adopted market mechanisms including new models of institutional financing and tuition fees in context with the stratification of Russian society. She concludes her chapter with the suggestion to policy makers to ensure that proposed educational policies match the actual socio-economic conditions in the country.

In the third section, we have included chapters focusing on socio-cultural and ecological approaches to education. When we use the term *eco-social justice*, we mean an educational approach that analyzes the increasing destruction of the world's diverse ecosystems, languages and cultures by the globalizing, and ethnocentric forces of Western consumer culture. Eco-justice scholars and educators study, support, and teach about the ways that various cultures around the world actively resist these colonizing forces by protecting and revitalizing their commons, that is, the social practices and traditions, languages, and relationships with the land necessary to sustain their communities. By emphasizing the commons (and its enclosure or privatization), Eco-justice perspectives understand social justice to be inseparable from and even imbedded in questions regarding ecological wellbeing. Eco-justice education thus emphasizes educational reform at the public school, university, and community levels as a necessity in stemming the tide of both cultural and ecological destruction.

Chet Bowers focuses primarily on how current educational reform proposals and practices reinforce the basic cultural assumptions underlying the consumer- and technology-dependent lifestyle now being globalized. Four double binds are identified as undermining the possibility of an eco-justice future: how universities promote the values and assumptions underlying the industrial consumer-dependent culture, the way computers undermine the intergenerational knowledge essential to a sustainable future, the emancipatory theories of education that are ethnocentric and based on liberal assumptions that have contributed to deepening the ecological crises, and the way the scientism of many scientists contributes to the ideology supporting the industrial culture now being globalized. The chapter ends with a series of recommendations for educational reforms addressing eco-justice issues.

Kelly Young reviews the environmental education literature and traces the existence of Indigenous Knowledge (IK) and Traditional Ecological Knowledge (TEK) within the forms of the sustainable environmental knowledge and practices that have been developed globally. Young emphasizes that IK and TEK formed the basis for the pre- and post-contact environmental education movement in North America. Young's chapter focuses on a profile of recently published work about IK and TEK in environmental education, including recently published literature on eco-justice education. In particular, several broad categories are explored: (a) ecosystems, agriculture and natural resources management, and training informed by IK and TEK; (b) curriculum development and place-based experiential education informed by IK and TEK; and (c) First Nations storytelling and its importance in environmental education.

Andrejs Kulnieks' chapter discusses the connection between Aboriginal languages and the landscapes they originate within. He explores this connection by describing the process of translating the Latvian poet and writer Imants Ziedonis' untitled poem and illustrating the difficulties that arise through the process of translation and cross-cultural communication. This description demonstrates the importance of moving toward the complexity that eco-poetic writing can inspire while acknowledging the importance of recognizing the wealth of experience and knowledge that multilingual students bring with them to the classroom.

Karleen Pendleton Jiménez addresses the issue of the *deficits* of the privileged. While the cultural and resource deficits of marginalized children have been thoroughly investigated to gain greater understanding of their exclusion from systems of education, the deficits of the privileged need further exploration. Jiménez is concerned with questions such as what resources or literacies do privileged students lack that result in the difficulties they encounter when receiving instruction on social oppression? Through an investigation of both critical pedagogy and cognitive theory, possible causes for their struggles are offered, in addition to an examination of potential pedagogical practices. Issues of language, power, and (dis)comfort are central to the discussion and to the role that educators present to their students.

Two

In Your Care:
School Administrators and their Ethical and Professional Responsibility toward Students across Sexual-Minority Differences[1]

André P. Grace

8:00am
I'm tired this morning
Yesterday I cleaned up vomit in the lunchroom
And dealt with an angry teenager
Spewing curses at me as he punched his locker door
Each day brings its challenges

Today James wants to meet with me
He would like to set up a Gay-Straight Alliance Club
His mom has already phoned
She said that she hopes the club can start up soon
I love her eagerness
James has the same enthusiasm

Every child should have a mother who cares that much
Every child should have a teacher who cares that much
Every teacher should see James
Every teacher should see every child
Respecting and accommodating
The characteristics that make them different

So be the caring teacher
Be the caring school administrator
Love the whole adolescent
Even when they dare to say
Especially when they dare to say
I am different
I am queer

Those of us who have worked as school administrators know the rigors and the demands of our educational and cultural work. Each day is people-intensive as we variously deal with happy children, hurting children, children in trouble, concerned parents, colleagues, school-district personnel, school trustees, community members, and other educational interest groups. Indeed, as my poem indicates, each day brings it challenges. But perhaps one of the greatest challenges is honing our ability to see students and teachers who are different from us. It is easy to see and work with people who are like us in terms of their relational characteristics and the norms they value. However, it is not so easy to see, respect, and accommodate those who are different from us.

When we are able to respect and accommodate differences in students and teachers, including linguistic, ethnocultural, and sexual differences, we have the potential to be caring school administrators who engage in ethical leadership. As Starratt (2004) sees it, ethical leaders are responsible, authentic, and present in their work in schools and communities; they have an ethical and civic responsibility to revitalize citizenship by advocating for diversity and inclusion. Starratt equates being a responsible leader with intervening in school life and alleviating or preventing harm. He also equates it with being a self-directed learner.

> As an *educator*, the leader is an educated person who continues to learn more about the human condition, about the social, political, cultural, and natural worlds that make up the curriculum the school intends to teach, . . . [which includes a focus on] responsive pedagogies for various student populations. (p. 51)

To be an authentic leader, Starratt emphasizes the importance of dialoguing across differences. Authentic school administrators speak to and dialogue with those in their care. Starratt maintains that it is difficult to be an authentic leader. He concludes that authenticity "is always a relative achievement, always at risk, always in dialogue with the other in actualizing itself, always amplifying or diminishing in the face of daily circumstances" (p. 75). Nevertheless, being an authentic leader, like being a responsible leader, is necessary for school administrators to be present. For Starratt, being present requires us to be wide-awake, focusing on our verbal and body language: "Presence enables us to look at the other and let the other speak to us" (p. 87).

To help school administrators become ethical leaders, I have organized this chapter with three purposes in mind: to assist school administrators to build their knowledge of inclusive Canadian law, legislation, and educational policy; to help them build awareness of social and cultural issues affecting lesbian, gay, bisexual, and trans-identified (LGBT) and other sexual minorities; and to help them engage in school practices inclusive of sexual minorities. I discuss aspects of the educational and cultural work of school administrators, noting complexities and perceptions of their role that require them to be both transactional and transformational leaders. I provide an overview of moves to protect individual rights in the history of inclusive citizenship in Canada. I review legal and legislative progress, and I provide a selected chronology of pivotal moments in gay liberation in Canada. I reflect on the contemporary status of sexual minorities in Canadian education as I discuss certain policy changes prompted by Supreme Court judgments that have respected guarantees in the *Canadian Charter of Rights and Freedoms*. I provide a list of steps that school administrators can take to assist their self-directed learning and resource building in relation to becoming caring leaders who focus on inclusive education for sexual minorities. I conclude with an assessment of sexual-minority affairs in Canada and suggestions for future educational and cultural work.

SCHOOL ADMINISTRATORS, WORK MATTERS, AND ROLE PERCEPTIONS

When I think about my principal during Jesuit high school, I do not remember an ethical leader who was responsible, authentic, and present to every student. Instead I remember a rigid and uncaring man who was intolerant of students whom he could not categorize as "Catholic gentlemen" in that all-boys school setting. In his words and actions, it was evident that such young gentlemen could only fit the heteronormative mold. Those he held up were middle-class for the most part, and they appeared unquestioningly committed to their religious faith. This principal was my religion teacher in Grade Eleven. I often tell the story about one of my personal experiences in a class that he led about human love and desire and their expression in a Catholic context. During the class, my friend Joshua confronted Father with a question about homosexuality. Father had been discussing chastity, which he described as a call to celibacy for all Catholics outside the sanctity of marriage. Joshua raised his hand and asked, "What about homosexuality, Father?" The principal and teacher-priest turned crimson red, rocking back and forth. Just as we thought he was lost for words, he blurted out, "Well, there is just no place to put it!" Demonstrating the lack of control that is a common pubescent trait, Joshua interjected, "Well Father, I can think of two places!" That reply earned him a week's suspension. However, no one dared to question the teacher-priest's reply or the lack of control and caring his crass, homophobic answer denoted.

After three years and nearly four thousand class periods, this is my most indelible memory of my high-school experience. As a gay youth, I felt shame, anguish, and despair that day, feelings that haunted me for many years to come. I tell this story to remind school administrators of their ethical and professional responsibility to care for every student, including sexual-minority students. School administrators assume this responsibility by virtue of their position in public education. Their professional lives are never easy as each day brings many challenges and burdens. However, when they are responsive and responsible in dealing with *all* students across differences, they can experience joy in their work. To feel this joy in a meaningful and deserved way, school administrators need to be both transactional and transformational leaders. To be a transactional leader, they need to know Canadian and provincial/territorial legislation and laws that frame an inclusive and accommodating Canadian culture and society. They also need to know how to apply this knowledge to the development and implementation of educational policy that can help them create inclusive schools. To be a transformational leader, school administrators have to believe, as inclusive Brazilian educator Paulo Freire (2004) did, that change needed to make better schools and a better world is difficult but possible. They need to know that, with this belief, comes a responsibility to insert the self into the world. Freire explains:

> With curious subjectivity, intelligence, and interference
> into the objectivity to which I dialectically relate, my
> role in the world is not simply to apprehend [or

> critically question] what occurs, but to intervene as the
> active subject of occurrences. I am not a mere object of
> history but equally its subject. In the world of history,
> of politics, of culture, I *apprehend* not simply to *adapt*
> but [to intervene and] to *change*. (p. 60)

Unfortunately, too few school administrators choose to intervene when it comes to addressing the challenges facing sexual-minority students and teachers as they mediate life in schools. In interviews conducted nationally for my research, many sexual-minority students and teachers told me that they consider school administrators to be a key barrier to being visible in schools, the students' learning places and the teachers' workplaces. This reality raises an important question: What is the ethical and professional responsibility of school administrators toward sexual-minority students and teachers? The answer should be obvious. Their responsibility lies in being there for sexual-minority students just as they would for every other student; it lies in supporting sexual-minority teachers as persons and professionals employed in their schools. When school administrators deliberately ignore or dismiss sexual-minority issues in schools, they commit an act of intolerance. When they act to protect sexual-minority students and teachers from harm, they engage in an ethical practice that respects and accommodates sexual minorities. The law can help them in this practice, and the principal can turn to the police and those responsible for dealing with hate/bias crimes for assistance. For example, if an individual makes a homophobic remark or ridicules sexual-minority persons in a school as a public space, then, in accordance with Section 319 (1) of the *Criminal Code of Canada*, that individual is guilty of an offense (CCC, 2006a). This section acknowledges that such homonegative public communication can provoke others to engage in acts of symbolic or physical violence toward sexual-minority students and teachers. Furthermore, when an individual engages in an act of violence against a person on school property, and such an act is based on hate, prejudice, or bias toward the victim's sexual orientation or gender identity, that individual has committed a hate/bias crime under Section 718.2 of the *Criminal Code* (CCC, 2006b). With sufficient evidence, the police can lay charges in both cases.

If school administrators are to be ethically and professionally responsible, then they need to separate exclusionary private *morals* from public *ethics* in dealing with sexual-minority students and teachers. In doing so, freedom of religion, is not jeopardized; indeed Section 2 of the *Charter* guarantees this freedom. Still, Section 1 of the *Charter* insists that there can be no hierarchy of rights in Canada. This means institutional rights such as the rights of denominational schools cannot supersede individual rights. Thus school administrators working in publicly funded separate schools have to find ways to respect and accommodate sexual-minority individuals within the parameters of their institution's religious philosophy and educational practice (Grace & Wells, 2005).

As a member of a sexual minority, I don't care about being accepted by conservative faith-based groups. I know their traditional morals usually get in the way of accepting sexual-minority persons. However, I do care about being respected and accommodated in public institutional spaces. After all, I am a Canadian who is entitled to the rights and privileges of citizenship that the *Charter* protects. With regard to schools, I want school administrators to have the personal courage and the professional fortitude to respond openly to the needs of the sexual-minority youth placed in their care and the sexual-minority teachers employed in their schools. School administrators need to remember that sexual-minority students and teachers have been historically disenfranchised because some educators have allowed private and institutional morality to interfere with their public responsibility to meet the needs of all students and teachers in their care. In a post-*Charter* Canada, they have to transgress such exclusion and intervene to make Canadian schools inclusive and accommodating places that truly operate in the spirit of the *Charter*.

THE EVOLUTION OF SEXUAL-MINORITY RIGHTS IN CANADA

The individual rights of Canadians are protected under Section 15 of the *Charter*, which came into effect in 1985. As noted, Section 1 of the *Charter* tells us that there can be no hierarchy of rights in Canada. This legislated reality challenges us to mediate differences in respectful and responsive ways. Following the tenets of the *Charter*, K-12 education, as a mainstream Canadian institution, must engage in public ethics that protect and respect the diverse characteristics of persons including race, gender, gender identity, national or ethnic origin, color, religion, sex, age, mental or physical disability, and sexual orientation. While protection against discrimination on the ground of sexual orientation has arguably been provided since the *Charter* was enacted, the Supreme Court of Canada clearly confirmed sexual orientation as a ground analogous to other personal characteristics in 1995 in *Egan and Nesbit v. Canada* (MacDougall, 2000). In keeping with Section 15 of the *Charter*, protecting sexual-minority students and teachers from bias, prejudice, and discrimination is part of the responsibility of Canadian K-12 education. Being that education is a provincial/territorial jurisdiction, the ministries of education and the teachers' associations in every province and territory have to accept this responsibility and be there for every student and teacher. This requires both building and sharing sexual-minority knowledge and resources. Moreover, it requires providing opportunities to principals, teachers, and guidance counselors to engage in professional development that has two clear aims: (a) building awareness and understanding of sexual-minority issues, and (b) addressing issues in ways that abet just and inclusive education. This work is central to overcoming societal, cultural, and individual ignorance. After all, ignorance often leads to fear and misunderstanding, which, in turn, can lead to symbolic or physical violence. Symbolic violence includes shaming, harassment, name-calling, and rightist politico-religious denunciation; physical violence includes a spectrum of criminal acts like assault and battery, rape, and murder. Incidents of violence are well documented in Janoff's (2005) book *Pink Blood: Homophobic Violence in Canada*. In his statistical study, Janoff includes a necrology of victims (1990-2004) who were variously beaten, kicked, strangled, suffocated, stabbed, shot, burnt, bludgeoned, dismembered, run over, or thrown off buildings. Of concern to school administrators, teachers, and other educational interest groups, he notes that more than 40% of the perpetrators of these hate crimes were homophobic teenagers. In terms of violence directed toward sexual-minority youth and young adults, the 2004 Ping national survey, which analyzed data gathered from 1 358 Canadians between the ages of thirteen and twenty-nine, indicated that 23.8% had witnessed acts of symbolic and/or physical violence directed toward a sexual-minority person their own age (Wells, 2005).

GAY LIBERATION IN CANADA: LEGAL AND LEGISLATIVE PROGRESS

In 2002 Canadians celebrated the twentieth anniversary of the patriation of our Constitution from Britain, which enabled the Federal Government to control future amending of the Constitution solely through the Canadian Parliament. That pivotal event in 1982 was coupled with the entrenchment of the *Charter* in the Constitution.

Section 15, which, as noted earlier, came into effect in 1985, includes constitutional protection from discrimination on the ground of sexual orientation.[2] Since then, Canadian Courts have protected the *Charter* and the individual rights of Canadians. This judicial process has involved a persistent and ongoing questioning of the unifying nature of our Constitution and the inclusive nature of our *Charter*. The *Charter*, which is arguably Prime Minister Pierre Elliott Trudeau's greatest legacy to our nation, was central to his vision of building a Just Society advocating inclusion and reflecting the diversity that is metaphorically described as the Canadian mosaic. Key decisions by the Supreme Court of Canada acknowledging and accommodating sexual orientation have proliferated, particularly since the mid-1990s. Canadian research indicates that successful efforts of sexual-minority individuals to attain rights in legislative, educational, and other sociocultural contexts are inextricably linked to progress made in the legal arena. However, while acknowledging the significant impact of the *Charter* in aiding legal and legislative progress for sexual-minority Canadians, Lahey (1999) notes a key factor impeding our full Canadian citizenship: lesbians, gays, and others across sex, sexual, and gender differences lack constitutional personhood. This exclusion limits exercising our full legal capacities as human beings and limits progress that can be made in social, economic, and political contexts. It has historically placed restrictions not only on material contexts like rights in terms of inheritance, but it has also, on a much deeper and important level, restricted our rights and responsibilities as persons as we mediate life in our circles of intimate relationships and beyond.

One of the three most crucial of all Supreme Court of Canada decisions advancing citizenship rights, as ranked by Peter W. Hogg, the former Dean of Osgoode Hall Law School at York University, Toronto, is the decision in *Vriend v. Alberta* that confirmed equality rights for lesbian and gay Canadians (Saunders, 2002). Delwin Vriend, an openly gay educator at Kings College, Edmonton, Alberta, had been dismissed in 1991 on the pretext that his employment violated that conservative institution's religious policy. The Supreme Court of Canada handed down its long-awaited decision in *Vriend* on April 2, 1998. The Supreme Court's decision was in the educator's favor in his legal challenge to have sexual orientation read into the provincial human-rights legislation known as the *Alberta Individual Rights Protection Act* at the time he was fired.[3] In its judgment, the Supreme Court deemed that Act unconstitutional. Most importantly, in confirming equality rights for lesbian and gay Canadians, the *Vriend* decision provided both an impetus and a demand for teacher federations and associations to design and implement inclusive policies and practices that address the needs of sexual-minority teachers and students in Canadian schools. *Vriend* ultimately had repercussions for Alberta and other Canadian provinces and territories that had not yet moved on their own to extend provincial/territorial human-rights legislation to prohibit discrimination against lesbians and gays. Overall, *Vriend* has done more though than require provinces and territories to include sexual orientation as a prohibited ground of discrimination in their human-rights legislation. It has challenged Canadian people to rethink a social, cultural, educational, and historical mindset that has excluded or erased fellow citizens because their ways of being and loving do not fit within the confines of a heteronormative society. As well, it has provided them cause to reexamine their attitudes, values, beliefs, and actions in relation to lesbian and gay people whom the Supreme Court of Canada has accorded the right to live and work free from discrimination in safe and secure surroundings.

Vriend and other legal and legislative moves that have assisted lesbians and gays in their struggle to attain the rights and privileges of full Canadian citizenship indicate significant progress in building a Just Society that acknowledges and accommodates sex, sexual, and gender differences.[4] Canada has come a long way since December 22, 1967 when then Justice Minister Pierre Elliott Trudeau proposed amendments to the *Criminal Code* that resulted in the decriminalization of homosexuality. In spearheading this law reform, Trudeau moved Canada away from state control of the individual freedoms embodied and embedded in sexuality, a move best summed up in his poignant and memorable statement, "The State has no business in the bedrooms of the nation" (Goldie, 2001, p.18). The amendments passed in 1969. Prior to this liberating historical event, a Canadian citizen could be jailed simply for being an admitted practicing homosexual. As Warner (2002) points out, the threat or reality of incarceration provides just one example of the historical abuse, mistreatment, and exclusion of sexual-minority Canadians. He provides other examples. In 1953, on the heels of the hidden Holocaust in which many lesbians and gays had been persecuted and slaughtered in Nazi concentration camps, Canada's *Immigration Act* was amended to declare homosexuals a prohibited class whose entry into the country could be denied. As well, in its own expression of McCarthyism in the post-World War II era, the Canadian

Government prohibited homosexuals from holding positions in foreign affairs, the military, and the Royal Canadian Mounted Police. Indeed, until the early 1960s, the federal Department of External Affairs summarily dismissed homosexuals found working in its midst.

While the amendments to the *Criminal Code* in 1969 did not result in much legal or legislative progress abetting gay liberation in the 1970s and 1980s, these decades mark an important time of prolific lesbian-and-gay community building in Canada, increased consciousness of sexual-minority rights, and celebration of pride in same-sex orientation (Warner, 2002). Indeed what might be called a gay MTV effect became a pervasive cultural phenomenon as gays and lesbians flocked to Montreal, Toronto, and Vancouver to live in communities in the areas of these cities that became known as gay ghettos. As the following selected chronology of the progress of the gay-liberation movement in Canada indicates, most legal and legislative progress has occurred since the mid-1990s. In the wake of *Egan and Nesbit v. Canada*, which resulted in the Supreme Court of Canada acknowledging sexual orientation as an analogous character of person in Section 15 (1) of the *Charter*, there have been significant advances in the human and civil rights of sexual-minority Canadians. Thus, even though subsequent changes in social disposition and cultural behavior toward sexual-minority citizens have been slow among the populace and across educational and other institutions, the chronology shows that, in recent years, sexual-minority Canadians have had good reason to celebrate on *National Coming Out Day* in Canada (October 11th) (CBC 2003a, 2003b, 2005a, 2005b, 2006; Saunders, 2002; SCC, 2004).

GAY LIBERATION: CANADIAN TIMELINE

1965   E. Klippert was sentenced to jail for acknowledging that he was gay, was unlikely to change his sexual orientation, and had had sex with men over a 24-year period. He was confined to prison for an indefinite time period and labeled a "dangerous sex offender" by the Supreme Court of Canada. His incarceration incited debate about Canada's treatment of homosexuals under the *Criminal Code*.

1967   Federal Justice Minister Pierre Elliott Trudeau proposed amendments to the *Criminal Code* to change laws against homosexuality.

1969   Homosexuality is decriminalized.

1971   E. Klippert is finally released from prison.

1977   Québec became the first Canadian jurisdiction to include sexual orientation in its provincial human-rights code, stating it was illegal to discriminate against homosexuals in areas of housing, employment, and public accommodation.

1979   The Canadian Human Rights Commission recommended that sexual orientation be added to the *Canadian Human Rights Act*.

1980   Bill C-242 was defeated and sexual orientation was not added to the listing of characters of person protected from discrimination in the *Canadian Human Rights Act*.

1982   The *Canadian Charter of Rights and Freedoms* formed a unique section of the revitalized Canadian Constitution that was patriated from Britain.

1985   Section 15 of the *Charter* (the equality provision protecting individual rights) came into force.

1985   The Parliamentary Committee on Equality Rights released a report (*Equality for All*) that recommended the *Canadian Human Rights Act* should include sexual orientation as a form of illegal discrimination.

1986   Ontario became the second Canadian jurisdiction to include sexual orientation in its provincial human-rights code.

1992   *Haig v. Canada* upheld a lower court ruling that stated Section 3 of the Canadian Human Rights Act violated Section 15 of the *Charter* by not including sexual orientation as a character of person to be protected from discrimination. As a result of this ruling, sexual orientation was read into the Act and the Canadian Human Rights Council began accepting complaints based on sexual orientation. However, the bill to change the Act was not passed until 1996.

1992   The Federal Court removed the ban on homosexuals being allowed to serve in the Canadian military.

1995   *Egan and Nesbit v. Canada* was the first case in the Supreme Court of Canada to deal directly with sexual orientation under Section 15 of the *Charter*. J. Egan and his partner J. Nesbit had sued the Government of Canada for the right to claim a spousal pension under the *Old Age Security Act*. The Act defined spouse in terms of opposite-sex relationships. The outcome of the case was not in favor of the plaintiff, and spousal benefits were denied. However, the Supreme Court was unanimous in its agreement that *sexual orientation* was an analogous and protected category under Section 15 of the *Charter*. It also declared that an opposite-sex definition of partnerships contravened Section 15 of the *Charter*.

1996 Bill C-41 was proclaimed, which amended the *Criminal Code of Canada* to ensure that stricter penalties were introduced for any crimes motivated by bias, prejudice, or hate.

1996 Bill C-33 amended the *Canadian Human Rights Act* to include sexual orientation in Section 3 of the Act.

1998 As a result of the decision in *Vriend v. Alberta*, sexual orientation was read into the Alberta human-rights legislation. Most importantly, equality rights were granted to lesbian and gay Canadians.

1999 Bill C-78 was proclaimed, making it the first federal legislation to provide outright same-sex benefits for civilian and uniformed government employees and Members of Parliament.

1999 *M v. H* led to legal recognition of same-sex relationships. M and H had been a lesbian couple for over 10 years. In 1992, upon dissolution of their partnership, M sued H for spousal support under the *Ontario Family Law Act*. The Act defined spouse in terms of opposite-sex partners. The Ontario Court of Queen's Bench ruled that the definition violated the *Charter*, and that the phrase "a man and a woman" should be replaced with "two persons." H appealed, but the Ontario Court of Appeal upheld the decision. Neither M nor H continued with the case, but the Ontario Attorney General appealed the decision to the Supreme Court of Canada. In 1999 the Supreme Court ruled that Ontario's definition of spouse was unconstitutional and gave Ontario six months to change the Act.

2000   Bill C-23 was proclaimed. This omnibus legislation extended social and tax benefits and obligations in all federal statutes to include same-sex couples.

2001   Bill C-11, the new *Immigration and Refugee Protection Act*, was passed. Section 12 (1) of the new Act recognizes "common law partners," including same-sex partners, as members of the family class for the first time.

2002   In *Chamberlain v. Surrey School District No. 36*, the Supreme Court of Canada, in a 7-2-majority decision, ruled in favor of James Chamberlain, a Surrey, BC kindergarten teacher who sought to use three children's books that depicted same-sex families in his classroom. The Court ruling emphasized the responsibility of the School Board to carry out their public duties in accordance with strictly secular and nonsectarian principles, which includes a responsibility to avoid making policy decisions on the grounds of exclusionary beliefs.

2002   The Ontario Superior Court ruled that the provincial government must register gay and lesbian marriages, making it the first time that a Canadian court had ruled in favor of recognizing same-sex marriages under the law.

2002   The Québec Superior Court found the opposite-sex definition of marriage discriminatory and in violation of the *Charter*.

2003   The BC Supreme Court of Appeal ruled in favor of a redefinition of marriage that includes same-sex couples, citing that any other form of recognition falls short of true equality. The Court suggested that the redefinition of marriage should read "the lawful union of two persons to the exclusion of all others."

2003   Svend Robinson's Private Member's Bill C-250 was passed, expanding Section 318 of the *Criminal Code of Canada* so that the definition of *identifiable group*, which refers to any section of the public distinguished by colour, race, religion or ethnic origin, would also include sexual orientation. Bill C-250 made it illegal to incite hate propaganda against gays and lesbians.

2004   On December 9th in the Reference re Same-Sex Marriage, the Supreme Court of Canada held that the proposed legislation to extend the capacity to marry to persons of the same sex is consistent with the *Charter*. The Court maintained that this judgment was in keeping with "one of the most fundamental principles of Canadian constitutional interpretation: that our *Constitution* is a living tree which, by way of progressive interpretation, accommodates and addresses the realities of modern life" (SCC, 2004, p. 2). Moreover, the Court held that "the guarantee of religious freedom in Section 2 (a) of the *Charter* is broad enough to protect religious officials from being compelled by the state to perform civil or religious same-sex marriages that are contrary to their religious beliefs" (p. 3).

2005   On June 28th Bill C-38, the *Civil Marriage Act*, passed a third and final reading in the House of Commons. On July 20th, thirty-four years to the day that Everett Klippert was released from prison, Bill C-38 was passed by the Canadian Senate and became law. Canada became the fourth country to recognize same-sex marriage after the Netherlands, Belgium, and Spain.

2006   On December 6, the Conservative government of Prime Minister Stephen Harper brought forward a motion asking Parliament to revisit the same-sex marriage legislation. The motion was defeated 175-123 in a Parliamentary vote the next day, with the Prime Minister stating that he didn't see reopening the question in the future.

Sexual-Minority Issues in Canadian Education

The social history evidence before me clearly discloses that gay men and lesbian women have been treated as less worthy and less valued than other members of society. Canadian law has accepted that homosexuality is not a mental illness or a crime but rather an innate characteristic not easily susceptible to change. Stigmatization of gay men rests largely on acceptance of inaccurate stereotypes – that gay men are mentally ill, emotionally unstable, incapable of enduring or committed relationships, incapable of working effectively and prone to abuse children. Scientific studies in the last fifty years have discredited these stereotypes. . . . The record before me is rife with the effects of historic and continuing discrimination against gays. The evidence in this record clearly demonstrates the impact of stigmatization on gay men in terms of denial of self, personal rejection, discrimination and exposure to violence. . . . It is one of the distinguishing strengths of Canada as a nation that we value tolerance and respect for others. All of us have fundamental rights including expression, association, and religion. . . . We, as individuals and as institutions, must acknowledge the duties that accompany our rights. Mr. Hall has a duty to accord to others who do not share his orientation the respect that they, with their religious values and beliefs, are due. Conversely, for the reasons I have given, the Principal and the Board have a duty to accord to Mr. Hall the respect that he is due as he attends the prom with his date, his classmates and their dates.

The preceding excerpts are from the judgment of Justice Robert MacKinnon in the Marc Hall case (pp. 5-14, as cited in Grace & Wells, 2005). The judgment approved the application for an interlocutory injunction that provided an immediate order allowing Marc to attend his Catholic high-school prom with the partner of his choice. The decision came on May 10, 2002, just a few hours before his prom, enabling Marc to attend with his boyfriend Jean-Paul Dummond.

Sexual-minority students like Marc Hall and sexual-minority teachers have been marginalized in Canadian education as the expected replicator of a heteronormalized society and its heterosexualizing culture (Grace, 2006; Grace & Benson, 2000; Grace & Wells, 2001, 2004, 2005, & in press). However, with equality rights of Canadians enshrined in Section 15 of the *Charter*, sexual-minority teachers and students have increasingly turned to the Courts to use the force of law to fight for their rights in schools and other educational settings. Thus the force of law has become a way to counter the exclusionary force of history and, as indicated, that history is a record of denying the rights and privileges of full citizenship to sexual-minority Canadians. Consequently, sexual-minority citizens have never been as visible, vocal, safe, and secure in sociocultural contexts as those whose sex, sexual, and gender differences go unquestioned (Grace, 2001). The preceding excerpts from the judgment of Justice Robert MacKinnon provide a conspectus of this history of disenfranchisement.

Have post-1982 legal and legislative changes in Canada translated into full access and accommodation for sexual-minority teachers and students? They have not. While these changes have laid a basis for increased access and accommodation for sexual minorities in culture and society, the transformation of Canadian K-12 education into a fully inclusive institution remains a slow, incremental process. Sexual-minority teachers and students still confront heterosexism, sexism, homophobia, and transphobia daily in the generally conservative climate and culture of schools. Since support for sexual-minority rights in Canada coexists with continuing disapproval of sexual-minority citizens on political and moral grounds, sexual-minority teachers and students remain in a paradoxical struggle to be cared about in a caring profession. Indeed there has been a profound silencing of homosexuality in Canadian classrooms (MacDougall, 2000).

The 1998 *Report on Education in Canada*, which failed to provide any focus on sex, sexual, and gender differences, states, "Education reflects and influences the social, economic, political, and cultural changes happening around it" (Council of Ministers of Education, Canada, 1998, p. 3). At this juncture, Canadian K-12 education as a key public institution is being asked to respond to a prevalent and pervasive focus on legal and legislative changes with respect to acknowledging and accommodating sex, sexual, and gender differences. Indeed issues regarding these differences have made their way into schools, and sexual-minority teachers and students are increasingly expressing their needs and demanding their human and civil rights. One thing is now clear in K-12 schools in Canada: Gay is *NOT* going to go away. Thus changes to Canadian laws and legislation in relation to sex, sexual, and gender differences are requiring changes to educational policies and practices. The Alberta Teachers' Association (ATA) is proving to be a leader in this regard. Following the *Vriend* decision in 1998, the ATA moved quickly to begin protecting sexual-minority students, passing a resolution at its 1999 Annual Representative Assembly (ARA) to include sexual orientation as a category protected against discrimination in its *Code of Professional Conduct*. Then, at its 2000 ARA, ATA members began providing protection to sexual-minority teachers by voting to include sexual orientation as a category of person protected by equality provisions in its *Declaration of Rights and Responsibilities for Teachers*. At its 2003 ARA, the ATA became the first teachers' association in Canada to include gender identity in its *Code of Professional Conduct*, thus protecting transidentified students. In 2004, the ATA provided the same protection to transidentified teachers. In 2005, the ATA passed a resolution to enable and support the establishment of Gay-Straight Alliance groups in Alberta high schools (Wells, 2005). In 2006, the ATA developed policy directives that the ARA passed to urge the Alberta Department of Education to provide curricula and educational resources that address sexual-minority issues, and to urge provincial school boards to develop district policies to address the health and safety of sexual-minority students and teachers, as well as employment concerns of sexual-minority staff (ATA, 2007). This policy work continues through the ongoing initiatives of the ATA's Sexual Orientation and Gender Identity Sub-committee, which is affiliated with the Association's Diversity, Equity, and Human Rights Committee.

With inclusive education across sex, sexual, and gender differences mandated by the ATA, *all* members of the Association have an ethical responsibility to act in light of these changes and demands, which serve to recognize, respect, and honor the dignity and worth of sexual-minority individuals. However, this can be most stressful work and any teacher (or, for that matter, any member of any educational interest group) might be fearful. For example, sexual-minority teachers could fear the repercussions of being out and visible in their workplaces. They could also fear becoming role models for sexual-minority students because there are those in society who would conflate this role with being a recruiter to some misconstrued gay cause. Straight teacher allies could fear being labeled homosexual if they visibly support sexual-minority colleagues and students. Thus, educators doing this work for social justice have to be courageous risk-takers.

However, beyond the practical fears that some teachers and some others with vested interests in K-12 education may have, and beyond the moral apprehensions of those citizens who do not understand and thus ignore or fear sexual-minority differences, everyone in education has to act in keeping with the constitutional guarantees respecting and accommodating sexual-minority citizens. This means that we all have to address sexual-minority issues in relation to the social (being and interacting) and cultural (acting and doing) fabrics of schools as the workplaces of teachers and the learning environments of students.

BEING A CARING SCHOOL ADMINISTRATOR:
GETTING STARTED ON SEXUAL-MINORITY INCLUSION

When sexual-minority students and teachers tell me that they perceive school administrators as a barrier to their freedom, comfort, and inclusion in school settings, my first instinct is not to get angry at principals as authority figures and mediators of life in schools. After all, I have been a school administrator. I know the demands of the job. I know that every day is a political adventure and an exercise in negotiating power and interests. Moreover, I know that addressing sexual-minority issues means working in the problematical intersection of the moral and the political. Many school administrators are uninformed and unprepared when it comes to engaging in this difficult work.

Becoming informed is the first step in working successfully toward sexual-minority inclusion. Building knowledge of sexual minorities takes many school administrators into new territory with respect to role-related learning. So when sexual-minority students and teachers tell me that school administrators leave them out, my first inclination is to ask two questions: What do school administrators need to know in order to include sexual minorities in meaningful and deliberate ways in schooling and school culture? How might school administrators be supported in this educational and cultural work? In working to answer these questions, I have developed guidelines to help school administrators get started.

— Work everyday to see, speak to, and interact with every student and teacher across sexual-minority differences.

— Set a caring tone and use an ethic of respect to accommodate sexual-minority differences in your school.

— Use language that is inclusive and sensitive around issues of sexual-minority differences.

— Educate yourself about the realities of sex, sexual, and gender differences, and different constructions of family. As a corollary, learn about heterosexism, sexism, homophobia, transphobia.

— Educate yourself about the history of Canadian and provincial/territorial laws and legislation that have abetted sexual minorities in efforts to achieve the rights and privileges of citizenship. See, for example, Lahey (1999) and MacDougall (2000).

– Learn about the social and cultural realities of living as a member of a sexual minority in Canada. See, for example, Janoff (2005). As well, check Egale Canada (2007). Egale Canada was founded in 1986 to advocate for Canadian sexual-minority citizens. This national organization engages in political action to achieve more equitable laws for sexual minorities; intervenes in legal cases that have an impact on sexual-minority human rights and equality; and increases public education and awareness by providing information to individuals, groups, and the media. The Egale acronym stands for equality for gays and lesbians everywhere.

– Assist your teachers to engage in similar education and learning, and provide them with opportunities for professional development so they can build knowledge of sexual minorities and learn about age appropriate ways to address sexual-minority issues and concerns. For example, see workshops developed by Wells (2003).

– Build a resource base in your school that will provide you with material to help you mediate conflict with those within and outside the school who resist sexual-minority inclusion. The resource base will also be useful to teachers who want to engage in pedagogical and cocurricular practices inclusive of sexual minorities. The following resources provide helpful starting points: *Seeing the Rainbow: Teachers Talk about Bisexual, Gay, Lesbian, Transgender and Two-Spirited Realities* (CTF & EFTO, 2002); *Lessons Learned: A Collection of Stories and Articles about Bisexual, Gay, Lesbian and Transgender Issues* (CTF, 2005); Schrader and Wells's (2005) annotated essay of sexual-minority resources for use in schools; and, the Alberta Teachers' Association's Sexual Orientation and Gender Identity Website, which was developed by Wells (2004). This website is an encompassing resource for educators. It provides suggestions, guidelines, and an extensive resource base to help teachers address sexual-minority issues and concerns in their schools, classrooms, and community environments.

– Check with your teacher association and school district to see what educational policies have been developed to assist and support you and your teachers in educational and cultural work to create a school that respects and accommodates sexual minorities. If such policies are not in place, then advocate and work to have policies inclusive of sexual minorities developed and implemented. Remember, policy enables protection.

– If you are an administrator in a Catholic school, then check with your diocese to see if they have pastoral guidelines for working with sexual-minority youth. For example, in November 2004, the education commission of the Ontario Conference of Catholic Bishops released *Pastoral Guidelines to Assist Students of Same-Sex Orientation* (OCCB, 2004). This document, which acknowledges the ontological naturalness of being gay or lesbian, was developed to help school chaplains, guidance counselors, principals, and teachers address the "pastoral challenge" of counseling and caring for lesbian and gay students (Swan, 2004, p. 4).

– If you are an administrator in a Catholic school district that has a policy recommending reparative therapy as a possible treatment for unhappy sexual-minority youth, then educate yourself about the dangers of reparative therapy as stated by the Canadian Medical Association and an array of mainstream national and international mental-health associations (Grace, 2005; Grace, in press). As well, read critiques of Courage, a Catholic apostolate that promotes sexual-reorientation therapy in religious and psychotherapeutic forms (Grace, 2005).

– Intervene in your school by supporting students who want to initiate a Diversity Club or Gay-Straight Alliance Club. Help them find a teacher-facilitator and provide them with advice around safety and security issues. To develop guidelines see, for example, Wells (2006).

– Intervene to enable sexual-minority teachers to have their needs met in relation to their welfare and work, and their personal safety and professional security. Learn about teachers' association initiatives and sections of collective agreements that provide them with individual protections in keeping with the *Charter*. As well, explore websites such as the one developed by the Gay and Lesbian Educators of British Columbia (GALE-BC) (2007). GALE-BC was formed in 1990 as a community-based educational advocacy and resource group. As part of its mandate, GALE-BC emphasizes the need to work toward the full inclusion of sexual-minority students, parents, teachers, and administrators in the BC educational system. GALE-BC is the largest community-based sexual-minority educational organization in Canada. It actively supports Gay-Straight Alliances in BC Schools.

This list is certainly not exhaustive, but it is a substantive starting point for building knowledge of sexual minorities and developing inclusive educational resources. I have found these interventions useful in my work with school administrators as well as pre-service and practicing teachers. The upshot in educating yourself about sexual-minority differences is this: Knowing about these differences aids the work of creating truly safe, caring, and inclusive schools.

CONCLUDING PERSPECTIVE: PRESSING NEEDS

Progressive moves in Canadian law and legislation provide a framework to develop institutional supports and cultural practices, enabling the accommodation of sexual-minority citizens in education and other sociocultural contexts. Even so, in dispositional and practical terms, Canadian culture and society lag behind the law and legislation in building the kind of inclusive environment that legal judgments and legislative acts have guaranteed. Despite some progress in education, there is still a pressing need to focus on diversity, equity, welfare, and inclusion in relation to sexual-minority students and teachers who need personal and educational supports. Addressing this need requires that school administrators, teachers, and other interest groups including parents, politicians, and church groups become better educated regarding sex, sexual, and gender differences, and the rights of sexual-minority citizens with respect to these differences. Such community education is timely and vital. It is part of building an inclusive ethical pedagogy and a Just Society. It is part of according sexual-minority persons the respect and rights of full citizenship that every Canadian is due.

NOTES

1 This chapter builds on a featured speaker's paper that I presented to the Canadian Teachers' Federation at the *Building Inclusive Schools: A Search for Solutions* Conference, Ottawa Marriott Hotel, Ottawa, ON, November 2005. That presentation was entitled *Lesbian, Gay, Bisexual, and Trans-identified (LGBT) Teachers and Students and the Post-Charter Quest for Ethical and Just Treatment in Canadian Schools.*

2 *Sexual orientation* is defined here as sexual desire and need for affectional or erotic partners of the same, opposite, or either sex. Therefore, both heterosexuals and homosexuals have a sexual orientation. Sexual orientation is distinct from gender identity, e.g. a person born a biological male but whose gender identity is that of a female can be oriented to either a male or a female person as the object of personal desire and need. It is essential to note: "Definitions of sexual orientation may vary, in part, due to the fact that many cultures have a wide range of perceptions and attitudes about sexual behavior depending on factors such as gender, religion, and social status" (Ferguson & Howard-Hamilton, 2000, p. 286; see also Espin, 1984; Smith, 1997). It must also be kept in mind that not every society has created sociological categories or defined people according to their sexual desire or behavior. In other words, "gay" or "homosexual" are not universal designations with similar meanings everywhere (Cintrón, 2000, p. 307). *Gender identity* is defined here as the gender (a psychological and/or socially constructed state that is distinct from biological sex, i.e. female or male) to which an individual identifies; a sense of being a woman or a man; a sense of being masculine or feminine based on desired ontology or kind of being, not biological sex; gender identity has a personal and emotive sense to it. For further explication of LGBT and other sexual-minority terminology, see Wells and Tsutsumi (2005).

3 The current revised provincial human rights legislation in Alberta is entitled the *Human Rights, Citizenship and Multiculturalism Act*

4 The Supreme Court has yet to hear any case involving the human or civil rights of bisexual, transgender, or transsexual citizens (Lahey, 1999).

References

Alberta Teachers' Association (ATA). (2007). *A history of ATA sexual orientation and gender identity (SOGI) initiatives* [Brochure]. Edmonton, AB: Author.

Canadian Broadcasting Corporation (CBC). (2003a). *B.C. Court backs same-sex marriages.* Retrieved February 25, 2004, from http://www.cbc.ca/storyview/CBC/2003/05/01/samesex_bc030501

Canadian Broadcasting Corporation (CBC). (2003b). *MPs vote to protect gays under hate law.* Retrieved February 25, 2004, from http://www.cbc.ca/stories/2003/09/17/hate030917

Canadian Broadcasting Corporation (CBC). (2005a). *The Supreme Court and same-sex marriage.* Retrieved November 1, 2005, from http:www.cbc.ca/news/background/samesexrights/index.html

Canadian Broadcasting Corporation (CBC). (2005b). *Canada timeline: Same-sex rights.* Retrieved August 1, 2006, from http://www.cbc.ca/news/background/samesexrights/timeline_canada.html

Canadian Broadcasting Corporation (CBC). (2006). *MPs defeat bid to reopen same-sex marriage debate.* Retrieved February 25, 2007, from http://www.cbc.ca/canada/story/2006/12/07/vote-samesex.html

Canadian Teachers' Federation (CTF). (2005). *Lessons learned: A collection of stories and articles about bisexual, gay, lesbian, transgender and two-spirited realities.* Ottawa, ON: Authors.

Canadian Teachers' Federation & The Elementary Teachers' Federation of Ontario (CTF & ETFO). (2002). *Seeing the rainbow: Teachers talk about bisexual, gay, lesbian, transgender and two-spirited realities.* Ottawa, ON: Authors.

Cintrón, R. (2000). Ethnicity, race, and culture: The case of Latino gay/bisexual men. In V. A. Wall & N. J. Evans (Eds.), *Toward acceptance: Sexual orientation issues on campus* (pp. 299-319). Lanham, MD: American College Personnel Association.

Council of Ministers of Education, Canada (CMEC). (1998). *Report on education in Canada.* Toronto: Author.

Criminal Code of Canada (CCC). (2006a). *Hate propaganda.* Retrieved August 1, 2006, from http://laws.justice.gc.ca/en/C-46/267514.html

Criminal Code of Canada (CCC). (2006b). *Purposes and principles of sentencing.* Retrieved August 1, 2006, from http://laws.justice.gc.ca/en/C-46/268353.html#rid-268362

Egale Canada. (2007). *Welcome to Egale Canada.* Retrieved February 25, 2007, from http://www.egale.ca/index.asp?lang=E

Espin, O. M. (1984). Cultural and historical influences on sexuality in Hispanic/Latina women: Implications for psychotherapy. In C. Vance (Ed.), *Pleasure and danger: Exploring female sexuality* (149-164). London: Routledge.

Ferguson, A. D., & Howard-Hamilton, M. F. (2000). Addressing issues of multiple identities for women of color on college campuses. In V. A. Wall & N. J. Evans (Eds.), *Toward acceptance: Sexual orientation issues on campus* (pp. 283-297). Lanham, MD: American College Personnel Association.

Freire, P. (2004). *Pedagogy of indignation*. Boulder, CO: Paradigm Publishers.

Gay and Lesbian Educators of British Columbia (GALE-BC). (2007). Retrieved February 25, 2007, from http://www.galebc.org

Goldie, T. (Ed.). (2001). *In a queer country: Gay & lesbian studies in the Canadian context*. Vancouver: Arsenal Pulp Press.

Grace, A. P. (2001). Being, becoming, and belonging as a queer citizen educator: The places of queer autobiography, queer culture as community, and fugitive knowledge. *Proceedings of the 20th Annual Conference of the Canadian Association for the Study of Adult Education, Laval University, Québec City, PQ*, 100-106.

Grace, A. P. (2005). Reparative therapies: A contemporary clear and present danger across minority sex, sexual, and gender differences. *Canadian Woman Studies, 24*(2, 3), 145-151.

Grace, A. P. (2006). Writing the queer self: Using autobiography to mediate inclusive teacher education in Canada. *Teaching and Teacher Education, 22*, 826-834.

Grace, A. P. (in press). The charisma and deception of reparative therapies: When medical science beds religion. *Journal of Homosexuality*.

Grace, A. P., & Benson, F. J. (2000). Using autobiographical queer life narratives of teachers to connect personal, political and pedagogical spaces. *International Journal of Inclusive Education, 4*(2), 89-109.

Grace, A. P., & Wells, K. (2001). Getting an education in Edmonton, Alberta: The case of queer youth. *Torquere, Journal of the Canadian Lesbian and Gay Studies Association, 3*, 137-151.

Grace, A. P., & Wells, K. (2004). Engaging sex-and-gender differences: Educational and cultural change initiatives in Alberta. In J. McNinch & M. Cronin (Eds.), *I could not speak my heart: Education and social justice for gay and lesbian youth* (pp. 289-307). Regina, SK: Canadian Plains Research Centre, University of Regina.

Grace, A. P., & Wells, K. (2005). The Marc Hall prom predicament: Queer individual rights v. institutional church rights in Canadian public education. *Canadian Journal of Education, 28*(3), 237-270.

Grace, A. P., & Wells, K. (in press). Gay and bisexual male youth as educator activists and cultural workers: The queer critical praxis of three Canadian high-school students. *International Journal of Inclusive Education*.

Janoff, D. V. (2005). *Pink blood: Homophobic violence in Canada*. Toronto: University of Toronto Press.

Lahey, K. A. (1999). *Are we persons yet? Law and sexuality in Canada*. Toronto: University of Toronto Press.

MacDougall, B. (2000). *Queer judgments: Homosexuality, expression, and the courts in Canada*. Toronto: University of Toronto Press.

Ontario Conference of Catholic Bishops (OCCB). (2004). *Pastoral guidelines to assist students of same-sex orientation*. Toronto: OCCB.

Saunders, P. (2002). *The Charter at 20*. Retrieved August 5, 2005, from http://www.cbc.ca/news/features/constitution/

Schrader, A., & Wells, K. (2005). Queer perspectives on social responsibility in Canadian schools and libraries: Analysis and resources. *School Libraries in Canada Online, A Journal of the Canadian Association for School Libraries, 24*(4). Retrieved August 4, 2006, from http://www.schoollibraries.ca/issues/9.aspx

Smith, A. (1997). Cultural diversity and coming-out processes. In B. Greene (Ed.), *Ethnic and cultural diversity among lesbians and gay men: Psychological perspectives on lesbian and gay issues – Vol. 3* (pp. 279-300). Thousand Oaks, CA: Sage.

Starratt, R. J. (2004). *Ethical leadership*. San Francisco: Jossey-Bass.

Supreme Court of Canada (SCC). (2004, December 9). *Reference re same-sex marriage (2004 SCC 79; file no.: 29866)*. Retrieved December 9, 2004, from http://www.lexum.umontreal.ca/csc-scc/en/rec/html/2004scc079.wpd.html

Swan, M. (2004, December 6). Ont. offers help for gay students. *Western Catholic Reporter*, 4.

Warner, T. (2002). *Never going back: A history of queer activism in Canada*. Toronto: University of Toronto Press.

Wells, K. (2003). *Building safe, caring and inclusive schools for lesbian, gay, bisexual and transgender students: Professional development workshop series for Alberta teachers, facilitator's guide*. Edmonton, AB: Alberta Teachers' Association.

Wells, K. (2004). *Sexual orientation and gender identity* [Alberta Teachers' Association's Sexual Orientation and Gender Identity Educational Website]. Retrieved July 31, 2006, from http://www.teachers.ab.ca/Issues+In+Education/Diversity+and+Human+Rights /Sexual+Orientation/Index.htm

Wells, K. (2005). *Gay-straight student alliances in Alberta schools: A guide for teachers*. Edmonton, AB: Alberta Teachers' Association.

Wells, K. (2006). *The gay-straight student alliance handbook: A comprehensive resource for K-12 teachers, administrators, and school counsellors*. Ottawa, ON: The Canadian Teachers' Federation.

Wells, K., & Tsutsumi, M. (2005). *Creating safe and caring schools for lesbian, gay, bisexual, and trans-identified students: A guide for counsellors*. Edmonton, AB: The Society for Safe and Caring Schools and Communities.

THREE

SCHOOL ADMINISTRATORS AS PUBLIC INTELLECTUALS: RETHINKING LEADERSHIP PREPARATION

Yvette Daniel

> Leadership for social justice investigates and poses solutions for issues that generate and reproduce social inequities.
>
> – Tillman & Dantley (2006, p. 17)

Educational leaders are expected to be transformative intellectuals. They navigate a labyrinth of expectations as they try to balance competing demands (Shields, 2004). There is no shortage of literature on this topic; in fact, even to reference a few here might do injustice to the proliferation of the literature and research on the changing role of school administrators – leaders, principals, superintendents and others – in a milieu of reform and restructuring in our schools.[1] However, much of the current literature has focused on pedagogical issues, and not much attention has been given to the institutional basis of educational restructuring that would equip school leaders with the critical tools needed to address the complex issues of social justice in school settings (Daniel & Griffith, 2004).

Throughout my career in public education, I have spent considerable time in schools, and have worked closely with school and board administrators. Furthermore, I worked in an administrative capacity, albeit for a very short time, and I have experienced the constraints and the possibilities of being in the role of a public intellectual. The daily demands of running a complex institution leave little time for praxis. However, in a milieu of increasing diversity and demographic shifts, the task of leadership for social justice cannot be left to chance. It is not possible to continue to live with "isolated stabs at inequities or see them as management challenges" (Marshall, 2004, p. 4). We cannot continue to live with the notion of color-blindness or deficit thinking if school leaders, as public intellectuals, are going to transform schools. We need to rethink leadership education and training, to step beyond the traditional, taken-for-granted Principals' Qualification Programs (PQPs) in Ontario and the Masters' degree that most candidates acquire merely to meet the minimum qualifications for leadership roles in the system. I am more convinced than ever of the need for substantial change, especially when I witness candidates rush to fulfill the minimum requirements of their final research paper; sometimes barely mentioning the concept of social justice when writing on transformative moral leadership. What are the chances that these candidates will become public intellectuals dedicated to transformative practices, or to what extent will they perpetuate the status quo of schooling as it currently exists? Grogan (2004) in a testimonial of appreciation for William Foster's work in this area argues that "local educational leadership is being circumscribed by an administrative mentality that is pervasive in the United States and elsewhere today"(p. 222).

Education for leadership in our schools must be transformed to ensure that school administrators at all levels are public intellectuals capable of transformative action. I argue that the problem lies, first and foremost, with the conservative nature of schooling. Kozik-Rosabal (2000) frame the issue this way: "Schools respond to the political dictates of the groups in power; they do not usually shape or lead our societal visions for the future" (p. 370). Second, the fault does not rest with mostly well-intentioned professionals but, rather, in our inability to provide them with the appropriate skills and strategies through redesigned leadership preparation programs. Such programs need to draw people from nontraditional contexts into educational leadership, cultivate new skills for teaching in a diverse milieu, and "infuse school leadership preparation with lessons from outside the narrow bonds of K-12 education" (Hess & Kelly, 2005, p.177).

Therefore, I first articulate in this chapter the notion of public intellectuals as it applies to educational leadership, and explicate its implications within the four frames within which leadership is manifested in organizations. Next, in order to lay the groundwork for public intellectuals to be able to redesign educational practices, I present Kumashiro's (2000) schema for anti-oppressive education, interweaving it with key concepts such as equity audits (Skrla, Scheurich, Garcia, & Nolly, 2004), deficit thinking (Grogan, 2004, Shields, 2004, Skrla & Scheurich, 2001), and pedagogical silences (Kozik-Rosabel, 2000, Shields, 2004). However, these concepts will remain in the realm of the theoretical unless adequate programs for leadership preparation for social justice become part of the discourse in policy and in practice. I forward examples of initiatives in the U.S., not as templates to be copied, but as suggestions that policy-makers and all those involved in leadership education can adopt and adapt to create a viable venue for leadership for social justice, specifically in Ontario.

FRAMES FOR UNDERSTANDING THE ROLE OF PUBLIC INTELLECTUALS IN ADDRESSING SOCIAL JUSTICE ISSUES

Schools are sites that link the intellectual activity taking place within to broader societal issues beyond the buildings walls. Therefore, critical interrogation of current educational practices is a moral imperative for school leaders committed to implementing social justice practices within their institutions. Dantley and Tillman (2006) argue:

> Implied in the idea of transformative leadership is the exchange of new ideological and theoretical frames and practices for the more celebrated profession-forming ones that have traditionally informed the field of educational leadership. Inherent also in notions of transformative leadership are the exigencies of individual and institutional change. These ideas of change, however, are based on a critical theoretical and moral frame that dares to interrogate the rituals as well as the underlying presuppositions and assumptions that craft administrative practices in schools. (p. 22)

Critical interrogation for individual and institutional redesign (Maxcy, Crow, Roy, & Cormier, 1992) takes place within the constraints of the four aspects of the organization; structures, politics, human resources and symbolic awareness. These four aspects are derived from the concept of frames articulated by Bolman and Deal (1997, 2002) that is widely used in educational administration, especially when rethinking school policies and practices. Frame analysis allows administrators to understand that a variety of perspectives must be employed to make sense of the complex and nonlinear organization of schooling; thus their role as public intellectuals should be viewed through multiple lenses. It is even more compelling to note the interdependence and the interrelationships between frames, "like a mobile, it is hard to touch one frame without setting off a reaction in all the others" (Seashore-Louis, Toole, & Hargreaves, 1999, p. 259).

The *structural frame* focuses on analysis, design, and strategy. It is based upon a rational approach that holds people accountable for the responsibilities they undertake in a formal structure, but extends to informal ways as well. The principal is called upon to coordinate the efforts of individuals and groups within the organization through policies and rules. School structures are not static; they are in a state of constant flux and adaptation (Morrison, 2002). As the diversity in our schools increases, principals and school officials, in particular, must consider the ways in which the complex structures of schools require that changes do not happen in isolation – all changes to these structures occur within a complex web of relationships.

The *political frame* "points out the limits of authority and the inevitability that resources are almost always too scarce to fulfill all demands" (Bolman & Deal, 2002, p. 3). The political frame considers the manner in which the school under the stewardship of the principal creates internal and external supports to change current practices in ways that will challenge extant inequities. In the process of implementing change, the leader requires the skills to manage political issues that affect power relationships and status this change provokes. Seashore-Louis et al (1999) argue that "the language of educational change is full of political terms; agenda setting, stakeholders, coalitions, political will, arenas, conflict resolution, resource allocation, political pressures, and constituencies" (p. 262). As administrators take on the role of critical agents for change, they have to negotiate these political frames in skillful and innovative ways.

The *human resources frame* examines the role of people collectively within the organization as they learn to change their practices, solve problems, and support changes through the use of different images and metaphors, parallel instead of linear processing, and effective problem-solving and behavior strategies that include sustained interaction and mutual support. This frame underscores the significance of individual needs and motives within a social system. Administrators have to employ strategies of shared decision making; provide opportunities for participation; and work toward enlisting commitment and involvement from staff, students, and community stakeholders. Administrators play a significant role when the source of thinking and acting is diffused throughout the organization through deep changes in beliefs and practices.

The *symbolic frame* is also referred to as the cultural perspective for viewing organizations. Each school and school board or school district has its own distinct culture that determine "the way we do things around here." Bolman and Deal (2002) posit that "symbols govern behavior through shared values, informal agreements, and implicit understandings" (p. 4). These myths, rituals, and symbols could, potentially, lead to actions that foster inequities. Therefore, the central question in this frame focuses on the culture of the school and the school board (or school district) in addressing these inequities. Individuals use different schemas to interpret their experiences and, hence, the meaning derived from that experience is not always shared. Bolman and Deal (2002) argue that to deal with ambiguity and uncertainty people create symbols and stories to provide understanding and that myths, rituals, and ceremonies give people the meaning they seek.

These four organizational frames are interrelated and cannot be treated in isolation in our analysis. They are an integral part of the organizational structure and climate of educational institutions. Every school principal, therefore, has to reevaluate generic implementation policies for addressing inequities within his or her organizational structures and climate. Thus, as the four frames are employed in exploring these critical roles, it is important to be cognizant of the complexity and the interconnectivity of these frames in the lived reality of schools. Recognizing this complexity also calls attention to the limits and possibilities for public intellectuals in organizations where transformative practices can occur without fear of reprisal. Educational institutions are relatively resistant to change; hence long-term policy planning, implementation, and leadership preparation are required if social justice as a theoretical construct will have a real impact on students in our schools.

In this section, I briefly explicated the notion of public, or transformative, intellectuals as it relates to the task of working for social justice within the four frames of organizations. School administrators, as public intellectuals face the challenge of negotiating these frames. In order to facilitate this process, they must, first and foremost, construct counternarratives (Grogan 2004) by deconstructing deficit thinking practices that are prevalent in our institutions, critiquing pedagogical silences, and undertaking the uncomfortable task of performing equity audits. By doing so, school administrators can begin to work from Kumashiro's (2000) anti-oppressive schema for educational change.

DECONSTRUCTING METANARRATIVES

The dominant discourses and practices of educational leadership are nested in structuralist metanarratives of human capital resource management that emphasize homogenization, supervision, and administration. The focus on efficiency and effectiveness in our current milieu privileges compliance to accountability measures instead of critical reflection. Even as we serve a more heterogeneous student population (in terms of race, ethnicity, social class, gender, country of origin, native language, sexual orientation and disabilities) than ever before, there are increasing pressures to ensure effective education for all. In the U.S., the *No Child Left Behind Act,* with its implications for high stakes accountability systems, and initiatives in Ontario such as EQAO tests, with the subsequent publications of results, have brought issues of responsibility for educating all children to the forefront. Therefore, educational leaders "have had to ponder both the rhetoric and reality of how to address questions of diversity in schools" (Riehl, 2000, p. 56). School leadership has to face the challenge of restructuring by using a different metaphor; leadership as design (Maxcy et al, 1992) where leaders are designers and artists required to engage in a process of *creating* unique responses by redefining the taken-for-granted assumptions about schooling and society. One way of redesigning lies in interrogating of the notion of deficit thinking, overcoming pathologies of silence and conducting equity audits.

PATHOLOGIES OF SILENCE AND DEFICIT THINKING

At a conference venue last year I heard a school district superintendent quip, "For me, all children are the same" when questioned about the number of aboriginal students suspended from schools in his jurisdiction. Comments of this nature by educators are misguided attempts at equality because they feel uncomfortable dealing with difference that Shields (2004) argues are *pathologies of silence*. On the one hand, educators are silent about these differences, or, on the other hand, they engage in deficit thinking that is equally harmful.

In Valencia's (1997) influential treatise on the topic of deficit thinking, he argues that the most common explanation for school failure among a substantial proportion of low SES and minority students is attributed to generalization based upon misconstrued assumptions about alleged internal deficiencies (such as cognitive or familial deficiencies, home culture, SES, and others). Thus, in this paradigm, the responsibility for failure is attributed to external factors rather than a critical examination of the education system itself (Grogan, 2004, Riehl, 2000 Shields, 2004, Skrla & Scheurich, 2001). These assumptions shrouded in deficit thinking have led to proliferation of terms like *at-risk students*. In some parts of Ontario, schools in lower SES and those serve a diverse student population are labeled *compensatory education schools*. Mostly, deficit thinking "allows inequities to be explained away as normal and inevitable" (Skrla & Scheurich, 2001, p. 244).

First and foremost, public intellectuals must admit and uncover the stubborn presuppositions of deficit thinking in our habits of minds or *habitus* that impede change. These presuppositions form the habits of mind for most school administrators, despite their otherwise good intentions to work in the best interests of the students they serve. Shields (2004) argues:

> The challenge for educators, I believe, is to recognize how our habitus restricts equity and social justice and then find ways to overcome these constraints. To do this, we must learn to acknowledge and validate difference without reifying it or pathologizing it. (p. 113)

In Skrla and Scheurich's (2001) study of four large school districts, superintendents spoke with candor about deconstructing these metanarratives; the first step, they found, is shifting one's frames of reference. They realized how these views were shared by the majority of educators in their districts.

> Likewise, a central office administrator in Brazosport criticized earlier deficit attitudes of herself and others and said that she and other administrators felt "noble" about working in high-poverty schools because they kept the "warm, safe, and on a regular schedule" and that they

> thought the poor academic performance of the students
> was "inevitable and not anyone's fault." (p. 252).

It is not easy, as I write this chapter, to admit that I have witnessed and also participated in such discourses in the past while working at a large metropolitan inner-city school. Therefore, I can understand how easy it is to fall prey to the prevalence of deficit thinking cloaked in a rational and simplistic discourse, not to mention the difficult task of conscious and critical reflection necessary to dismantle these frames of reference.

EQUITY AUDITS

In recent accountability measures, the emphasis has been placed on numbers and comparative reporting within a bifurcated and reductive thinking model. In the literature on accountability, the debate is polarized into two camps: those that are for and those against these measures. However, Skrla et al (2004) reconceptualize equity audits, not as an end point in data collection and analysis, but as a starting point in the discussion on inequities and the development of an action plan for change relative to the needs identified through the auditing process. Equity audits could assist us in moving beyond technical fixes and examining deeply rooted issues that the data manifest. This process is not comfortable and, as such, partly indicates the entrenched fear of putting these issues on the table, for doing so requires leaders to confront the realities of inequitable education that had often remained invisible due to silences or deficit thinking. Skrla et al offer a set of three dimensions that together offer a straightforward formula for equity auditing that is expressed as: Teacher Quality Equity + Programmatic Equity = Achievement Equity. This audit requires an examination of the evidence for teacher quality equity or inequity for a single school or a school district. Equally important is an audit of programmatic equity examined through the quality of programs and student placements in the jurisdiction under study and the resulting disaggregating of data on achievement equity. In Ontario, for example, there is very little disaggregating of data, either by race, class or any other variable. When questioned about this gap, the most common response is, "For us all students are equal." Public intellectuals must confront these inequitable practices in an attempt to create socially just practices in our school system. The task is not easy for leaders as they negotiate the challenges within the structural, political, human resources and symbolic (cultural) frames of the messy reality of their daily work. Deconstructing deficit thinking, uncovering pathologies of silence and conducting equity audits prepare the terrain upon which a framework of anti-oppressive education is constructed (Kumashiro, 2000).

FOUR APPROACHES TO ANTI-OPPRESSIVE EDUCATION

Kumashiro suggests four approaches to anti-oppressive pedagogies: (a) Education for the Other; (b) Education about the Other; (c) Education that is critical of privileging and Othering; and (d) Education that changes students and society. By Other, he means "other than the norm" in terms of race, SES, gender, and sexuality. Individuals who are part of the dominant discourse and have "seldom walked through the land of the other" (Rusch, 2004, p. 32) are less comfortable because it is difficult to understand "that the world is normed by and for them" (Rusch, 2004, p. 32).

Kumashiro describes and critiques each approach and recommends the use of an amalgam of these approaches. In leadership preparation programs, these approaches should be studied, discussed, and practiced in our quest to redesign schools that promote equity and social justice. The first approach, "Education for the Other," focuses on improving the experiences for students who are *othered* in schools, by acknowledging pathologies of silence and transforming *habitus* and the assimilationist ideologies within which schools operate. Educators must combat this oppression by recognizing that schools are harmful spaces and work toward the goal of transforming our schools into helpful, affirming, therapeutic, and supportive spaces through the building of relationships and community (Shields, 2004).

The second approach, "Educating about the Other," addresses the distortions and omissions in the school curriculum. Thus, the curriculum should integrate *otherness* into the curriculum throughout the year. Equity audits are useful in order to recognize the inequities in the curriculum, teacher quality, program structure, and achievement levels of "Education for the Other" and "Education about the Other." Both these approaches, despite their various strengths do not bring about structural and systemic changes.

The third approach, "Education that is critical of privileging and Othering," examines societal structures to understand how ruling ideologies are transmitted through hegemonic practices, thereby providing a venue from which to critique social inequalities. In this approach, administrators are called upon to develop and practice the tenets of Friere's critical pedagogy through analytical and critical thinking skills. However, raising consciousness in itself will not necessarily lead to social change if learning is not translated into actions.

The fourth approach, "Education that changes students and society," is based on the premise that "oppression originated in discourse" (p. 40). Kumashiro suggests using a poststructuralist approach to look beyond these approaches to overcome resistance to change and learning "to participate in the ongoing, never-completed construction of knowledge" (p. 43). Students must learn to always look beyond what they know and to ask questions and consider what has not yet been considered or formulated. Kumashiro's framework for anti-oppressive education serves as a foundation for practice in rethinking leadership preparation for a social justice agenda in education.

REDESIGNING LEADERSHIP PROGRAMS

In this section, I examine initiatives that have been taken in some parts of the U.S. toward leadership preparation that fosters the development of transformative intellectuals. Following this, implications for the Ontario context will be considered.

INNOVATIVE PROGRAMS IN EDUCATIONAL LEADERSHIP

Some researchers have raised serious doubts that traditional university-based administration and leadership programs can prepare transformative intellectuals, mainly because they fail to link content to practice (Grogan & Andrews, 2002, Hess & Kelly, 2005). Furthermore, most university professors are far removed from the realities of schools. An urgent need exists for collaboration between higher education, the professional organizations, and school districts themselves to provide preparation outside the conventional classroom formats (p. 248). However, despite numerous calls for change, most new programs merely tinker with existing ones under a new packaging (Hess & Kelly, 2005). Murphy (2006) bemoans the fact that despite the huge amounts of energy and resources devoted to reforming educational leadership programs, much of the change has been on the margins.

In the U.S. a set of National Standards was developed by The Interstate School Leaders Licensure Consortium (ISLLC) to certify educational administrators. These National Standards are enforced through testing and have been the cause of a lively debate among scholars (Anderson, 2001). Nonetheless, there are several initiatives that work within the boundaries of these National Standards to develop preparation programs and courses that place social justice and equity as their guiding principles. The University Council for Educational Administration (UCEA) is a consortium of major research universities with doctoral programs in educational leadership and policy. UCEA's influential academic journal, *Educational Administration Quarterly*, its conferences, and collaborative research projects focus on leadership for social justice. Recently, an on-line journal, *Journal of Research on Leadership Education*, is accessible free of charge on its website. In its first issue there are several articles that call for a need for educational leaders who can produce systemic change (Murphy, 2006, Valverde, 2006, Walker, 2006, Silverberg & Kottkamp, 2006). The key message of the first issue is that ethical and moral leadership must be fostered in preparation programs for school officials to become agents of change.

One nontraditional program is of interest for this discussion. The New Leaders for New Schools (NLNS) (Hess & Kelly, 2005) aims to recruit talented and committed people, who, otherwise, are not drawn to or are rejected from traditional leadership training programs. The program has strict admission procedures, and candidates who have displayed exceptional qualities could be nominated to participate in this program. The curriculum is designed around three strands, transformational leadership, instructional leadership, and organizational leadership, with a residency in area public schools rounding out the program. Instead of job shadowing in the traditional sense, NLNS candidates actually work in schools and are required to target two or three challenges. These challenges are concrete deliverables; all residents must work with three teachers and show evidence of increased student achievement, must oversee a team to ensure a focus on the core business of student achievement, and must start an initiative to tackle a building wide problem and document its success. Hess & Kelly (2005) point out that "this type of documented competency assessment is alien to traditional school administration internships and ensures that residents are ready to take on their own school after completion" (p.170).

Although NLNS is widely touted as an exceptional program, it has run into difficulties due to statutory and political challenges. One challenge is the licensure system that requires it to contract with traditional schools or risk that these candidates might not find appropriate job placements. In each city, NLNS is required to adapt its curriculum to meet the licensure requirements of that particular state.

It is not possible to discuss several other exemplary programs here, such as Harvard University's Urban Superintendency program, or the University of Washington's Danforth Education Leadership program (Jackson & Kelley, 2002). None of these programs are perfect models, nor do we expect them to be. However, it is important to highlight some of the key characteristics of these programs to serve as exemplars in other contexts.

Most of these programs are more demanding, employ stringent and careful selection and screening procedures, and design a more coherent and focused curriculum around themes or strands, instead of a format of isolated modules typically found in traditional curricula for leadership development. Jackson and Kelley's (2002) analysis has identified a model for the design of effective preparation programs. The three main components – students, faculty, and the knowledge base – are the three anchors, represented as the three vertices of this program development triangle. Students are recruited after a careful screening process, faculty includes academics, researchers, and practicing administrators, and the knowledge base consists of core and critical knowledge. In designing these programs, it is essential to question not only what counts as knowledge, but also, more importantly, what knowledge is needed (Riehl, Larson, Short, & Reitzug, 2000). Moreover, state legislated standards are also taken into consideration. Students, faculty, and knowledge base are linked throughout the program's structure, the process of developing a vision for content and design, and the instructional strategies that focus on the particular issues of developing transformative leaders. All aspects are developed through careful collaboration through a visioning and re-visioning process. Through a commitment of time and resources, as well as a focused vision, it is possible to move toward systemic changes in the way leadership preparation is conceptualized and articulated.

All of the aforementioned aspects of leadership preparation require a theory of action (Argyris & Schon, 1974) so that the quest to develop leadership for social justice does not remain espoused theory. It is important to change the deeply entrenched assumptions in a profession that has not given social justice issues the highest priority. Regardless of the location and context of these programs, there are some principles that are important in promoting social justice as the main theme in leadership development (Cambron-McCabe, 2006). First, "the practice for effective leadership intervention for equity" will require individuals to take risks; therefore, different strategies must be employed so that people who have a commitment to social justice and want to learn how to address inequities, as outlined in the previous sections, gain access to these programs (p. 117). Furthermore, collaboration between the different stakeholders is also crucial in training all administrators, not just those who are entering the profession. Next, scholars who employ rigor in their research need to step forward and become involved in the policy process as leaders who can implement these changes at the conceptual, theoretical, and practical levels. Lastly, refocusing preparation programs means more than repackaging or tinkering with existing curricula, but starting afresh from a zero-based curriculum strategy (Murphy, 2006) in order to prevent a mismatch between the rearticulated foundations – what the program stands for – and the curriculum. Existing courses could always be reintegrated as needed.

THE LANDSCAPE OF ONTARIO'S LEADERSHIP PREPARATION

In Ontario, the traditional Principals' Qualification Programs (PQP) are provided by the various faculties of education, the Ontario Principals' Council (OPC), Ontario College of Teachers (OCT), and the Elementary Teachers Federation of Ontario (ETFO). A on-line search revealed that most PQPs have identical formats: Part One consisting of modules of study that focus on topics such as legal issues, school operations, human resource management followed by a practicum component that provides a structured leadership experience. Part Two of the program also consisting of modules that examine leadership, staff development, school planning, and school program development. The format and topics adhere to traditional forms of leadership and administration preparation. A cursory look at Education Leadership Canada, a division of OPC revealed that it, too, offers multiple professional development opportunities for current and aspiring school principals. Courses offered through its summer institute for 2006 include topics such as; Leadership that makes a difference, Supporting Math Education, The Juggling Act, Literacy Development, and Improving Numeracy and Literacy Results.

The first step in developing an innovative model is an in-depth research and review to examine the particulars of the various principal and other leadership programs in Ontario. This research should map out the characteristics of the different programs to identify strengths, weaknesses, and gaps. Next, a framework for leadership for social justice could be developed based upon examples in the U.S. and through university, district, and community collaboration to establish centres for leadership for social justice specifically for the Ontario context. Although funding for research here is not as extensive as in the U.S., researchers could seek support from the Ministry of Education, Social Science and Humanities Research Council of Canada, University-based Research Grants, Council for Ministers of Education. In Ontario, it is also necessary to conduct equity audits using the data generated by standardized testing to establish a culture of disaggregating data according to the different variables, such as race, class, gender, sexual orientation, disability, and others. Leaders must be supported in confronting the inequities and the silences within the constraints of the structural, political, human resources, and symbolic frames so that they might eventually redesign these existing frames. Anchoring the theme of social justice and equity in preparation programs will enable school leaders to "understand their ethical and moral obligations to create schools that promote and deliver social justice" (Grogan & Andrews, 2002, p.250). Although education in Canada is the responsibility of each province, a national agenda that promotes leadership preparation for equity and social justice is necessary.

CONCLUSION

The commitment to preparing leaders who are transformative intellectuals is an imperative that should be on the forefront of our national and provincial policy agendas. In this chapter, I contend that the discourse of accountability and measurable outcomes could be used to further the social justice agenda through innovative leadership preparation. School leaders have to create synergy within the four frames of organizational structures; moreover, they cannot lapse into a comfort zone of compliance. Through leadership preparation that prioritizes social justice, school administrators, as public intellectuals, have an important role to play in redesigning educational institutions by deconstructing prevalent the metanarratives and rethinking education within an anti-oppressive framework. Leadership preparation programs that move away from the traditional positivist, managerialist discourse are needed in order to turn these espoused theories into theories in action that involve risk-taking and a transformation of habitus. Current literature offers examples of preparation programs that have abandoned these traditional structures that are no longer viable. School administrators as public intellectuals, who with a commitment, passion, a capacity for continuous self-reflection, and fortitude can create spaces where all students are successful, not only on test scores, but also in learning to live in a truly democratic society.

NOTES

[1] For the purpose of this article, given the limits of space, school administrators refers to school superintendents, school principals, school leaders, board officials and others. The author is aware of the many distinctions between these roles; however, these differences are not taken up in this chapter.

References

Argyris, C. & Schon, D. (1974). *Theory in practice: Increasing professional effectiveness*. San Francisco: Jossey Bass.

Anderson, G. (2001). Disciplining leaders: A critical discourse analysis of the ISLLC National Examination and Performance Standards in educational administration. *International Journal of Leadership in Education*, *4*(3), 199-216.

Bolman, L. & Deal, T. (2002). *Reframing the path to school leadership: a guide for teachers and principals*. Thousand Oaks, California: Corwin Press.

Bolman, L., & Deal, T. (1997). *Reframing Organizations: Artistry, choice and leadership*. San Francisco: Jossey Bass.

Cambron-McCabe, N. (2006). Preparation and development of school leaders: Implications for social justice policies. In C. Marshall & M. Oliva (eds.). *Leadership for Social Justice: Making Revolutions in Education* (pp. 110-129), New York: Pearson.

Daniel, Y., Griffith, A. (2004). Institutional change and the principalship in an era of educational reform. *Canadian and International Education*, *33*(1), June 2004, 7-30.

Dantley, M., & Tillman, L. (2006). Social justice and moral transformative leadership. In C. Marshall & M. Oliva (eds.) *Leadership for social justice: Making revolutions in education* (pp. 16-30). New York: Pearson.

Foster, W. (1986). *Paradigms and promises: New approaches to educational administration*. Buffalo, NY: Prometheus Books.

Grogan, M. (2004). Keeping a critical, postmodern eye on educational leadership in the United States: In appreciation of Bill Foster. *Educational Administration Quarterly*, *40*(2), April 2004, 222-239.

Grogan, M. & Andrews, R. (2002). Defining preparation and professional development for the future. *Educational Administration Quarterly*, *38*(2), 233-256.

Hess, F. & Kelly, A. (2005). An innovative look, a recalcitrant reality: The politics of principal preparation reform. *Educational Policy*, *19*(1), 155-180.

Jackson, B. & Kelley, C. (2002). Exceptional and innovative programs in educational leadership. *Educational Administration Quarterly*, *38*(2), 192-212.

Kozik-Rosabel, G. (2000). "Well, we haven't noticed anything bad going on," said the principal: Parents speak about their gay families and schools. *Education and Urban Society*, *32*(3), 368-389.

Kumashiro, K. (2000). Toward a theory of anti-oppressive education: Four approaches to anti-oppressive education. *Review of Educational Research*, *70*(1), Spring 2000, 25-53.

Marshall, C. (2004). Social justice challenges to educational administration: Introduction to a special issue. *Educational Administration Quarterly*, *40*(1), Feb 2004, 3-13.

Maxcy, S., Crow, G., Roy, S., & Cormier, S. (1992). Leadership as design in school restructuring. *The International Journal of Educational Management*, *6*(6), 20-28.

Morrison, K. (2002). *School leadership and complexity theory.* New York: Routledge Falmer.

Murphy, J. (2006). Some thoughts on rethinking the pre-service education of school leaders. *Journal of Research on Leadership Education.* Retrieved on June 12, 2006, http://www.ucea.org/JRLE/pdf/vol 1/issue 1/Murphy.pdf

Riehl, C. (2000). The principal's role in creating inclusive schools for diverse students: A review of normative, empirical, and critical literature on the practice of educational administration. *Review of Educational Research*, *70*(1), 55-81.

Riehl, C., Larson, C., Short, P., & Reitzug, U. (2000). Reconceptualizing research and scholarship in educational administration: Learning to know, knowing to do, doing to learn. *Educational Administration Quarterly*, *36*(3), 391-427.

Rusch, E. (2004). Gender and race in leadership preparation: A constrained discourse. *Educational Administration Quarterly*, *40*(1), 14-46.

Seashore-Louis, K., Toole, J., & Hargreaves, A. (1999). Rethinking school improvement. In J. Murphy & K. Seashore-Louis (eds.) *Handbook of Research on Educational Administration* (2nd ed.) (pp. 251-276). San Francisco: Jossey-Bass Publishers.

Shields, C. (2004). Dialogic leadership for social justice: Overcoming pathologies of silence. *Educational Administration Quarterly*, 40(1), 109-132.

Silverberg, R. & Kottkamp, R. (2006). Language Matters. *Journal of Research on Leadership Education.* Retrieved on June 10, 2006, http://www.ucea.org/JRLE/pdf/vol 1/issue 1/Kottkamp.pdf

Skrla, L. & Scheurich, J. (2001). Displacing deficit thinking in school district leadership. *Education and Urban Society*, *33*(3), 235-259.

Skrla, L. Scheurich, J., Garcia, J., & Nolly, G. (2004). Equity audits: A practical leadership tool for developing equitable and excellent schools. *Educational Administration Quarterly*, *40*(1), 133-161.

Valencia, R. (1997). *The evolution of deficit thinking: Educational thought and practice.* London: Falmer.

Valverde, L. (2006). Needed: Leadership for liberation – A Global portrait painted in shades of brown. Retrieved on June 10, 2006, http://www.ucea.org/JRLE/pdf/vol 1/issue 1/Valverde.pdf

Walker, A. (2006). Leadership development across cultures. *Journal of Research on Leadership Education.* Retrieved on June 10, 2006, http://www.ucea.org/JRLE/pdf/vol 1/issue 1/Walker.pdf

FOUR

CREATIVITY IN SCHOOL DISCIPLINE: USE OF NON-SUSPENSION ALTERNATIVES BY HIGH SCHOOL VICE-PRINCIPALS

Ken Brien

School administration research regularly finds that vice-principals are typically responsible for school discipline in high schools (e.g., Barger, 1999; Mertz & McNeely, 1999; Weller & Weller, 2002). In particular, they must often respond to serious student misconduct cases referred to them by teachers and other school personnel. When doing so, vice-principals must consider all disciplinary options available to them. Suspension is a long-standing disciplinary sanction for serious student misconduct. In a recent study of high school vice-principals in three Canadian provinces (Brien, 2004), I asked respondents to describe the extent to which existing laws and policies allowed or encouraged the use of disciplinary measures other than suspensions to respond to serious student misconduct. The results from that study form the basis for this chapter.

Vice-principals face many challenges in choosing and implementing a variety of disciplinary measures. Can vice-principals use anything besides suspensions when disciplining students? To what extent can they apply creativity in cases of serious student misconduct? In what ways do laws and policies help or hinder them in applying consequences that are specifically tailored to the students and contexts involved in each situation? This chapter will attempt to address these questions. It will begin by reviewing the legal responsibilities and tensions faced by school administrators with respect to student discipline. This will be followed by a discussion of the reasons for and drawbacks of suspending students from school using legal, pedagogical, ethical, and practical perspectives. Following a report on my study findings, the chapter will discuss the extent to which laws and policies support the use of disciplinary alternatives to suspensions. It will show that, while vice-principals are willing to use creative alternatives to suspensions, they also face significant barriers and obstacles in doing so.

LEGAL RESPONSIBILITIES FOR STUDENT DISCIPLINE

Schools derive their responsibility and authority to discipline students from statute law, common law, and constitutional law. *Statute law* for education comes primarily from provincial school law, but other sources such as the federal *Youth Criminal Justice Act* (YCJA) (2002) also contain provisions relevant to school discipline. *Common law* refers to the body of law created by courts and judges in making decisions and used as precedents for later cases. *Constitutional law* in Canada is found in a variety of sources, of which the *Canadian Charter of Rights and Freedoms* (1982) is the most significant for school discipline. Educators must deal with two primary legal principles in the administration of student discipline in schools: the duty to maintain a safe and orderly learning environment for *all* students and the duty to protect the rights of *individual* students. Keel (1998) listed a wide range of disciplinary measures available to educators. Many corrective measures that deal with minor disruptions – such as reprimands, brief detentions, and loss of privileges – are not referred to in any legislation, except as part of the general statutory duty to maintain a safe and orderly learning environment. For more serious incidents, the application of discipline measures raises legal issues such as due process rights, human rights, or constitutional rights. Such measures include search and seizure, suspension and expulsion, and exclusion of intruders from school property. School officials must understand the full range of legal frameworks governing their actions in the administration of school discipline.

Provincial education statutes hold teachers, and especially principals, responsible for maintaining proper discipline in their schools (Keel, 1998). For example, Section 20 of the Alberta *School Act* (2000) requires that a principal must "maintain order and discipline in the school and on the school grounds and during activities sponsored or approved by the board." Furthermore, in light of growing concerns about the need to protect and promote human rights considerations in schools, a recent amendment to the *School Act* also sets out the following requirement for school boards: "A board shall ensure that each student enrolled in a school operated by the board is provided with a safe and caring environment that fosters and maintains respectful and responsible behaviours" (s. 45[8]). Similarly, the New Brunswick Department of Education's (2001) *Policy 703* is intended to ensure a positive learning and working environment for everyone involved in schools. Among its statement of principles, *Policy 703* defines a positive learning and working environment as one in which "pupils have the right to be taught and to learn without being disrupted by others and have the responsibility not to disrupt the learning of others." The significance of this type of legal duty of school boards with respect to student discipline cases recently achieved public prominence in a case from British Columbia. The B.C. Court of Appeal ruled in 2005 that a school board was guilty of violating a student's human rights when Jubran, a high school student, was repeatedly subjected to verbal and physical harassment by fellow students in spite of consistent efforts by school administrators to investigate and respond to each reported case of harassment (*School District No. 44 [North Vancouver] v. Jubran*). This case illustrates the important fact that teachers and principals not only have a duty to discipline students, but that their measures also must be effective in correcting student misconduct, particularly if the safety or wellbeing of other students is at risk.

Provincial statutes impose a corresponding duty upon students to submit to the authority of their teachers and principals. For example, Section 12(e) of the Alberta *School Act* (2000) requires that a student shall "account to the student's teachers for the student's conduct." In Ontario, provincial regulations made pursuant to the *Education Act* (1990) state that: "Every pupil is responsible for his or her conduct to the principal of the school that the pupil attends" (*Operation of Schools – General*, 1990, s. 23[4]). Section 14 of the New Brunswick *Education Act* (1997) lists several duties of pupils, including this clear, concise statement: "It is the duty of a pupil to . . . comply with all school policies" (s. 14[1][h]). In practice, this means that vice-principals, exercising the authority and responsibility delegated to them by principals, have both the duty and the authority to take necessary disciplinary measures to establish and maintain a safe and orderly learning environment in their schools.

Although provincial laws have the most direct application to public education, there are federal statutes that high school vice-principals must consider when responding to cases of serious student misconduct. Perhaps the most important of these is the YCJA (2002), a federal criminal statute applying to persons aged twelve to seventeen years, the age range corresponding to most high school students. Certain actions committed by students may not only violate school rules, but also rise to the level of criminal offenses. These may include assault, theft, and possession of prohibited items such as weapons and drugs. When investigating allegations that students may have committed such offenses at school, vice-principals must be careful that in administering school discipline they do not jeopardize possible criminal proceedings that may be warranted by the circumstances. In particular, vice-principals must heed the requirements under the YCJA regarding the admissibility of statements made by youth to a person in authority. Failure to do so may cause such statements to be ruled inadmissible in a criminal trial.

The body of law in Canada is not limited to provincial and federal statutes. The interpretation of laws is the responsibility of courts and judges, whose decisions are recorded and published for use in subsequent cases. This creates a body of jurisprudence known collectively as the common law. In addition to their statutory responsibilities, school administrators also have common law duties with respect to school discipline. These include responsibilities arising from two important principles for teachers: *in loco parentis* and fiduciary roles of teachers. The prominent British jurist Sir William Blackstone articulated the *in loco parentis* principle in the eighteenth century and applied it to teachers (DeMitchell, 2002). Over the years, courts have held that teachers and principals have the authority to discipline students because, during the school day, teachers are standing in the place of parents and are, therefore, given the power to do what is reasonable in the circumstances (Alberta Civil Liberties Research Centre, 1996). In discipline matters, educators are expected to treat students in a manner similar to that of a kind, firm, and judicious parent (Bezeau, 2007). While Magsino (1995) observed some erosion of the importance of the *in loco parentis* principle in recent decades, particularly as teachers are increasingly viewed as agents of the state, Conte (2000) argued that the principle still applies to public schools, although in a more challenging context. He observed that, as a result of changes in family structures and in the influence of other social institutions, schools act in ways once reserved for the home and the community.

An important consequence of this common law principle is that courts will generally show deference to disciplinary decisions made by school officials. Keel (1998) pointed out that courts would normally not pass judgement on whether the decision made by an educator was right or wrong. Consider, for example, the following statement by Barclay J. of the Saskatchewan Court of Queen's Bench (*Lutes v. Prairie School Division No. 74*, 1992): "The Court should, subject to any *Charter* argument, refrain from ruling on the rightness or wrongness of the decision of the School so long as the School is acting within its jurisdiction in disciplining the student" (p. 237). Instead, courts will normally focus only on whether the teacher or school administration had the authority to make the decision and whether due process was followed (Keel, 1998, p. 129). Courts have cited both teachers' statutory duties to maintain safe and orderly schools and their *in loco parentis* role to uphold the legality of searches conducted by school officials for the purpose of enforcing school rules and protecting the safety of all students.

The fiduciary concept is another common law principle that affects the work of vice-principals in student discipline. In particular, courts have noted that the student-teacher or student-principal relationship is significantly different from that existing between police officers and ordinary citizens. Mr. Justice G. V. La Forest (1998), a retired justice of the Supreme Court of Canada, described the teacher-student relationship this way: "There is little doubt . . . that the teacher-student relationship is a fiduciary one" (p. 128). La Forest identified such concepts as trust, confidence, role modeling, and influence as key elements of the fiduciary relationship existing between teachers and students. These principles came into play in a well-known case that arose in Nova Scotia. In this case, a vice-principal acted on a tip that a student would be bringing drugs to a school dance. He searched the student in his office, located drugs on the student, and turned the drugs over to an RCMP officer who was present during the search. The Supreme Court of Canada made the following comments in their landmark *R. v. M.(M.R.)* (1998) decision on searches of students by school officials:

> Students know that teachers and school authorities are
> responsible for providing a safe school environment
> and   maintaining   order   and   discipline   in   the

school.... Teachers and principals are placed in a position of trust that carries the onerous responsibilities of teaching and of caring for the children's safety and well-being.... This reduced expectation of privacy coupled with the need to protect students and provide a positive atmosphere for learning clearly indicate that a more lenient and flexible approach should be taken to searches conducted by teachers and principals than would apply to searches conducted by the police.

The Court recognized that the fiduciary role of teachers complemented their statutory responsibilities to support the authority of teachers and principals in the administration of student discipline.

With the proclamation of the *Charter* in 1982, Canadian courts gained expanded authority and responsibility to review provincial and federal legislation to ensure that they are consistent with constitutional principles. Since public schools are created and operate under provincial law, the actions of school administrators while exercising their statutory authority are subject to *Charter* scrutiny. A key requirement affecting vice-principals is found in Section 7 of the *Charter*: "Everyone has the right to life, liberty, and security of the person and the right not to be deprived thereof except in accordance with the principles of fundamental justice." Other provisions that may become relevant in discipline matters include freedom of expression and association (s. 2) and equality rights (s. 15). Vice-principals must ensure that their decisions on discipline matters consider all relevant constitutional principles so that they respect students' *Charter* rights. This becomes especially important when considering suspensions or other measures that may affect a student's right to an education.

SUSPENSIONS OF STUDENTS

Suspension of students is a long-standing sanction applied by school administrators for misconduct; however, there are legal, pedagogical, ethical, and practical factors that vice-principals need to consider when making suspension decisions. Vice-principals must face the tension between the expectation to give more support to disruptive students and the expectation to remove them from school for the benefit of other students. Gunn (1994) observed that parents, school board members, and educators themselves have frequently questioned the effectiveness of suspensions. For example, suspensions for truancy are particularly ill-suited consequences, even if legally authorized (Keel, 1998).

LEGAL ISSUES

One area of school law that affects school administrators is the suspension of students. In general, provincial education statutes give principals the power to suspend students (Giles, 1988; Keel, 1998; Mackinnon, 1994). Even so, school law sets limits on lengths of suspensions, defines the offenses for which suspensions are authorized, and prescribes the process to be followed by school officials when imposing suspensions.

In many Canadian provinces, there are statutory limitations on the length of suspensions imposed by principals. In Canada, Keel (1998) pointed out that limits for any single suspension by a principal range from a low of three days in Saskatchewan (*Education Act*, 1995, s. 154[1][a]) to twenty days in Ontario (*Education Act*, 1990, s. 306[2]). A typical limit is five consecutive school days, as in Alberta and New Brunswick (Alberta *School Act*, 2000, s. 24; New Brunswick *Education Act*, 1997, s. 24). If students are to be removed from schools for longer periods, then principals must make a case to their superintendents or school boards who are generally authorized to suspend or expel students for the rest of the school year and, in some jurisdictions, even longer.

Besides restrictions on the allowable length of school suspensions, education statutes may also specify the student offenses for which suspensions are legally authorized. For example, the Ontario *Education Act* (1990) lists several offenses for which suspensions are mandatory and permits school boards to list additional discretionary suspension offenses. The Alberta *School Act* (2000, s. 24) provides two basic reasons for suspensions, but the New Brunswick *Education Act* (1997, s. 24) allows principals to suspend students simply "for cause." Under the New Brunswick Department of Education's (2001) *Policy 703*, each school is expected to create a positive learning environment plan that includes references to the types of situations and offenses for which suspension is an appropriate disciplinary response.

In addition to specifying the infractions for which suspensions are authorized and setting limits on their length, statutes and court rulings have described a range of procedural requirements for school administrators to follow when suspending students. On this matter, the landmark case in the United States was *Goss v. Lopez* (1975). The U.S. Supreme Court ruled that, for suspensions of ten days or less, students were entitled to minimal due process. The Court stated that students must be given oral or written notice of the charges against them, an explanation of the evidence against them, and an opportunity to present their side of the story. An Ontario court made a similar ruling in *Re Peel Board of Education and B. et al.* (1987). Reid J. ruled that students should, at a minimum, be given an opportunity to tell their side of the story before principals make the decision to suspend students. Where a longer suspension or expulsion is being considered, then the due process requirements are more rigorous, including such features as the right to a full hearing, the calling of witnesses, and representation by legal counsel. The general principle is that the greater the disciplinary sanction, the more rigorous the fairness or due process requirements (Keel, 1998, pp. 135-136; "School violence," 1994; Streshly & Frase, 1992).

Provincial legislation on suspensions and expulsions now typically includes provisions to protect students' and parents' rights to procedural fairness. For example, in Alberta, Ontario, and New Brunswick, principals are required to provide students or parents (or both) with written notice of the reasons for a suspension. These provinces also allow for students and parents to appeal some suspension decisions, either informally or formally to the principal, the superintendent, the school board, or even, in Alberta, to the Minister of Education. In addition, Canadian students and parents can apply to the courts for judicial review and the common law remedies available there (Keel, 1998, p. 133). Clearly, a decision by a vice-principal to suspend a student has the potential to trigger more legal consequences than many other disciplinary measures.

PEDAGOGICAL ISSUES

Suspension of students also has the potential to trigger pedagogical concerns for vice-principals. All teachers, including vice-principals, typically have a statutory duty to encourage student learning, and this duty is not limited to academic matters, nor are they relieved of this duty for students guilty of misconduct at school. For example, the Alberta *School Act* (2000) requires that "a teacher while providing instruction or supervision must . . . encourage and foster learning in students" (s. 18[1][d]). This requirement can create a dilemma when considering whether to suspend a student from school. How does the vice-principal encourage and foster student learning when telling a student to stay away from school for a period of time?

On one hand, if a student's disruptive behavior is interfering with the learning of others in the classroom or school, then vice-principals have a pedagogical duty to protect the learning environment. This may necessitate the removal of this student from the classroom and, perhaps, the school for a temporary period for the wellbeing of all. The presence of a dangerous or disruptive student is certainly not conducive to learning by all students in the school. Similarly, consider students who have made a series of poor behavior choices for which suspension from school was clearly presented as a logical consequence for these choices. In such cases, a pedagogical argument could be made that these students must be suspended so that they learn to live with the logical consequences of their choices. This would be consistent with the view that student learning includes more than just the academic curriculum delivered in schools.

On the other hand, there are many pedagogical difficulties that arise when students are suspended. For example, school administrators in Indiana, in the context of a statewide focus on school accountability and higher academic standards, reported that students who were suspended for several days would often fall behind in class and fail their courses (Hupp, 2004). Furthermore, suspended students are more likely to feel alienated from school, which often leads to failure and eventual withdrawal from school (Smale, Burger, & da Costa, 2005). Crump (2003) reported on efforts by California school districts to keep students who misbehave in school by attempting to create a climate where students feel they belong and by offering them tools to deal with their behavior problems. Clearly, student alienation and academic failure are serious pedagogical drawbacks to the use of suspensions.

ETHICAL ISSUES

Ethical issues, which relate closely to pedagogical considerations, also figure in a vice-principal's decision to suspend a student. For example, the ethical standards for Ontario teachers define *Care* to include "compassion, acceptance, interest, and insight for developing students potential" (Ontario College of Teachers, 2006, p. 9). Similarly, the Code of Professional Conduct of the Alberta Teachers' Association includes this requirement: "A teacher treats pupils with dignity and respect and is considerate of their circumstances" (Alberta Teachers' Association, 2004, p. 10). The Code of Professional Conduct of the New Brunswick Teachers' Association (n.d.) includes the following statement of principle: "Teachers have regard for the dignity, liberty, and integrity of students under their supervision and endeavor to convey to students some understanding of their own worth." In all of these ethical statements, it is clear that the focus is on the wellbeing of individual students. Therefore, in addition to their statutory duty to maintain order and discipline for the benefit of the school community as a whole, vice-principals are also ethically obliged to consider the impact of a suspension on the individual student involved. The impact of a suspension from school may have pedagogical, social, emotional, or psychological implications for the student. All of these must be considered by vice-principals as part of their ethical responsibilities towards pupils.

PRACTICAL ISSUES

There are also a number of practical issues associated with student suspensions. In the short run, a vice-principal will make a classroom teacher happy if a disruptive student is sent away for several days. A short-term suspension for a few days can provide a cooling off period for the student and the teacher, especially if student-teacher conflict precipitated the suspension. Similarly, if two students were suspended for a fight at school, a day or two of suspension might be required so that the students, parents, and school officials can work to resolve the issues that led to the fight without exposing the school to further escalation of the conflict. Moreover, in comparison with other discipline measures, such as detention or counseling or in-school suspension, a traditional suspension demands fewer school resources, at least in the short term.

However, suspensions do come with practical drawbacks too. To start, they may not be particularly effective for some students. For those students who are academically unmotivated, a three-day suspension is a legally authorized three-day holiday from school. These students may view the suspension as a reward for bad behavior, hardly a deterrent to further misconduct. Once these students return from suspension, their teachers will likely have to provide assistance to help them get caught up with their missed work, placing an extra burden on teachers. A related disadvantage of suspensions is that they may worsen the alienation from school felt by some students. Teachers working to encourage and motivate these students may find that a period of suspension increases the alienation and undermines their previous efforts.

Another practical drawback for vice-principals in suspending students is the loss of parental support. While parents may be aware of their children's difficult behavior and may support school efforts to improve the behavior, they will normally prefer that schools find ways to deal with their children at school. Instead, when a vice-principal decides to suspend a student, parents are more likely to take an adversarial stance in opposition to the school and defend their children's behavior. The reasons for this reaction may range from legitimate concerns about their children's educational welfare to more selfish concerns about the inconvenience of providing supervision to their children during the school day. Regardless of the motivations, vice-principals must be prepared for parental resistance to suspensions. This resistance can escalate, especially in the American context, to legal challenges by parents, with all the attendant costs, complications, and consequences for vice-principals.

The overriding practical consideration for vice-principals in suspension decisions is that students do not lose their right to an education. Contrary to the wishes of many harried teachers and vice-principals, suspended students do not just disappear – eventually they come back! Keel (1998) pointed out that compulsory attendance laws not only require students to attend school to a specified age, they also require schools to provide an education for all students at least until they reach school-leaving age. For example, Section 8(1) of the Alberta *School Act* (2000) states that every student who meets age and citizenship requirements in a given school year "is entitled to have access in that school year to an education program in accordance with this Act." Indeed, even if an Alberta student is expelled by a school board following the required statutory processes, the board may expel a student from a school only if "the student has been offered another education program by the board" (s. 25[1][b]). While a suspension may provide a temporary reprieve for schools, vice-principals and other school officials must use the suspension period to come up with a suitable educational program for suspended students. This plan may include a costly specialized alternative program or simply a transfer to a different school.

A striking example of this arose recently in Britain. Halpin and Webster (2004) reported that the British government was preparing to require all schools, including its top grammar schools, to accept some very disruptive students. These were students who had been permanently excluded from their previous schools. Halpin and Webster cited concerns by then-Education Secretary Charles Clarke that too many such students were being concentrated into undesirable schools. Clarke commented that "all schools . . . should share a collective responsibility for ensuring that vulnerable, hard-to-place children . . . are admitted to a suitable school as quickly as possible." Since finding alternative educational programs for suspended students may be difficult and expensive for schools, vice-principals need to ensure that they have considered and tried as many alternatives to suspension as possible.

CREATIVITY AND THE USE OF ALTERNATIVE DISCIPLINARY MEASURES

But what does creativity have to do with an administrative task like student discipline? To begin with Marshall's (2005) insight, creativity and learning theory are both essentially about connection-making. Marshall, in a discussion about curricular integration, argued that creativity is similar to learning in that it too finds and makes unexpected connections between concepts and meanings. Let me demonstrate a small measure of creativity by comparing the work of two very different professionals: provincial court judges and high school vice-principals. In both settings, the decision-maker has to consider the appropriate response in cases of misconduct by an offender. Furthermore, the range and choice of sanctions available to the decision-maker may be greatly constrained. Moreover, the decision-maker needs to consider the rights and wellbeing of both the offender and any others affected by the decision. For both categories of decision-makers, there is a sanction that might be considered standard or traditional, particularly by outsiders: suspension for vice-principals and imprisonment for judges. It is interesting that the sentencing principles of federal law explicitly encourage the use of alternatives to imprisonment: "All available sanctions other than imprisonment that are reasonable in the circumstances should be considered for all offenders" (*Criminal Code*, 1985, s. 718.2[e]). The intent is that imprisonment be used a last resort in sentencing offenders and that all reasonable alternatives to imprisonment be considered when possible and available.

While education legislation typically does not contain such explicit use of alternatives to suspension, many school administrators and policy makers have argued that suspensions and expulsions are also supposed to be a last resort (Crump, 2003). For example, Crump reported on alternatives used in California districts such as mentoring teams, Saturday classes, and peer conflict resolution programs. Hupp (2004) listed alternatives used in Indiana such as cleaning bathroom walls, random drug tests, anger management counseling, community service projects, and court-ordered alternative programs. Districts experiencing soaring suspension and expulsion rates, often due to zero tolerance policies, have sought these types of disciplinary alternatives. For some students, the nature of their disruptive or violent conduct has led some jurisdictions to create alternative educational programs, often away from the normal school setting to allow for the removal of these students from regular classes and, at the same time, to provide them with an opportunity to receive a public education (e.g., Bickerstaff, Leon, & Hudson, 1998; Breunlin, Cimmarusti, Bryant-Edwards, & Hetherington, 2002; Carpenter-Aeby, Salloum, & Aeby, 2001). Reed and Himmler (1985) observed that vice-principals have two types of resources for dealing with student misconduct: formal organizational sanctions and personal presence. Their study found that vice-principals preferred to use their personal presence before applying organizational sanctions. The main reason for this choice was that most of their formal sanctions, such as parental involvement, extra assignments, and suspensions, were only moderately effective.

When vice-principals try to use alternatives to suspension, they may face obstacles. Of course, the presence of obstacles should not eliminate creative efforts. Indeed, Lindstrom (1997) identified perseverance as a key characteristic of any creative activity. He maintained that the ability to persevere develops through dealing with situations presenting both ambiguity and multiple solutions. Other characteristics of any creative activity listed by Lindstrom included trying new solutions by combining ideas in unexpected ways, considering the influence of the work and thoughts of others, and adopting a variety of perspectives for tasks and problems. The obstacles faced by vice-principals may include opposition from parents and students or even from teachers, other school personnel, district administrators, and trustees. For example, after-school detention, another long-standing practice in schools, was recently banned in Scotland after a high school student filed a lawsuit claiming that it was a violation of her human rights as described in the European Convention on Human Rights (Kelbie, 2003). Time out, another short-term option, also came under intense scrutiny by education officials in Minnesota after complaints from parents and special education activists (Stern, 2002). Corporal punishment, once a standard discipline tool in earlier centuries and decades, has fallen out of favor in many jurisdictions. In the Canadian context, many provinces and school boards had already outlawed the practice before the Supreme Court of Canada ruled that corporal punishment by teachers was unacceptable (*Canadian Foundation for Children, Youth and the Law v. Canada*, 2004).

RECENT STUDY FINDINGS

During the 2002-2003 school year, I conducted a study of high school vice-principals in Alberta, New Brunswick, and Ontario (Brien, 2004). One element of my study was to learn the extent to which existing laws and policies supported high school vice-principals in their use of alternatives to suspensions to deal with serious student misconduct. This topic was part of a larger study examining the effects of laws and policies on high school vice-principals in carrying out their responsibilities for student discipline. Responses to survey questions about alternatives to suspensions were received from 281 vice-principals in the three provinces.

Participants were asked to respond to three statements concerning alternatives to suspensions:

- *Apart from suspensions,* provincial law allows me enough disciplinary options to fulfill my level of responsibility for student discipline.

- *Apart from suspensions,* school district policies allow me enough disciplinary options to fulfill my level of responsibility for student discipline.

- *Apart from suspensions,* school policies allow me enough disciplinary options to fulfill my level of responsibility for student discipline.

Respondents were asked to indicate the extent to which they agreed with these statements using a standard Likert scale of responses: strongly disagree, disagree, not certain, agree, and strongly agree. Space was also provided on the questionnaire to encourage participants to provide written explanations for their choices. Their responses provided data that allowed for interprovincial comparisons and overall findings with respect to alternatives to suspensions as permitted by laws and policies at three levels of the school system.

In response to the first question, a majority of respondents in all three provinces agreed that provincial law allowed them enough disciplinary options apart from suspensions (72% overall), although there was less agreement from New Brunswick respondents (65%) compared to those in the other two provinces (73% ON, 72% AB). This difference was more pronounced in the responses to the second question about school district policies. While 76% of respondents agreed that policies at this intermediate level allowed them enough non-suspension alternatives, only 59% of New Brunswick vice-principals expressed agreement, compared to 84% and 77% agreement from Alberta and Ontario participants respectively. A statistical test known as chi-square performed on the data showed this difference to be statistically significant ($p < 0.05$). This result suggests that the difference in responses from New Brunswick has less than 5% probability of being due solely to chance. In other words, it appears that the differences can be attributed to variations in how vice-principals in the three provinces perceive the effects of district policies on their ability to use alternatives to suspensions. As one New Brunswick vice-principal commented: "The district level is where practice is disheartening. Administrators need to be permitted to administer. Instead, we are second-guessed and given directives on issues that should be the clear domain of the school." At the school level, overall agreement to the statement came from 77% of respondents, with similar levels of agreement for each province (83% AB, 76% ON, 73% NB). These results suggest that, at the school level, vice-principals are allowed and, perhaps, even encouraged to use their professional judgement and creativity to select and implement appropriate disciplinary sanctions in response to student misconduct.

For each of the survey questions described above, respondents were invited to offer explanatory comments for their responses. Respondents offered many comments on the topic of non-suspension disciplinary options. Examination of these comments uncovered the following themes:

- Vice-principals will attempt a variety of non-suspension alternatives.

- Suspension is often the only available disciplinary tool.

- Use of alternative disciplinary options is limited by lack of resources and external support.

- Their comments suggested the existence of both external and internal obstacles to using alternatives to suspensions.

Vice-principals reported that laws and policies generally do not mention any alternatives to suspensions. When they attempt alternative strategies, such as counselling, moral suasion, detention, in-school suspension, or community service, and students do not comply, then they have no choice but to impose suspensions as a last resort. Many respondents expressed frustration with the lack of resources to use in-school suspensions or even detentions. Budget cuts and collective agreement restrictions were cited as reasons for the lack of support programs or staff for alternative disciplinary options. Creative approaches such as school clean-up and other community service required the support and cooperation of parents, students, and even custodial unions. The following comments from respondents illustrated these concerns:

- We do feel, when it comes to district policy (maybe provincial), that we are very limited in our options apart from suspensions. I get the comment from parents often, "Isn't there anything else you can do?" (NB vice-principal)

- I feel the problem is not the policy but money. We have a policy concerning in-school suspension but no money to fund the program. As a result, students are suspended who might otherwise be placed in ISS [in-school suspension] for a week. (NB vice-principal)

- We basically have 3 tricks in our discipline bag . . . detention, in-school suspension, some might call it study hall, and suspension. That does not give much flexibility. I recently assigned a girl who had made a mess the task of cleaning the cafeteria and although her parents agreed, I was approached by the custodians' union that this girl was doing their job. Parents are often unwilling to accept any consequences for their child's actions and are frequently very critical. It is very difficult to deal with student discipline amidst all this adversity. I have no problem dealing with kids, but the adults often drive me nuts. (ON vice-principal)

- Disciplinary options – $$$ not enough. I am not a proponent of suspensions *but* sometimes this seems to be the only option – not enough school personnel – not enough support from Social Services – not enough parent support – most involve $$$. (NB vice-principal)

Without the necessary support and resources and in spite of the recognized drawbacks, vice-principals were often forced to use suspensions.

DISCUSSION AND CREATIVITY IMPLICATIONS

A common thread throughout their comments was that vice-principals would attempt to find disciplinary measures to protect the learning environment of their schools and also to meet the needs of individual students facing disciplinary action. This required a balancing of interests and priorities. A New Brunswick vice-principal expressed the following concern: "We are too timid in education to exclude students who persistently disrupt the education of others. We've gone too far in protecting individual rights." On the other hand, an Alberta vice-principal commented: "Always discipline students from the perspective of helping them to succeed!" Similarly, an Ontario vice-principal observed: "My philosophy always makes the student's growth the centre of the decision. Sometimes the hard line will inspire growth but sometime small adjustments with the soft touch will go much farther." These competing demands require vice-principals to have access to a range of educational and disciplinary options, but scarce resources and other obstacles often make these options unavailable.

However, external factors were not the only obstacle to the use of alternatives to suspensions; the comments from the survey respondents suggested that some internal reasons exist for not considering alternatives to suspensions A particularly important factor for respondents was lack of time. A common thread through the questionnaire responses from all three provinces was the heavy workloads of vice-principals. This would clearly affect their decision-making processes in disciplinary matters. Koru (1993) portrays vice-principals as exceptionally busy: always on their feet, walking around, maintaining visibility, working in reactive mode, constantly shifting gears, and frequently engaged in verbal encounters. Consider Marshall's (1985) description of busy vice-principals as "street level bureaucrats" forced to select which discipline problems to deal with seriously and which to ignore. Compare also Reed and Himmler's (1985) observation that "load on the system" was a significant factor in deciding the process used by vice-principals to remediate incidents of student misconduct. Reed and Himmler found that, on busy days, when vice-principals had many discipline and other problems to deal with at the same time, they would attempt to deal summarily with misconduct cases. Similarly, Paquette and Allison (1998) remarked that school administrators must work in *real time*, characterized by fractured, fragmented professional lives. As a result, according to Paquette and Allison, school administrators cannot subject all their decisions to the painstaking analysis of judicial workers.

But the internal limitations on the use of creative disciplinary measures go beyond time constraints. Considerations of fairness and consistency are important to any teacher, and especially to vice-principals, when making discipline decisions. Furthermore, in the increasingly litigious climate in which teachers and administrators work, creative choices in discipline sanctions may lead to accusations of unfairness and inconsistency. As pointed out earlier, school administrators are subject to the principles contained in the *Charter* when exercising their statutory duties. In particular, Section 15 of the *Charter* guarantees all persons equal benefit and equal protection of the law. Thus, if students receive different consequences for similar offenses, and if the severity of these consequences is *perceived* to be different, whether by the offenders, their parents, other students, teachers, or others, then vice-principals will face criticism and resistance in their efforts to administer discipline creatively. A recent Nova Scotia case illustrated the type of public criticism that school officials can face when suspension is expected but does not occur. As reported by the CBC ("Students call for suspension in choking case," 2006), a large group of students and parents staged a demonstration in front of their junior high school when a student accused of choking another student was not suspended. The protesters carried signs with slogans such as "fair rules for everyone" and described cases where other students had been suspended for allegedly less serious infractions. Recall the comparison made earlier in this chapter between vice-principals and provincial court judges. Just as suspension is the expected consequence for serious student offenses, often judges are similarly expected to impose jail terms for many offenses. In spite of the legislated expectation to consider a range of options, with imprisonment to be reserved only for the most serious cases, judges are regularly criticized by commentators and the public for choosing options such as conditional sentences instead of jail terms.

The alternative to creativity and choices of sanctions tailored to the specific needs associated with the situation and individuals involved is commonly referred to as the *zero tolerance* approach. While a full discussion of zero tolerance policy in student discipline is beyond the scope of this chapter, its emphasis on consistency, clarity, and certainty offers a definite appeal for vice-principals whose work context does not encourage creative decision-making. Indeed, Hawkins (1998) advocated a completely different approach from the use of creativity, preferring instead the use of precedent in a manner similar to that used by courts. He listed the advantages of the use of precedent in legal and administrative decision-making; these included ready access to a repertoire of accustomed ways of handling decisions, a device to make decision-making quicker and easier, and a refuge when the exercise of discretion was questioned. While precedent may be an appealing tool for efficiency and consistency in discipline matters, it contrasts sharply with the pedagogical and ethical commitments of educators to seek creative solutions to meet student needs.

There is no question that it is much easier to use the same consequences for all types of misconduct rather than trying to find creative solutions custom tailored to each student. The following comment by an Ontario vice-principal illustrated this point: "I am not a 'big fan' of suspensions! Counselling, mentoring, etc takes more time but is more effective in the long run. It is more work *not* to suspend." Some respondents claimed that suspension was their only disciplinary tool. Consider this comment from an Ontario vice-principal: "Suspension is really the only 'club' I hold over the students re discipline, without suspension I do not believe I could fulfill my level of responsibility." When lesser or intermediate sanctions such as detentions or in-school suspensions are not available, vice-principals can find themselves in a difficult situation when responding to student misconduct. A colleague of mine, a former vice-principal and now principal, used to tell our staff that he often felt that his only disciplinary options were "a tissue and a sledgehammer." Vice-principals will attempt to save the sledgehammer (suspension) for the most serious cases, but can only use the tissue (talking, counselling, persuasion) so many times before it loses its effectiveness. Indeed, even suspensions can lose their effectiveness for some students if vice-principals use them too frequently or too early in the intervention cycle with students. For this reason, it is important to develop an adequate range of disciplinary options to enable vice-principals to consider the full range of these options to respond to student misconduct within the legal and regulatory frameworks that govern our schools.

CONCLUSION

This chapter examined the use of creativity by high school vice-principals, particularly with respect to alternatives to suspensions. It began with a review of the legal responsibilities of educators, particularly high school vice-principals, for student discipline. They must deal with two complementary and, at times, conflicting obligations: the duty to protect the wellbeing of all students and, at the same time, the duty to protect the rights of individual students. Since the use of suspension is a well-established disciplinary tool of vice-principals, it was important to examine a range of factors that vice-principals must consider when making suspension decisions. Finally, this chapter reported the findings of a recent study concerning the extent to which existing laws and policies support the use of alternatives to suspensions. Respondent vice-principals from three Canadian provinces expressed the desire to use a variety of alternatives, but they also described a variety of impediments to their use. Examples from other jurisdictions suggest that effective and creative alternatives exist and can be used by vice-principals and others with the desire, ability, encouragement, and resources to do so.

References

Alberta Civil Liberties Research Centre. (1996). *Rights and responsibilities in Canada: Navigating through Alberta's schools.* Calgary, AB: Author.

Alberta Teachers' Association. (2004). *Teaching in Alberta A teacher education learning resource.* Edmonton, AB: Author.

Barger, B. E. (1999). A study of novice assistant principals: Dilemmas of working with discipline. *Dissertation Abstracts International, 59*(7), 2259A. (University Microfilms No. AAT 9841801)

Bezeau, L. M. (2007). *Educational administration for Canadian teachers* (7th ed.). Fredericton, NB: Author. Retrieved on June 2, 2006, from http://www.unb.ca/education/bezeau/eact/

Bickerstaff, S., Leon, S. H., & Hudson, J. G. (1998). Preserving the opportunity for education: Texas' alternative education programs for disruptive youth. *Education & Law Journal, 8*, 359-406.

Breunlin, D. C., Cimmarusti, R. A., Bryant-Edwards, T. L., & Hetherington, J. S. (2002). Conflict resolution training as an alternative to suspension for violent behavior. *Journal of Educational Research, 95*, 349-357.

Brien, K. (2004). *School discipline in a legal and regulatory environment: Perspectives of high school vice-principals.* Unpublished doctoral dissertation, University of Alberta, Edmonton, AB.

Canadian Charter of Rights and Freedoms, Part I of the *Constitution Act, 1982,* being Schedule B to the *Canada Act 1982* (U.K.), 1982, c. 11. Retrieved on June 2, 2006, from http://laws.justice.gc.ca/en/charter/index.html

Canadian Foundation for Children, Youth and the Law v. Canada (Attorney General), [2004] 1 S.C.R. 76, 2004 SCC 4 (CanLII). Retrieved on June 2, 2006, from http://www.canlii.org/ca/cas/scc/2004/2004scc4.html

Carpenter-Aeby, T., Salloum, M., & Aeby, V. G. (2001). A process evaluation of school social work services in a disciplinary alternative educational program. *Children & Schools, 23*(3), 171-181.

Conte, A. E. (2000). *In loco parentis:* Alive and well. *Education, 121*(1), 195-200.

Criminal Code, R.S.C. 1985, c. C-46. Retrieved on June 2, 2006, from http://laws.justice.gc.ca/en/C-46/index.html

Crump, G. (2003, Apr. 10). Discipline revisited: Seeking alternatives to suspension and expulsion, districts try to keep problem students in school. *The Sacramento Bee.* Retrieved on Sept. 16, 2007, from http://www.sacbee.com/content/news/v-print/story/6429438p-7381537c.html

DeMitchell, T. A. (2002). The duty to protect: Blackstone's doctrine of in *loco parents:* A lens for viewing the sexual abuse of students. *Brigham Young University Education & Law Journal, 2002*(1), 17-52.

Education Act, R.S.O. 1990, c. E.2. Retrieved on June 2, 2006, from http://www.canlii.org/on/laws/sta/e-2/20060412/whole.html

Education Act, S.N.B. 1997, c. E-1.12. Retrieved on June 2, 2006, from http://www.canlii.org/nb/laws/sta/e-1.12/20060412/whole.html

Education Act, S.S. 1995, c. E-0.2. Retrieved on June 12, 2006, from http://www.canlii.org/sk/laws/sta/e-0.2/20060412/whole.html

Giles, W. H. (1988). *Schools and students: Legal aspects of administration.* Toronto: Carswell.

Goss v. Lopez, 419 U.S. 565 (1975).

Gunn, J. (1994). Disruptive students from a school district perspective. In W. F. Foster (Ed.), *Education & law: Education in the era of individual rights* (pp. 60-66). Georgetown, ON: Canadian Association for the Practical Study of Law in Education.

Halpin, T., & Webster, P. (2004, Nov. 18). Top schools will be forced into taking unruly pupils. *The Times Online.* Retrieved on Sept. 16, 2007, from http://www.timesonline.co.uk/article/0,,2-1363731,00.html

Hawkins, K. (1998). Law and discretion: Exploring collective aspects of administrative decision-making. *Education & Law Journal, 8,* 139-160.

Hupp, S. (2004, Dec. 2). Moving beyond "zero tolerance." *The Indianapolis Star.* Retrieved on Sept. 16, 2007, from http://www.cyc-net.org/today2004/today041203.html

Keel, R. G. (1998). *Student rights and responsibilities: Attendance and discipline.* Toronto: Emond Montgomery.

Kelbie, P. (2003, Jan. 7). Classrooms ban detention after pupil cites human rights. *The Independent.* Retrieved on Sept. 16, 2007, from http://education.independent.co.uk/news/article138178.ece

Koru, J. M. (1993). The assistant principal: Crisis manager, custodian, or visionary? *NASSP Bulletin, 77*(556), 67-71.

La Forest, G. V. (1998). Off-duty conduct and the fiduciary obligations of teachers. *Education & Law Journal, 8,* 119-137.

Lindstrom, L. (1997). Integration, creativity, or communication? Paradigm shifts in Swedish art education. *Arts Education Policy Review, 99*(1), 17-24. Retrieved Nov. 16, 2005, from Academic Search Elite.

Lutes v. Prairie View School Division No. 74 (1992), 101 Sask. R. 232 (Q.B.).

Mackinnon, M. (1994). The disruptive student: School board perspective. In W. F. Foster (Ed.), *Education & law: Education in the era of individual rights* (pp. 67-85). Georgetown, ON: Canadian Association for the Practical Study of Law in Education.

Magsino, R. (1995). The family: Parents' and children's rights. In R. Ghosh & D. Ray (Eds.), *Social change and education in Canada* (3rd ed.) (pp. 290-309). Toronto: Harcourt Brace Canada.

Marshall, C. (1985). Professional shock: The enculturation of the assistant principal. *Education and Urban Society, 18,* 28-58.

Marshall, J. (2005). Connecting art, learning, and creativity: A case for curricular integration. *Studies in Art Education, 46*(3), 227-241. Retrieved Nov. 16, 2005, from Academic Search Premier.

Mertz, N. T., & McNeely, S. R. (1999, April). *Through the looking glass: An up front and personal look at the world of the assistant principal.* Paper presented at the Annual Meeting of the American Educational Research Association, Montreal, QC. (ERIC Document Reproduction Service No. ED 435 124)

New Brunswick Department of Education. (2001). *Policy 703: Positive learning environment.* Fredericton, NB: Author. Retrieved on Sept. 16, 2007, from http://www.gnb.ca/0000/pol/e/703A.pdf

New Brunswick Teachers' Association. (n.d.). *Code of professional conduct.* Fredericton, NB; Author. Retrieved on Sept. 17, 2007, from http://www.nbta.ca/code_of_ethics.html

Ontario College of Teachers. (2006). *Foundations of professional practice.* Toronto: Author. Retrieved on Sept. 10, 2007, from http://www.oct.ca/publications/PDF/foundation_e.pdf

Operation of Schools – General, R.R.O. 1990, Regulation 298. Retrieved on June 2, 2006, from http://www.canlii.org/on/laws/regu/1990r.298/20060412/whole.html

Paquette, J., & Allison, D. (1998). Decision-making and discretion: The agony and ecstasy of law and administration. *Education & Law Journal, 8,* 161-181.

R. v. M.(M.R.), [1998] 3 S.C.R. 393, 1998 CanLII 770 (S.C.C.). Retrieved on June 2, 2006, from http://www.canlii.org/ca/cas/scc/1998/1998scc84.html

Re Peel Board of Education and B. et al. (1987), 59 O.R. (2d) 654 (H.C.).

Reed, D. B., & Himmler, A. H. (1985). The work of the secondary assistant principalship: A field study. *Education and Urban Society, 18,* 59-84.

School Act, R.S.A. 2000, c. S-3. Retrieved on June 2, 2006, from http://www.canlii.org/ab/laws/sta/s-3/20060412/whole.html

School District No. 44 (North Vancouver) v. Jubran, 2005 BCCA 201 (CanLII). Retrieved on June 7, 2006, from http://www.canlii.org/bc/cas/bcca/2005/2005bcca201.html

School violence: Expulsions and the duty of fairness. (1994). *EduLaw for Canadian Schools, 6,* 1-2.

Smale, W. T., Burger, J., & da Costa, J. (2005). Early school leaving: Implications for school administrators. In H. D. Armstrong (Ed.), *Examining the practice of school administration in Canada* (pp. 421-460). Calgary, AB: Detselig.

Stern, S. (2002, Dec. 3). Timeout rooms under scrutiny. *The Christian Science Monitor.* Retrieved on Sept. 16, 2007, from http://www.csmonitor.com/2002/1203/p15s01-lecl.htm

Streshly, W. A., & Frase, L. E. (1992). *Avoiding legal hassles: What school administrators really need to know.* Newbury Park, CA: Corwin Press.

Students call for suspension in choking case. (2006, May 23). *CBC News*. Retrieved on Sept. 16, 2007, from http://www.cbc.ca/ns/story/ns-giusti20060523.html

Weller, L. D., & Weller, S. J. (2002). *The assistant principal: Essentials for effective school leadership*. Thousand Oaks, CA: Corwin Press.

Youth Criminal Justice Act, S.C. 2002, c. 1. Retrieved June 2, 2006, from http://laws.justice.gc.ca/en/Y-1.5/index.html

FIVE

DEVIANCE AND THE EARLY SCHOOL LEAVER

William Smale

Too often the concept of juvenile justice becomes confused with the system of courts, probation officers, social workers, detention centres, police officers, and those who devote special attention to the legal problems of the youth or our society. Juvenile justice, however, is better defined as *fair and reasonable treatment for all children.* The point to be made is not that these persons and institutions have failed, but every teacher must remember teachers are very much a part of the juvenile justice system. Indeed, teachers play a central role because they stand *in loco parentis.*

– Giles & Proudfoot (1994, p. 124)

This chapter explores young offenders' attitudes about early school leaving. The first section of this chapter provides an historical overview of the juvenile justice system in Canada in order to provide a basis for understanding the *Youth Criminal Justice Act* (YCJA). Understanding the students' world also requires an understanding of the justice system which governs their environment, a system that Giles and Proudfoot (1994) believe has relevance for teachers. The second section presents the findings in relation to the following research question: What demographic and crime-related factors, if any, contributed to the participants dropping out of high school? The findings are discussed in relation to a variety of theoretical and empirical research literature and perspectives. The name of the sponsoring institution has been changed for legal and ethical reasons, and any identifying information has been eliminated. Based on a summary of the results, I will conclude by indicating how these findings improve our awareness of the contextual circumstances surrounding the problem of drop-outs.

THE JUVENILE JUSTICE SYSTEM: AN HISTORICAL OVERVIEW

Before the nineteenth-century, Canada had no legal structure in place to deal with juvenile delinquency and children had few legal rights. Wayward adolescents were held accountable for their actions and subjected to the same, sometimes harsh punishments administered to adults. This approach to juvenile delinquency was based on the Crime Control Model, which emphasized societal protection and incarceration. This punitive resolution to delinquency was eventually replaced by a system perceived to be more suitable. The nineteenth-century was a period of changing perceptions about youth and delinquency: Juvenile courts were established, alternatives to incarceration were imposed, the roots of the modern youth probation system were laid down, reformatories were built, and laws were enacted to distinguish young offenders from adult offenders (Bala, 1997).

The *Juvenile Delinquents Act* (JDA), premised on positivist criminology, came into force in 1908 and offered a new perspective on youth crime and punishment. The view contended that adolescents were not criminals, but engaged in delinquent behavior because they came from the wrong side of the tracks. This view maintained that external forces affecting socialization, such as lack of parental care, discipline, education, and money, were to blame for deviancy, and that rehabilitation could be attained only through suitable governmental interventions (Bala, 1997). Thus, the JDA followed a philosophy promoting the use of informal legal procedures and indeterminate custodial dispositions to rehabilitate insufficiently socialized delinquents (Corrado, 1992).

The JDA's underlying and guiding philosophy was based upon the principle of child-welfare, often called *parens patriae*, a Latin term meaning "parent of the country," which implied a perception of the state as a kindly surrogate parent who dealt with the juvenile delinquent in a nonadversarial manner (Hartnagel & Baron, 1995; Milner, 1995; MSGCS, 1997). Under this welfare model, the state no longer dealt with delinquents as criminals, but as misdirected children requiring help, guidance, and proper supervision (MSGCS, 1997). The JDA received two main criticisms. First, the legal rights of young persons were often overlooked, particularly in minority, immigrant, urban poor, and other marginalized groups. Second, judges, police, probation officers, and other members of the juvenile justice system possessed significant discretionary powers that were reflected in every stage of the judicial process, but most obviously in the custodial setting (Bala, 1997). For example, authorities were allowed to incarcerate young persons for as long as authorities deemed necessary, irrespective of the type of crimes committed. Delinquents were released from custody only when they had reached adult status or demonstrated their apparent "rehabilitation" to correctional officials.

By the 1960s, the act was being examined and challenged on many fronts. The JDA had several opponents and critics, such as Lovekin's and McGrath's critiques in 1961 (see Hartnagel & Baron, 1995), due to its arbitrary, lenient, and informal nature. Public concern and controversy resulted in the federal government releasing a report entitled *Juvenile Delinquency in Canada*. This 1965 report initiated extensive discourse and progressive reform because of its faultfinding nature, but the *Young Offenders Act* (YOA) was not tabled in Parliament until 1981. Besides the federal government's report, another catalyst for change was the introduction of human rights for children. The *Canadian Charter of Rights and Freedoms* was proclaimed in 1982 and clearly contradicted the JDA. Lack of due process and rights for youths was inconsistent with Section 15(1) of the *Charter*, which states:

> Every individual is equal before and under the law and
> has the right to equal protection and equal benefit of
> the law without discrimination and, in particular,
> without discrimination based on race, national or
> ethnic origin, colour, religion, sex, age or mental or
> physical ability.

In 1984, the JDA was replaced by the federal YOA, which reflected the *Charter* and assumed that young persons were accountable for their behavior. The YOA was the federal government's conclusive resolution to twenty years of scholarly research, discussion and working papers, recommendations, concessions, and arduous negotiations. Moreover, this act was also a microcosm of the changing values and attitudes within Canadian culture towards young persons in trouble with the law, especially those convicted of violent offences (MSGCS, 1997). The new act, passed unanimously in the House of Commons, offered a different philosophy than that of the JDA (Hudson, Hornick, & Burrows, 1988). The YOA's guiding philosophy was based on a justice model of crime. This approach to youth justice was grounded on (a) the supposition that punishment should be consistent with the crime, and (b) the principle of natural justice (Corrado, 1992; MSGCS, 1997). Accordingly, the YOA was founded on the axioms of responsibility, accountability, and the protection of society (Bala & Lilles, 1982; Stauffer, 1981; Wilson, 1982). While still preserving the concept of *parens patriae*, the courts were now required to emphasize the legal rights of youths, from their initial contact with police to their final stages of appeal (Corrado, 1992; Schissel, 1993).

The YOA diverged considerably from the *parens patriae* orientation of the JDA by recognizing the constitutional and legal rights of young persons. The new YOA was intended to bring the youth justice system more in line with the criminal or adult justice system (Schissel, 1993). It was, according to Bala (1997), "clearly criminal law, not child-welfare legislation" (p. 34). The YOA's philosophy is outlined in Section 3(1), which explicates the following fundamental principles: (a) young people will be held accountable for their criminal behavior and will be charged for the same crimes as adults; however, they will not always be held accountable in the same way as adults; (b) to protect society, young persons may be supervised, disciplined, and controlled if they are found guilty of a criminal offense; (c) young persons have special needs because they may not be mature enough to fully understand the consequences of their actions; and as a result, they require guidance and assistance; (d) judicial proceedings should be avoided, and alternate measures imposed for those young persons who have committed crimes of a nonviolent nature; (e) young people are afforded the same rights and freedoms as adults and are entitled to the maintenance of their freedom consistent with the protection of society; and (f) young persons should be removed from their homes only when parental supervision is inappropriate or nonexistent.

By the late 1980s, few legalists, politicians, or community members had much faith in the act, and many were criticizing it for three main reasons. First, the maximum sentence for an indictable offense was only three years, which many considered inadequate for serious and violent crimes. Second, difficulties occurred in transferring youths to the adult court system where they would face stiffer sentences, or *dispositions*, as they are euphemistically called in the YOA. Third, access to information on young offenders was extremely restricted and confidential (Bala, 1997; Bala & Kirvan, 1991; Creechan & Silverman, 1995; Sampaio, 1996). The right to total protection of privacy for young persons was enshrined in the act, a stricture extended to all public and private organizations. In addition, Section 38 of the YOA prohibited the news media from publicly broadcasting or naming any victim, witness, or family member, as the young person could be identified by implication if the media did so. In 1992 and 1995, the governments of the day responded to the public concern and outcry by lengthening the maximum sentences to five and ten years, respectively (Bala, 1997). In addition, the 1995 amendments to Section 38 (1.13) provided for greater information sharing among professionals such as school officials and teachers (Alberta Education & Alberta Justice, 1996; Bala, 1997; Canadian School Boards Association, 1996).

The last attempt at overhauling the YOA was introduced in 1998, following more of the same criticisms noted above. On May 12th, 1998, the federal government announced plans to replace the fourteen year old controversial YOA with the *Youth Criminal Justice Act* (YCJA). Legislation was drafted to address five primary contextual factors: tougher treatment for extremely violent and repeat young offenders; alternatives to the court system for less serious and first-time offenders; increased public identification of those young offenders who have established a pattern of violent offenses or face adult sentences; less public financial support for those parents capable of paying their own legal costs; and a greater emphasis on crime prevention and early childhood intervention (Bindman & Bronskill, 1998; McIlroy & Feschuk, 1998; Mulawka, 1998). Like the *Criminal Code of Canada*, the YCJA is a federal statute dealing with criminal legislation; unlike the *Criminal Code*, the YCJA applies to young persons aged twelve to seventeen. Young persons under age twelve are not held criminally responsible for their actions; consequently, they are not prosecuted under the act but, instead, by child welfare legislation. A branch of the provincial government has responsibility for child welfare. The law of the land in Canada establishes a system of youth courts, procedures, and dispositions independent and distinct from the adult court system; nevertheless, the youth court system provides the same guarantees, rights, and freedoms as those granted to adults and holds youths responsible for their actions. Furthermore, because of their age and maturity level, young persons have broader rights not necessarily guaranteed to adults under the *Charter*. For example, young persons may have a lawyer present during bail, transfer, sentence, and disposition procedures (Cunningham & Griffiths, 1997).

The disposition phase of criminal proceedings is carried out uniformly by youth court judges across the country; however, substantial provincial variation exists in the administration of the act. For example, in some provinces, young persons aged twelve to fifteen appear in the family division of the provincial court while those aged sixteen to seventeen appear in its criminal division. Sanctions rendered by youth-court judges vary considerably depending on the nature and extent of the crime or crimes committed. The provisions set out in the YCJA allow for a full assessment of youths by the court. For the more serious offender, the judge may request a detailed psychiatric, medical, or psychological assessment which may include a predisposition report (PDR), pursuant to Sections 40 of the YCJA. The assessments noted above are designed to aid the courts in sentencing. Section 40(1) of the YCJA stipulates that "before imposing sentence on a young person found guilty of an offence, a youth justice court (a) shall, if it is required under this Act to consider a pre-sentence report before making an order or a sentence in respect of a young person," require the preparation of a pre-sentence report. According to Bala (1992), these assessments are not binding on the courts, but are frequently influential.

Although the YCJA emphasizes alternative measures for less serious offenders, those found guilty of violent crimes or otherwise perceived to be a risk to society are incarcerated in secure-custody facilities. Unlike the multilevel classification system for adults, the young offender secure custody system generally has only one designation: maximum security. The harshest and most intrusive disposition imposed by a youth-court judge is to order the young person into one of these institutions. The twelve participants of the present study fell into that group. All twelve participants had been referred by provincial youth-court judges to a term of secure custody and, in general, the youths represented a risk to either the community or themselves. Moreover, several of these youth had been identified as being chronically violent young offenders. Secure custody is intended as a last-ditch effort for transformation and rehabilitation; usually all other legal avenues and options have been exhausted.

Collective Characteristics of Participants

This section presents background information related to the participants in this study and is guided by the following research question: What demographic and criminal factors, if any, contributed to the young offenders' dropping out of high school? Various methods were employed to gather the data and are explained in this study in both aggregate and individual forms. Furthermore, many background characteristics of the participants are detailed below, and when practical, these are compared with national statistics.

The study group consisted of twelve male adolescents from a single secure-custody detention facility, all of whom had been sentenced in youth court. According to Statistics Canada (2000) data, 25 186 youths were placed in custody in 1998-1999, and about half of these young offenders were sentenced to a secure-custody detention facility. The institution selected for this study was governed and operated by the provincial government and was one of several young offender detention facilities located in the province. The correctional facility provided residential and educational programs for young offenders serving dispositions and for those who had been sentenced and were awaiting additional criminal charges. Residential programs at the correctional institution included alcoholics anonymous, victim awareness, drug and alcohol counseling, group counseling, individual drug-and alcohol-awareness counseling, social counseling, psychiatric assessment and counseling, independent life skills, seven steps society, anger management, and school. The educational program administered by the local board of education included a full complement of administrators, teachers, educational assistants, and support staff.

Other important background factors in relation to the respondent group of young offenders are compositional variables such as race and ethnicity. In the present study, "ethnic origin" refers to the "ethnic or cultural group(s) to which the respondent's ancestors belong" while "visible minority" refers to "persons, other than Aboriginal peoples, who are non-Caucasian in race or non-white in colour" (Statistics Canada, 2001a). According to Canadian census data for 1996, approximately one in three residents were of multiple ethnic origin, and one in nine was a member of a visible minority. The twelve participants in the present study generally reflected that racially and ethnically diverse ratio: nine were Caucasian, two were Black, and one was Oriental. Ethnic origin was coded from self-reports and institutional documents.

The North American literature suggested that ethnic minority groups, particularly students of Hispanic descent (e.g., Chicanos, Cubans, and Puerto Ricans), were more inclined than the general population to have higher dropout rates (e.g., Bean & Tienda, 1990; Ensminger & Slusarcik, 1992; McMillen, Kaufman, Hausken, & Bradby, 1993). Several scholars, including Rumberger (1987, 1995) and Steinberg, Blinde, and Chan (1984), reported that students from non-English speaking families were also at higher risk than other students for school failure. As well, research findings showed that schools with high concentrations of ethnic minority groups had significantly higher dropout rates than other schools (e.g., Fine, 1991; McNeal, 1997). However, few differences between ethnic groups exist once structural characteristics such as SES are accounted for (e.g., Alexander, Entwisle, Horsey, 1997; Frank, 1990; Kaufman & Bradby, 1992; McMillen et al., 1993; Rumberger, 1995).

Ethnic status also affects early school leaving in Canada. The literature indicated that a disproportionate number of Canadian students with ethnic ancestry are dropping out of mainstream secondary schools. Leaving the formal educational system is still the major obstacle to financial success for many Aboriginal (First Nations, Inuit and Métis) people in Canada. For instance, Jewison (1995) reported that approximately 76% of students residing in the Northwest Territories had dropped out of school before having received their secondary school diploma. Likewise, Employment and Immigration Canada (1990) noted that "dropout rates are particularly high among native youth (as high as 70 per cent in some areas)" (p. 10). This is an astounding statistic and suggests that a severe problem exists within this section of the population. Several other Canadian studies have reported similar findings (e.g., Anisef & Johnson, 1993; Brady, 1996; Gilbert, Barr, Clark, Blue, & Sunter, 1993; Hollander & Bush, 1996).

Before incarceration, all twelve participants had lived in Canadian urban centres. The research literature concerning geographical location and early school leaving is mixed: some evidence suggested, but did not conclusively demonstrate, that early school leaving may be linked to urban populations (e.g., Brennan & Anderson, 1990; DeYoung, 1994; Ekstrom, Goertz, Pollack, & Rock 1986; Figueira-McDonough, 1993; Rumberger & Larson, 1998), while opposing arguments noted that rural populations may place less emphasis on high school completion (e.g., Gilbert et al., 1993; Sullivan, 1988). However, Butlin (1999), relying on the SLF (1995) data, found that high school graduates from urban areas were far more likely compared to rural graduates to attend a postsecondary institution. Moreover, all twelve participants were single; only one participant had a child. Finally, the first language of all participants was English, and eleven of the twelve youths held Canadian citizenship. The findings from this study approach national census figures for 1996. For example, in Canada, approximately eight in ten residents had English or French as their mother tongue. In the present study, *mother tongue* refers to the "first language learned at home in childhood and still understood by the individual at the time of the census" (Statistics Canada, 2001b).

The following describes the family background characteristics and structural information of each participant. These data were derived exclusively from interview conversations. When interviewed, the participants ranged in chronological age from seventeen to nineteen years old; therefore, the study focused on the developmental stage of late adolescence to early adulthood. The mean age of the correctional facility young offenders – seventeen – generally mirrored that of the respondent group. Although just less than half of the participants were eighteen, they were still considered young offenders because their offenses had been committed as youths. According to Bala (1997), the date for establishing offender jurisdiction is the date the criminal act was committed. For example, if a person is approaching eighteen at the time of arrest and subsequently attends court after his or her birthday, the full disposition could be dealt with under the YCJA. However, once a young offender attains the age of eighteen, the courts have legal authority to direct that person to serve the remaining portion of his or her sentence in a correctional facility for adults. Amendments to the youth justice system over the last ten years have cleared the way for transferring youths, especially violent youths, to the adult system where they face longer dispositions and potential public identification. When interviewed, no participants in the present study had been scheduled for transfer proceedings.

Not surprisingly, all twelve participants had experienced school problems (e.g., truancy, low achievement, suspensions, expulsions, and early withdrawal). Slightly more than half of the participants had not completed grade nine before incarceration. Only five of the twelve participants had completed at least their first year of high school before dropping out. The dropout rates for this study are much higher than those reported in national census data. For example, in 1991, 3.8% of Canadian individuals aged fifteen to twenty-four had less than grade nine (Guppy & Davies, 1998), and, in 1996, 79% of young people between the ages of fifteen to nineteen declared themselves as full-time students. However, the findings from the School Leavers Survey (SLS, 1991) confirmed the trend reported in this study. The results of the national SLS study noted that almost one out of three school leavers had obtained only grade nine or less before prematurely leaving (Gilbert et al., 1993). Similarly, Gastright and Ahmad (1988), using data from a large American urban district, reported that 55% of the school districts' early school leavers had left high school before they had completed grade ten.

The data concerning the number of children in the participants' families revealed a wide distribution. Eleven participants reported at least one sibling, the range of the total cohort being from zero to ten-plus siblings. The respondent group had, on average, four siblings; however, several families were characterized by both half-siblings and step-siblings. For single-parent families in Canada, the 1998 average of 1.5 siblings does not approximate this study's findings (Statistics Canada, 2001c).

The proportion of family breakups among the participants' natural parents was considerably higher than it is among the general population. An astonishing eleven of the twelve early school leavers in the present study came from "broken" homes, although several participants had lived in blended families before being arrested. Using a qualitative approach, Okey and Cusick's (1995) study of twelve school dropouts confirmed the trend reported in this study. Their results revealed that only six of the twelve dropouts came from intact nuclear families (i.e., a social group consisting of both natural or biological parents). Considering that 84.2% of Canadian children live in two-parent families (Ross, Scott, & Kelly, 1996b), these rates are exceptional. The family structure of the participants' natural parents included four nominal level categories: married, never married, separated, and divorced. Six participants came from households characterized by divorce, three said that their natural parents were never married, two said that their parents were separated, while only one participant came from an intact nuclear family.

Besides the status of lone parent, the general familial pattern was that of common-law marriage, remarriage, and multiple marriages. Six participants came from homes marked by one-parent families, three came from homes marked by common-law arrangements, two came from homes marked by either remarriage or reconstituted families, while one participant lived in a traditional nuclear family. The figures noted above are much higher than those based on Canadian census data. For instance, in Canada it was reported that in 1996, one in seven families in private households were single-parent families (Statistics Canada, 2001d).

In general, children from single-parent families or children living independently are more likely to leave school early compared to children living in duel-parent families. For example, Sunter (1993), relying on data from the SLS (1991) study, noted that youths living independently were more than twice as likely to have dropped out of school as compared with their non-dropout counterparts. In a longitudinal study, Wright (1985) concluded that students living in dual-parent families were more likely to graduate from high school than their one-parent counterparts, father-only living arrangements being worse than mother-only. Finally, those students living without a parent or in a group home were least likely to graduate from school. Within the Canadian context, Radwanski (1987) further emphasized the importance of family structure in the dropout equation, pointing out that "young people from single-parent households are considerably more likely to drop out than those from homes in which both parents are present" (p. 74). Many other studies also provided valuable discussions regarding the association between family structure and early school leaving (e.g., Astone & McLanahan, 1991; Edmonton Public School Board, 1996; Gilbert et al., 1993; Gilbert & Orok, 1993).

The participants in the present study were also asked about their most recent living arrangements. Just under half of the participants had lived without a parent before incarceration. For discussion purposes, the informants' responses were grouped into four nominal level categories: living with the natural mother, living with the natural father, living with both natural parents, or living independently. Approximately two-thirds of the participants interviewed in the present study were either living in single-parent households or living independently before incarceration. Four of the five oldest participants had been residing with a parent. Furthermore, five participants had lived independently, and only one participant had lived in a traditional intact nuclear family. Participants in the present study differed noticeably during the early years of their lives from the general profile of children eleven years old and under in Canada. Data from the SLS (1991) study revealed that, respectively, only 15% and 7% of the population had lived in single-parent and no-parent families (Gilbert et al., 1993).

Most of the participants in the present study had been raised in single-parent families because of either separation, divorce, abandonment, or the death of a parent. Recent studies suggested that short-term social consequences of single-parent families included high rates of poverty and government subsidies such as welfare (e.g., Mitchell, 1991; Peng & Lee, 1993; Ross et al., 1996a; Shiono & Quinn, 1994; Vickers, 1994). Moreover, the long-term consequences of divorce and separation included higher rates of psychological, emotional, and behavioral problems (e.g., Astone & McLanahan, 1991; Driedger, 1998; Offord & Lipman, 1996; Ross, Roberts, & Scott, 1998; Shiono & Quinn, 1994), including higher rates of early school leaving (e.g., Gilbert & Orok, 1993; Goldschmidt & Wang, 1999; McLanahan & Sandefur, 1994). Furthermore, adolescents who have experienced family disruption through either separation or divorce are more likely than other youths to use drugs (e.g., Garnier, Stein, & Jacobs, 1997; Turner, Irwin, & Millstein, 1991), have health problems (e.g., Ross et al., 1998), and become involved with the youth justice system (e.g., Matsueda & Heimer, 1987; Sampson, 1987; Saner & Ellickson, 1996). The findings from the present study support those of the above literature. In identifying the reasons for leaving school early, family structure is an obvious consideration. The accumulated research literature clearly supported the notion that youths from structurally disadvantaged families (i.e., single-parent families) may be at greater risk for delinquency, school failure, and other social pathologies.

The following provides specific information concerning educational attainment, employment status, and household income of the participants' parents. This analysis was prompted by Ross et al. (1996b), who suggested that the important characteristics in determining the wellbeing of Canadian children included "household income and parents' labour-market status and education" (p. 32). The analysis concentrated on five general categories, including (a) natural mother's educational attainment, (b) natural father's educational attainment, (c) natural mother's employment status, (d) natural father's employment status, and (e) household income. For discussion purposes, all five categories were aggregated into one measure termed *family social status.*

In general, both parental education and household income were reported to be relatively low for the participants' families. The median level of education for the participants' parents was Grade 10.5. The parents' educational attainment was divided into three broad categories: school dropouts, high-school graduates, and postsecondary credentials.

When the participants were interviewed, most of their natural parents had not completed high school. Disaggregating the data reveals that three out of twenty-four parents had educational levels ranging between grade two and grade eight. Furthermore, thirteen of the twenty-four parents had educational levels ranging between grade nine and eleven; the remaining eight parents had educational levels ranging between grade twelve and university. This study's findings parallel research results of other studies. For example, Okey and Cusick (1995), who qualitatively studied the family context of twelve school dropouts, reported that fifteen of the twenty-four natural parents had not graduated from high school.

Some evidence in the literature suggested that the children of parents with a low level of education are more apt than other children to leave school early. For example, Radwanski (1987) emphasized this point: "The lower the level, occupational status and level of education of his/her parents, the greater is the statistical risk that any given student will not complete school" (p. 71). More recently, Goldschmidt and Wang's (1999) study relying on the database of the 1988 National Educational Longitudinal Study found evidence that parents' lack of education was highly correlated with the propensity of their child to drop out of school. Numerous other cross-sectional and longitudinal research-based studies have also shown a consistent relationship between low parental educational attainment and adolescent school leaving (e.g., Edmonton Public School Board, 1996; Gilbert & Orok, 1993; Janosz, Leblanc, Boulerice, & Tremblay, 1997; Okey & Cusick, 1995; Tanner, Krahn, & Hartnagel, 1995). Conversely, empirical evidence pointed to a nexus between highly educated parents and positive academic outcomes of offspring. For instance, de Brouker and Lavallée (1998), drawing on data from the International Adult Literacy Survey (IALS) for Canada conducted among 5 660 individuals in 1994, found that "young adults aged 26 to 35 whose parents did not complete high school have one less year of schooling than those whose parents graduated from high school" (p. 26). Other research also suggested a connection between parental educational attainment, particularly maternal educational attainment, and academic outcomes of children (e.g., Haveman & Wolfe, 1995; Spencer, Cole, DuPree, Glymph, & Pierre, 1993). Indeed, the literature also reported a relationship between parental involvement with their offspring's education and dropping out (e.g., Delgado-Gaitan, 1988; Ekstrom et al., 1986; Rumberger, Ghatak, Poulos, Ritter, & Dornbusch, 1990), particularly when this involvement did not include checking homework by the parent (Goldschmidt & Wang, 1999). Furthermore, research showed that children from homes where parental educational attainment was low or a low priority were more likely than other youths to become involved with the youth justice system (e.g., Figueira-McDonough, 1993; Jenkins, 1995; Saner & Ellickson, 1996).

The following analysis provides specific information concerning parents' employment status. Participants were asked in an open-ended manner to indicate their parents' current employment status. These data were then coded as either blue-collar, white-collar, or welfare. The findings reveal that four out of twenty-four parents were employed in white-collar occupations, twelve in blue-collar occupations, and eight were sustained by government assistance such as welfare. (According to Ross et al. (1996b), approximately 10% of Canadian children live in homes where welfare is the primary source of income.) As well, the literature has shown a consistent relationship between adolescent school leaving and parental occupational status (e.g., Gilbert & Orok, 1993; Okey & Cusick, 1995). Unfortunately, the cross-sectional research design of the present study is rather problematic in determining generational patterns. Future longitudinal studies designed to explore this area systematically would be useful.

As a crude indicator, the participants were also asked to rate their families' income level. Since this marker or guide may have missed other relevant financial information, caution must be exercised when interpreting the data. In a similar vein, Duncan, Brooks-Gunn, and Klebanov (1994) commented that "parental incomes are neither reported reliably by adolescents nor recalled reliably by retrospective studies" (p. 287). Nonetheless, this proxy measure is generally accepted by researchers in both qualitative and quantitative studies (Huston, McLoyd, & Garcia Coll, 1994). The families' household incomes were coded into three ordinal scaled categories: low, medium, and high household incomes. Five of the respondents described their parents' income as being in the medium range. The remaining seven participants considered their family's income to be low, while no participants reported a high household income. This study's findings agree with several recent reports stating that low household income is a predictor of early school leaving. For example, Okey and Cusick (1995), who studied the family context of twelve early school leavers, reported that ten participants had come from homes characterized by low incomes. (The findings of the NLSCY (1996) reported that a total of 24.6% of

Canadian children aged eleven years and under came from homes classified as "poor" (Ross et al., 1996b).) It may be cautiously concluded that only a small portion of the families in the present study had obtained financial independence. These findings are not surprising given that the overwhelming majority of the parents were neither supplemented by a second income nor had a high-school education.

While not unequivocal, the weight of the evidence from this research supports the literature's assertions that children from lower-income and poor families were more likely to have had educational difficulties (e.g., Gilbert et al., 1993; Lipps & Frank, 1997; Ross et al., 1996b) and to have dropped out of school (e.g., Bryk & Thum, 1989; Gilbert et al., 1993; Ross et al., 1996a; Vickers, 1994). On the other hand, empirical evidence pointed to a nexus between high SES families and postsecondary participation of offspring (e.g., Fournier, Butlin, & Giles, 1995; Looker, 1997; McGrath, 1996). Several other research-based studies have shown a strong correlation between low SES and delinquency (e.g., Farrington et al., 1990; Figueira-McDonough, 1993; Sampson & Laub, 1993). To some extent, the findings noted above parallel those of the present study. Clearly, research evidence underscored the connection between low family social status and parental educational attainment.

What follows describes the recidivism and the offending patterns of the respondent group. To investigate these issues, five indicators were examined: (a) offenders who were twelve to fifteen years old (Phase One), (b) number of previous convictions, (c) previous convictions for violence, (d) current convictions for violence, and (e) previous terms of detention. These data were derived from interviews with the participants and institutional documents. Most of the participants in the present study were recidivists with lengthy criminal records. In general, evidence in the literature suggested that youths with extensive criminal records were more likely than other offenders to reoffend in the future (e.g., Maguire, Flanagan, & Thornberry, 1988; Visher, Lattimore, & Linster, 1991). According to Statistics Canada (2000) data, "forty-two percent of young offenders sentenced in 1998/99 were considered recidivists." Although few federal recidivism studies have been conducted to date, provincial ministries have been the forerunners of such research, reporting rates from 44% to 82% (e.g., Leschied, Andrews, & Hoge, 1992; Sampaio, 1996).

Eleven participants in the present study had criminal records dating from Phase One convictions. Moreover, an extensive and longstanding body of literature has consistently documented that early delinquent behavior is a good predictor of later adult criminal behavior (Kandel et al., 1988; Loeber & Stouthamer-Loeber, 1987; White, Moffitt, & Silva, 1989). Furthermore, eight of the twelve participants had a record of multiple convictions, the average convictions among the group being approximately six each. Additionally, five of this study's participants had been classified as "chronic offenders." Research centering on chronic offending has routinely operationalized this term to mean six or more arrests (e.g., Loeber & Farrington, 1998).

Loeber and Farrington (1997), relying on several studies (i.e., Farrington & West, 1993; Huizinga, Loeber, & Thornberry, 1995; Wolfgang, Figlio, & Sellin, 1972), noted that "a minority of 'chronic' offenders account for a large proportion of all offenses" (p. 129). Likewise, Bala (1997), noted that "a relatively small portion of all adolescents are within the latter group of more serious, repeat offenders, but they are," he elaborated, "responsible for a disproportionately large amount of violent offences" (p. 18). Eleven of the twelve participants in this study had been convicted of at least one violent crime (i.e., armed robbery, assault, attempted murder, burglary with injury), and eight participants had a prior history of detention. It should be noted that the expression *previous term of detention* includes both open and secure custody. Predictably, a solid body of research evidence has shown that dropping out of school is linked to increased rates of juvenile delinquency (e.g., Binkley & Hooper, 1989; Fagan & Pabon, 1990; Janosz et al., 1997; Okey & Cusick, 1995; Stedman, Salganik, & Celebuski, 1988).

The following discussion indicates the primary reasons for the incarceration of the members of the respondent group. The findings revealed that 75% of the participants had been charged with multiple offenses. These data were derived exclusively from institutional records and were classified into a nominal level of measurement. The participants' current convictions are presented in order of prevalence and include eight categories reflecting a broad range of *Criminal Code* offenses. The following summarizes the aggregate of specific crimes committed by the participants: armed robbery (usually with a handgun or knife), fourteen convictions; theft under $5 000, nine convictions; breaking and entering, five convictions; wearing a disguise in the commission of an offense, four convictions; aggravated assault, three convictions; escaping custody and being unlawfully at large (UAL), three convictions; motor vehicle theft, two convictions; and other miscellaneous convictions such as accessory after the fact, highway traffic violations, and careless use of a firearm, five convictions.

The following provides specific information concerning the participants' criminal histories. The findings focus on five broad categories of crime: (a) sexual assault, (b) physical assault, (c) assault on an authority figure, (d), weapon use, and (e) escapes. The young offenders' criminal histories included not only previous offenses, but also most recent summary and indictable offenses. These data were gathered from two sources, including interviews with the participants and institutional documents. No participants had engaged in extrafamilial or intrafamilial sexual assault; however, two-thirds of the participants indicated a prior history of physical assault and aggression towards others. Not surprisingly, developmental studies of delinquency suggested a strong connection between physical aggression during childhood and subsequent violent and antisocial behavior (e.g., Haapasalo & Tremblay, 1994; Loeber, 1988; Moffitt, 1993; Stattin & Magnusson, 1989). In the present study, *antisocial behavior* means aggressive and delinquent behavior against societal norms (Loeber & Farrington, 1997; Stoff, Breiling, & Maser, 1997). Moreover, Hinshaw and Zupan (1997) noted that from a legal perspective, antisocial behavior is often called delinquency.

Institutional documents revealed that two of this study's participants had a history of assaultive behavior towards authority figures. Ten of the twelve participants had criminal histories involving weapons convictions, several of which involved knives, high-calibre handguns, handguns with large ammunition capacities, and other types of firearms. Weapon use was reported to be most prevalent in more serious offenses (indictable offenses) such as store robberies. Additionally, four of the twelve participants had escaped, or attempted to escape, while in custody. Finally, the literature generally supported the suggestion that both assaultive behavior towards authority figures and escaping custody may be clear indicators of both future subsequent aggression towards others and recidivism (e.g., Leschied et al., 1992).

Summary and Conclusion

The juvenile justice system in Canada retains many dispositional practices of the past. Custody appears to be the first option available for young persons found guilty of violent crimes or otherwise perceived to be a risk to the community. The harshest disposition that the courts can hand down is placement in a secure-custody detention facility. All participants in the present study fell into that category. The findings showed the respondent group was serving approximately thirteen months secure custody, approximately three times higher than the Canadian national average. Most of the participants were recidivists with lengthy criminal records dating from convictions obtained in their early teens. Slightly more than one-half reported that they came from low-income families, and break-ups between their natural parents were extremely common. Most of the participants reported living independently, and all had either dropped out of or been expelled from school.

This research represents another step in understanding the process of early school leaving. The study revealed the specific traits and perceptions of twelve young-offender dropouts. Hopefully, the findings from this study may help inform policy makers, teachers, and school administrators about the dropout problem in general. Specifically, the findings may assist these individuals in dealing with this unique subgroup of the dropout population. By establishing awareness of a specific group of dropouts and encouraging questions about our current theory and practice, I hope that this study may lead to solutions in future studies to the problem of early school leaving.

References

Alberta Education & Alberta Justice. (1996). *Young offender information sharing protocol.* Edmonton, AB: Author.

Alexander, K.L., Entwisle, D.R., & Horsey, C.S. (1997). From first grade forward: Early foundations of high school dropout. *Sociology of Education, 70*(2), 87-107.

Anisef, P., & Johnson, L. (1993). *The young adult learner: Fifteen to eighteen year old students in the Ontario English-language school system* (Vol. 1-2). Toronto: Queen's Printer for Ontario.

Astone, N.M., & McLanahan, S.S. (1991). Family structure, parental practices and high school completion. *American Sociological Review, 56*(3), 309-320.

Bala, N. (1992). The young offender act: The legal structure. In R.R. Corrado, N. Bala, R. Linden, & M. LeBlanc (Eds.), *Juvenile justice in Canada: A theoretical and analytical assessment* (pp. 20-73). Toronto: Butterworths.

Bala, N. (1997). *Essentials of Canadian law: Young offenders law.* Concord, ON: Irwin Law.

Bala, N., & Kirvan, M.A. (1991). The statute: Its principles and provisions and their interpretation by the courts. In A.W. Leschied, P.G. Jaffe, & W. Willis (Eds.), *The Young Offender's Act: A revolution in Canadian juvenile justice* (pp. 71-113). Toronto: University of Toronto Press.

Bala, N., & Lilles, H. (1982). *The young offenders act annotated.* Ottawa, ON: Solicitor General of Canada.

Bean, F., & Tienda, M. (1990). *The Hispanic population of the United States.* New York: Sage.

Bindman, S., & Bronskill, J. (1998, May 12). Ottawa maps changes to youth justice system: McLellan to scrap Young Offenders Act. *The Edmonton Journal,* p. A3.

Binkley, E.M., & Hooper, R.W. (1989). *Statistical profiles of students who dropped out of high school during the school year 1987-1988.* Nashville, TN: Davidson County Metropolitan Public Schools. (ERIC Document Reproduction Service No. ED 311 575)

Butlin, G. (1999). Determinants of postsecondary participation. (Statistics Canada, Catalogue No. 81-003-XIB-Quarterly). *Education Quarterly Review, 5*(3), 9-35.

Brady, P. (1996). Native dropouts and non-Native dropouts in Canada: Two solitudes or a solitude shared? *Journal of American Indian Education, 35*(2), 10-20.

Brennan, T., & Anderson, F. (1990). *A longitudinal study of factors producing high school dropout among handicapped and non-handicapped students.* Nederland, CO: Institutional Development and Economic Affairs Service. (ERIC Document Reproduction Service No. ED 334 762)

Bryk, A.S., & Thum, Y.M. (1989). The effects of high school organization on dropping out: An exploratory investigation. *American Educational Research Journal, 26*(3), 353-383.

Canadian Charter of Rights and Freedoms, Part I of the *Constitution Act, 1982*, being Schedule B to the *Canada Act 1982* (U.K.), 1982, c. 11. Retrieved on Apr. 10, 2006, from http://laws.justice.gc.ca/en/charter/index.html

Canadian School Boards Association. (1996). *Protocol and guidelines information sharing between school officials and young offenders personnel.* Ottawa, ON: Author.

Corrado, R.R. (1992). Introduction. In R.R. Corrado, N. Bala, R. Linden, & M. LeBlanc (Eds.), *Juvenile justice in Canada: A theoretical and analytical assessment* (pp. 1-20). Toronto: Butterworths.

Creechan, J.H., & Silverman, R.A. (1995). *Canadian delinquency.* Scarborough, ON: Prentice-Hall Canada Inc.

Cunningham, A.H., & Griffiths, C.T. (1997). *Canadian criminal justice: A primer.* Toronto: Harcourt Brace & Company.

de Brouker, P., & Lavallée, E. (1998). Getting ahead in life: Does your parents' education count. (Statistics Canada, Catalogue No. 81-003-XIB-Quarterly). *Education Quarterly Review, 5*(1), 34-40.

Delgado-Gaitan, C. (1988). The value of conformity: Learning to stay in school. *Anthropology and Education Quarterly, 19*(4), 354-381.

DeYoung, A.J. (1994). Children at risk in America's rural schools: Economic and cultural dimensions. In R.J. Rossi (Ed.), *Schools and students at risk: Context and framework for positive change* (pp. 229-251). New York: Teachers College Press.

Driedger, S.D. (1998, April 20). After divorce. *Maclean's: Canada's Weekly Newsmagazine, 111*(16), 39-43.

Duncan, G.J., Brooks-Gunn, J., & Klebanov, P.K. (1994). Economic deprivation and early childhood development. *Child Development, 65*(2), 296-318.

Edmonton Public Schools. (1996). *Early school leavers longitudinal study*: 1995. Edmonton, AB: Author.

Ekstrom, R.B., Goertz, M.E., Pollack, J.M., & Rock, D.A. (1986). Who drops out of high school and why? Findings from a national study. *Teachers College Record, 87*(3), 356-373.

Employment and Immigration Canada. (1990). *A national stay-in-school initiative.* Ottawa, ON: Ministry of Supply and Services Canada.

Ensminger, M.E., & Slusarcick, A.L. (1992). Paths to high school graduation or dropout: A longitudinal study of a first grade cohort. *Sociology of Education, 65*(2), 95-113.

Fagan, J., & Pabon, E. (1990). Contributions of delinquency and substance use to school dropout among inner-city youths. *Youth & Society, 21*(3), 306-354.

Farrington, D.P., Loeber, R., Elliott, D.S., Hawkins, J.D., Kandel, D.B., Klein, M.W., McCord, J., Rowe, D.C., & Tremblay, R.E. (1990). Advancing knowledge about the onset of delinquency and crime. In B.B. Lahey & A.E. Kazdin (Eds.), *Advances in clinical child psychology* (Vol. 13, pp. 283-342). New York: Plenum Press.

Fernandez, R.M., Paulsen, R., & Hirano-Nakanishi, M. (1989). Dropping out among Hispanic youth. *Social Science Research*, 18(1), 21-52.

Figueira-McDonough, J. (1993). Residence, dropping out, and delinquency rates. *Deviant Behavior, 14*(3), 109-132.

Fine, M. (1991). *Framing dropouts: Notes on the politics of an urban public high school.* Albany, NY: Sunny Press.

Fournier, E., Butlin, G., & Giles, P. (1995). Intergenerational change in the education of Canadians. (Statistics Canada, Catalogue No. 81-003- XPB). *Education Quarterly Review, 2*(2), 22-32.

Frank, J.R. (1990). High school dropout: A new look at family variables. *Social Work in Education, 13*(1), 34-47.

Garnier, H.E., Stein, J.A., & Jacobs, J.K. (1997). The process of dropping out of high school: A 19-year perspective. *American Educational Research Journal, 34*(2), 395-419.

Gastright, J.F., & Ahmad, Z. (1988). *Dropout causes and characteristics: Do local findings confirm national data?* Paper presented at the annual meeting of the American Educational Research Association, New Orleans, LA. (ERIC Document Reproduction Services No. ED 293 968)

Gilbert, S., Barr, W., Clark, M., Blue, M., & Sunter, D. (1993). *Leaving school: Results from a national survey comparing school leavers and high school graduates 18 to 20 years of age.* Ottawa: ON. Statistics Canada and Human Resources and Labour Canada.

Gilbert, S., & Orok, B. (1993). School leavers. (Statistics Canada, Catalogue No. 11-008E). *Canadian Social Trends*, (Autumn), 8-12.

Giles, T.E., & Proudfoot, A.J. (1994). *Educational administration in Canada* (5th ed.). Calgary, AB: Detselig Enterprises Ltd.

Goldschmidt, P., & Wang, J. (1999). When can schools affect dropout behavior? A longitudinal multilevel analysis. *American Educational Research Journal, 36*(4), 715-738.

Guppy, N., & Davies, S. (1998). *Education in Canada: Recent trends and future challenges.* (Statistics Canada, Catalogue No. 96-321-MPE No. 3). Ottawa, ON: Minister of Industry.

Haapasalo, J., & Tremblay, R.E. (1994). Physically aggressive boys from age 6 to 12: Family background, parenting behavior, and prediction of delinquency. *Journal of Consulting and Clinical Psychology, 62*(5), 1044-1052.

Hartnagel, T.F., & Baron, S.W. (1995). "It's time to get serious": Public attitudes toward juvenile justice in Canada. In J.H. Creechan & R.A. Silverman (Eds.), *Canadian delinquency* (pp. 47-59). Scarborough, ON: Prentice-Hall Canada Inc.

Haveman, R., & Wolfe, B. (1995). The determinants of children's attainments: A review of methods and findings. *Journal of Economic Literature, 33*(4), 1855-1857.

Hinshaw, S.P., & Zupan, B.A. (1997). Assessment of antisocial behavior in children and adolescents. In D.M. Stoff, J. Breiling, & J.D. Maser (Eds.), *Handbook of antisocial behavior* (pp. 36-50). New York: John Wiley & Sons, Inc.

Hollander, J., & Brush, B. (1996). Improving Grade 9 Native students' retention rates with a community based transition-years project. *Canadian School Executive,* 15(7), 17-20.

Hudson, J.H., Hornick, J.P., & Burrows, B.A. (1988). *Justice and the young offender in Canada.* Toronto: Wall and Thompson.

Huston, A.C., McLoyd, V.C., & Garcia Coll, C. (1994). Children and poverty: Issues in contemporary research. *Child Development, 65*(2), 275-282.

Janosz, M., Leblanc, M., Boulerice, B., & Tremblay, R.E. (1997). Disentangling the weight of school dropout predictors: A test on two longitudinal samples. *Journal of Youth and Adolescence, 26*(6), 733-762.

Jenkins, P.H. (1995). School delinquency and school commitment. *Sociology of Education, 68*(3), 221-239.

Jewison, C. (1995). Our students, our future: Innovations in First Nations Education in the NWT. *Education Canada, 35*(1), 4-11.

Kandel, E., Mednick, S.A., Kirkegaard-Sorensen, L., Hutchings, B., Knop, J., Rosenberg, R., & Schulsinger, F. (1988). IQ as a protective factor for subjects at high risk for antisocial behavior. *Journal of Consulting and Clinical Psychology, 56*(2), 224-226.

Kaufman, P., & Bradby, D. (1992). *Characteristics of at-risk students in the NELS: 88. National Educational Longitudinal study of 1988.* (DOE Publication No. NCES 92-042). Washington, DC: National Center for Educational Statistics. (ERIC Document Reproduction Service No. ED 349 369)

Leschied, A.W., Andrews, D.A., & Hoge, R.D. (1992). *Youth at risk: A review of Ontario young offenders, programs, and literature that supports effective intervention.* Toronto: Ministry of Community and Social Services.

Lipps, G., & Frank, J. (1997). The national longitudinal survey of children and youth, 1994-95: Initial results from the school component. (Statistics Canada, Catalogue No. 81-003- XPB). *Education Quarterly Review,* 4(2), 43-57.

Loeber, R. (1988). Natural histories of conduct problems, delinquency, and associated substance use: Evidence for developmental progressions. In B.B. Lahey & A.E. Kazdin (Eds.), *Advances in clinical child psychology* (Vol. 11, pp. 73-124). New York: Plenum Press.

Loeber, R., & Farrington, D.P. (1997). Strategies and yields of longitudinal studies on antisocial behavior. In D.M. Stoff, J. Breiling, & J.D. Maser (Eds.), *Handbook of antisocial behavior* (pp. 125-139). New York: John Wiley & Sons, Inc.

Loeber, R., & Farrington, D.P. (1998). Never too early, never too late: Risk factors and social successful interventions for serious and violent juvenile offenders. *Studies on Crime & Crime Prevention, 7*(1), 7-30.

Loeber, R., & Stouthamer-Loeber, M. (1987). Prediction. In H.C. Quay (Ed.), *Handbook of juvenile delinquency* (pp. 325-382). New York: John Wiley and Sons.

Looker, D.E. (1997). In search of credentials: Factors affecting young adults' participation in postsecondary education. *The Canadian Journal of Higher Education, 27*(2, 3), 1-36.

Maguire, K.E., Flanagan, T.J., & Thornberry, T.P. (1988). Prison labour and recidivism. *Journal of Quantitative Criminology, 4*(1), 3-18.

Matsueda, R.L., & Heimer, K. (1987). Race, family structure and delinquency: A test of differential association and social control theories. *American Sociological Review, 52*(6), 826-840.

McGrath, S. (1996). Correlates of post-secondary participation. In B. Galaway & J. Hudson (Eds.), *Youth in transition* (pp. 189-198). Toronto: Thompson Educational Publishing.

McNeal, R.B. (1997). High school dropouts: A closer examination of school effects. *Social Science Quarterly, 78*(1), 209-222.

McIlroy, A., & Feschuk, S. (1998, May 13). McLellan proposes youth justice changes: Violent offenders would be subject to special sentencing provisions. *The Globe & Mail*, p. A3.

McLanahan, S.S., & Sandefur, G.D. (1994). *Growing up with a single parent: What hurts, what helps.* Cambridge, MA: Harvard University Press.

McMillen, M.M., Kaufman, P., Hausken, E.G., & Bradby, D. (1993). *Dropout rates in the United States: 1992.* National Center for Educational Statistical Analysis. Washington, DC: Government Printing Office.

Milner, T. (1995). Juvenile legislation. In J.H. Creechan & R.A. Silverman (Eds.), *Canadian delinquency* (pp. 47-59). Scarborough, ON: Prentice-Hall Canada Inc.

Mitchell, A. (1991). The economic circumstances of Ontario's families and children. In R. Barnhorst & L.C. Johnson (Eds.), *The state of the child in Ontario* (pp. 22-47). Toronto: Oxford University Press.

Moffitt, T.E. (1993). Adolescence-limited and life-course persistent antisocial behavior: A developmental taxonomy. *Psychological Review, 100*(4), 647-701.

MSGCS. (1997). *Young offenders act process.* Ministry of the Solicitor General and Correctional Services, Research Services Unit. Toronto: Author.

Mulawka, B. (1998, June 1). A stab at youth reform: Changes to the YOA show Anne McLellan moving quickly up the liberal ladder. *Alberta Report*, 25(4), 6-7.

Natriello, G., McDill, E.L., & Pallas, A.M. (1985). School reform and potential dropouts. *Educational Leadership*, *43*(1), 10-14.

Offord, D.R., & Lipman, E.L. (1996). Emotional and behavioural problems. In Statistics Canada. *Growing up in Canada: National Longitudinal survey of children and youth* (pp. 119-126). (Statistics Canada, Catalogue No. 89-550-MPE, no 1). Ottawa, ON: Human Resources Development Canada.

Okey, T.N., & Cusick, P.A. (1995). Dropping out: Another side of the story. *Educational Administration Quarterly*, *31*(2), 244-267.

Peng, S.S., & Lee, R.M. (1993). *Educational experiences and needs of middle school students in poverty* (DOE Publication No. NCES 83-221b). Washington, DC: National Center for Education Statistics. (ERIC Document Reproduction Service No. ED 364 628)

Radwanski, G. (1987). *Ontario study of the relevance of education, and the issue of dropouts.* Toronto: Ontario Ministry of Education.

Ross, D.P., Roberts, P.A., & Scott, K. (1998). *Variations in child development outcomes among children living in lone-parent families.* (Working Papers No. W-98-7E). Hull, PQ: Applied Research Branch, Strategic Policy: Human Resources Development Canada.

Ross, D.P., Scott, K., & Kelly, M.A. (1996a). *Child poverty: What are the consequences?* Ottawa, ON: Centre for International Statistics. Canadian Council on Social Development.

Ross, D.P., Scott, K., & Kelly, M.A. (1996b). Overview: Children in Canada in the 1990s. In Statistics Canada (1996). *Growing up in Canada: National Longitudinal survey of children and youth* (pp. 15-46). (Statistics Canada, Catalogue No. 89-550-MPE, no 1). Ottawa, ON: Human Resources Development Canada.

Rumberger, R.W. (1987). High school dropouts: A review of issues and evidence. *Review of Educational Research*, 57(2), 101-121.

Rumberger, R.W. (1995). Dropping out of middle school: A multilevel analysis of students and schools. *American Educational Research Journal*, 32(3), 583-625.

Rumberger, R.W., Ghatak, R., Poulos, G., Ritter, P.L., & Dornbusch, S.M. (1990). Family influences on dropout behaviour in one California high school. *Sociology of Education*, 63(4), 283-299.

Rumberger, R.W., & Larson, K.A. (1998). Student mobility and the increased risk of high school dropout. *American Journal of Education*, *107*(1), 1-35.

Sampaio, P.A. (1996). *Membership of the task force on strict discipline for young offenders.* Toronto: The Ministry of the Solicitor General and Correctional Services.

Sampson, R.J. (1987). Urban black violence: The effects of male joblessness and family disruption. *American Journal of Sociology*, *93*(2), 348-382.

Sampson, R.J., & Laub, J.H. (1993). *Crime in the making: Pathways and turning points through life.* Cambridge, MA: Harvard University Press.

Saner, H., & Ellickson, P. (1996). Concurrent risk factors for adolescent violence. *Journal of Adolescent Health, 19*(2), 94-103.

Schissel, B. (1993). *Social dimensions of Canadian youth justice.* Toronto: Oxford University Press.

Shiono, P.H., & Quinn, L.S. (1994). Epidemiology of divorce. *The Future of Children, 4*(1), 15- 28.

Spencer, M.B., Cole, S.P., DuPree, D., Glymph., A., & Pierre, P. (1993). Self-efficacy among urban African American early adolescents: Exploring the issue of risk, vulnerability and resilience. *Development and Psychopathology, 5*(4), 719-739.

Statistics Canada. (2000). *Sentencing of young offenders* [On-line] *The daily.* Available: http://www.statcan.ca/Daily/English/000801/d000801b.htm.

Statistics Canada. (2001a). Population by ethnic origin, 1996 census [On-line]. Available: http://www.statcan.ca:80/english/Pgdb/People/Families /famil40b.htm.

Statistics Canada. (2001b). *Population by mother tongue, 1996 census* [On-line]. Available: http://www.statcan.ca:80/english/Pgdb/People/Population/def/defde mo18a. htm#notes.

Statistics Canada. (2001c). *Census families, number and average size* [On-line]. Available: http://www.statcan.ca:80/english/Pgdb/People/Families/famil40b.htm.

Statistics Canada. (2001d). *Census families in private households by family structure, 1991 and 1996 censuses* [On-line]. Available: http://www.statcan.ca:80/english/ Pgdb/People/Families/famil51a.htm.

Stattin, H., & Magnusson, D. (1989). The role of early aggressive behavior in the frequency, seriousness and types of later crime. *Journal of Consulting and Clinical Psychology, 57*(6), 710-718.

Stauffer, I. (1981). *The young offenders act: Proposed changes in the treatment of Canadian juvenile delinquents.* Ottawa, ON: National Legal Aid Research Centre.

Stedman, J.B., Salganik, L.H., & Celebuski, C.A. (1988). *Dropping out: The educational vulnerability of at-risk youth* (CRS Report for Congress 88 417-EPW). Washington, DC: Congressional Research Services. (ERIC Document Reproduction Service No. ED 300 495)

Steinberg, L., Blinde, P.L., & Chan, K.S. (1984). Dropping out among language minority youth. *Review of Educational Research, 54*(1), 113-132.

Stoff, D.M., Breiling, J., & Maser J.D. (1997). Antisocial behavior research: An introduction. In D.M. Stoff, J. Breiling, & J.D. Maser (Eds.), *Handbook of antisocial behavior* (pp. 115-124). New York: John Wiley & Sons, Inc.

Sullivan, M. (1988). *A comparative analysis of drop-outs and non-dropouts in Ontario secondary schools: A report to the Ontario study of the relevance of education and the issue of dropouts.* (Student retention and transition series: Ontario Ministry of Education). Toronto: Queen's Printer for Ontario.

Sunter, D. (1993). School, work, and dropping out. (Statistics Canada, Catalogue No. 75-001-E). *Perspectives on Labour and Income*, *5*(2), 44-52.

Tanner, J., Krahn, H., & Hartnagel, T.F. (1995). *Fractured transitions from school to work: Revisiting the dropout problem*. Toronto: Oxford University Press.

Turner, R.A., Irwin, C.E., & Millstein, S.G. (1991). Family structure, family processes, and experimenting with substance during adolescence. *Journal of Research on Adolescence*, *1*(1), 93-106.

Vickers, H.S. (1994). Young children at risk: Differences in family functioning. *The Journal of Educational Research*, *87*(5), 262-270.

Visher, C.A., Lattimore, P.K., & Linster, R.L. (1991). Predicting the recidivism of serious youthful offenders using survival models. *Criminology*, *29*(3), 329-366.

White, J.L., Moffitt, T.E., & Silva, P.A. (1989). A prospective replication of the protective effects of IQ in subjects at high risk for juvenile delinquency. *Journal of Consulting and Clinical Psychology*, *57*(6), 719-724.

Wilson, L. (1982). *Juvenile courts in Canada*. Toronto: Carswell.

Wright, E.N. (1985). *The retention and credit accumulation of students in secondary school: A follow-up from the 1980 Grade nine student survey*. Toronto: Toronto Board of Education, Research Service.

Youth Criminal Justice Act (2002). Retrieved May 5, 2006, from http://laws.justice.gc.ca/en/Y-1.5/index.html

ADULT AND HIGHER EDUCATION

Six

Curriculum Leadership Then and Now

William F. Pinar

Narratives are not only structures of meaning, but structures of power as well.

– Edward Bruner (1986, p. 144)

Not only is educational administration structured around the business model, wherein scores on standardized examinations represent the bottom line, measuring profit or loss, but the entirety of public education in the U.S. is also now cast in an inappropriate model that had its intellectual origins in the social efficiency movement, hegemonic during the 1920s (see Pinar et al., 1995, p. 95ff.). For the two decades following, social efficiency was eclipsed by child-centeredness and social reconstructionism, complementary (if also conflicting) wings of the Progressive education movement (Pinar et al., 1995, p. 103ff.). To begin to awaken from the nightmare that is the present – in which U.S. teachers are positioned in "gracious submission" by right-wing ideologues[1] – requires, I suggest, remembering the past.

To contribute to such remembrance, let us return for a moment to that postwar moment during which U.S. Progressivism reassembled itself before being defeated in the 1950s by an apparently unanticipated alliance between university arts and sciences professors and right-wing critics mobilized by Cold War politics (see Pinar, 2004, p. 65ff.). This postwar moment of progressive thinking in educational administration can be glimpsed through studying the 1946 *Yearbook* of the Association for the Supervision and Curriculum Development (ASCD).[2] To contrast that moment with our own, I will juxtapose fragments from that 1946 statement of curriculum leadership with key statements in Allan A. Glatthorn's (2000) *The Principal as Curriculum Leader*.[3]

While the province of educational administration is, of course, much broader than the supervision of the curriculum (now rephrased as curriculum leadership), it is the curriculum that preoccupies me. The curriculum is the intellectual and organizational centre of schooling. It is the curriculum on which the ideological struggle for the minds and political allegiances of U.S. school children has been focused (Zimmerman, 2002). The institutional authority of school administrators – the principal prominent among them – provides opportunities for those who can remember the historical calling of their vocation to play leadership roles in mobilizing resistance against the U.S. right wing's faith-based educational agenda (see Willis, 2006, p. 10), wherein controversial curriculum topics, among them evolution, global warming, stem cell research, and especially gay and lesbian subjects, are subjected to ideological screening. There was a time when curriculum leaders embraced curriculum controversy as paradigmatic of democratic living.

POST-WORLD WAR II AMERICA

The school is a great and moving force in a torn and worried world. It may be, without exaggeration, the last great hope of this nation.

– Fred T. Wilhelms (ASCD, 1946, p. 122)

With the end of World War II, U.S. educators, in solidarity with returning soldiers, felt entitled to "honorable discharges" from "wartime curriculums," ready to return to "the task of education for democratic living" (ASCD, 1946, p. 1). For the Progressives, recall, democracy was not only casting one's vote. For Progressives, democracy was an integrated psychological-social and intellectual process of solitary and social living articulated through education. Integral to subjective and social formation, the academic curriculum structured the education of the public. And that education – in the postwar period – was, we are told in the 1946 ASCD *Yearbook*, to be focused on "lasting peace," predicated upon making "true democracy operative for all people everywhere" (ASCD, 1946, p. 1).

Sounding almost like the current catechism (but with a different ideological intent), William Van Til summarizes the educational task in the postwar period: "In short, our major function should be to help young people understand and practice the democratic way of life in a technological age" (ASCD, 1946, p. 2).[4] The specific referent of the technological age was not the computer and its inflated educational potential. Rather, it was the atomic bomb, then, as now, threatening the "total destruction of civilization" (p. 5). Technology threatened peace even as it provided one curricular means for ensuring its permanence.

In 1946, there was little time to celebrate military victory or to rest after four catastrophic years of destruction, injury, and genocide. For U.S. Progressive educators, the postwar moment represented an opportunity to reaffirm their "struggle to bring school instruction to bear upon the significant social and individual problems of today" (ASCD, 1946, p. 3). In that "struggle," the supervisor and curriculum worker occupied "key positions" (p. 3).[5] These were intellectual as well as political positions, encouraging teachers to teach the dangers of (a) racism (p. 5), (b) the concentration of economic power, (c) the centralization of government, and (d) nationalism and imperialism (p. 7).

Technology and collective action (see ASCD, 1946, p. 7) comprised two educational tools the curriculum made available to students confronting the profound problems of postwar America. Van Til had no illusions about the nature of the problem: following George Counts (see Perlstein, 2000, p. 51), Van Til acknowledged that "today is the era of competing propagandas" (ASCD, 1946, p. 7). The supervisor and curriculum worker must consider such conflicts and trends if they are to formulate the "social foundations" of the "educational program" of the school (ASCD, 1946, p. 8). Not worried by the prospect of alarming a vociferous and powerful right-wing,[6] postwar supervisors embraced a curriculum of controversy so that students could "examine controversial issues with intelligence and foresight, to reserve judgments until evidence has been carefully weighed" (p. 8). In the contemporary period, even teachers' proposals to enrich the curriculum must be approved by a council that includes parents, a theme I return to in examining Glatthorn's book. Avoiding controversy today means right-wing censorship of the public school curriculum.

From these social and political issues associated with the Social Reconstructionists (see Riley, 2006), Van Til acknowledges the other wing of the Progressive education movement – child-centeredness – when he tells readers of the *Yearbook* that "a primary task for the postwar supervisor and curriculum worker then, is to understand these children and adolescents for whom our educational machinery exists" (ASCD, 1946, p. 8). Note two points: (a) that these those concepts – *children* and *adolescents* – are historically situated (see ASCD, 1946, p. 10; Baker, 2001; Lesko, 2001; Pinar, 2006a, pp. 15-42) and (b) that *students* represent the *raison d'être* for schooling.[7] In Glatthorn's text, there is acknowledgment of Howard Gardner's work (see Glatthorn, 2000, p. 60), an utilitarian endorsement of constructivism (2006, p. 6, 112ff.), but no historically situated developmental characterization of students; they are, simply, "learners," fated by definition to perform the curricular tasks that the "standards" require them to accomplish.

Van Til's opening chapter to the 1946 Yearbook concludes with a recapitulation of progressive education's pedagogical creed. The section head declares, "Our Commitment is to a Living Democracy," specifying an education that

> stresses the dignity and worth of the individual, calls for working together for shared purposes to extend associated living, continuously promotes the general welfare, and proceeds through the method of intelligence. (ASCD, 1946, p. 13)

"Associated living," a term recalling the theoretical commitments of Jane Addams and John Dewey, specified the social structure of democratic community, a social form in which individuals in association with each other employed intelligence to experiment for the sake of "general welfare."[8]

These educational commitments to democratic living extended – at least at a rhetorical level – to the organizational structure of the profession. The boundaries of those organizational hierarchies that structure the relationships between administrators and teachers seem blurred, at least as compared to those contemporary conceptions wherein the principal plays the key role in site-based school management and reform. In the *Yearbook's* second chapter, Marguerite Ransberger asks: "To whom shall American education turn for leadership during this transition period when new concepts must be gained and new insights developed?" (ASCD, 1946, p. 17), Ransberger's reply is: "Classroom teachers."

Administrators come second to teachers, but Ransberger allows that administrators "also rightfully play a role of leadership in the schools of our land. These are men and women who have training in financial affairs and are adept at meeting the public" (ASCD ,1946, p. 17). Here is a conception of administrators as, in effect, accountants and greeters, "a key liaison officer between the schools and the community" (p. 24), employees in service to classroom teachers. This conception is far from the CEO image accepted by too many indoctrinated into the business model of education.[9]

Also, in contrast to contemporary obsessions with standards and outcomes,[10] *leadership* meant not the implementation of politicians' agendas but, instead, "reading, exploring, of thinking in frontier areas." From such study (see Pinar, 2006a, pp. 109-120), school leaders were then to undertake the "responsibility" of "pointing the educational direction" (ASCD, 1946, p. 17). Who works "shoulder to shoulder" (p. 17) with administrators and the classroom teacher in this leadership capacity? Third on the list, then, are the supervisors.

In the 1946 *Yearbook*, the depiction of the supervisor is, let us say, hyperbolic. Two points are pertinent. First, it is remarkable to me that any administrative position could be described in such admiring terms. Given contemporary expectations, the absence of suspicion the description assumes is conspicuous. The second point concerns the specific descriptors employed: in reflecting (if in dramatic terms) the articles of faith of Progressive education (see ASCD, 1946, pp. 18-19), these provide a sharp contrast to descriptors of the business-executive/bureaucratic manager the contemporary supervisor is mandated to be. Sixty years ago, however, this administrator was imagined to be

> a frontier thinker, a philosopher, whose enthusiastic faith in democracy as a way of life is contagious. He is a dreamer, daring to dream of a world free of prejudice, hatred, and poverty. He is a man of action, working consistently in the classrooms of America to make his dreams come true. He is a friend, discovering in each individual with whom he works a personality worthy of recognition and understanding. He is a student of the social sciences noting and seeking to understand the trends of civilization. He faces the future courageously. The advent of the atomic age challenges but not does not completely daunt him. (p. 18)

No "realist" focused on calculation, instrumentality, and self-advancement, this version of the supervisor is committed to ending racism, poverty, and hatred.[11] S/he realizes that the school classroom, not the central-office bureaucracy, is the site of such civic educational action. No ideologue, however, the supervisor recognizes teachers as individuals as s/he confronts the past and imagines the future. Unfortunately, s/he is evidently limited to the social sciences; study of the humanities and arts does not seem paramount, as I would argue they are (see Pinar, 2004, p. 19). The supervisor's "sensitivity to new ideas" (ASCD 1946, p. 18) may compensate for these disciplinary limitations.

There is much more of note in the 1946 *Yearbook*, but I will conclude my remembrance of it and of the historical moment it evokes by citing Fred Wilhelms' concluding chapter. Wilhelms emphasizes that the supervisor is "an organizer of opportunity" (p. 119). Wilhelms then asks: "Opportunity for *what?*," The answer to this question is twofold:

1. Opportunity for teachers to learn what they need and want to learn.

2. Opportunity for teachers to lay their full part in policy-making. (p. 119).

To Summarize, Wilhelms is adamant that the "greatest task" of supervisors is "to serve ... teachers" (ASCD 1946, p. 122). In the nightmare that is the present, there is not even a rhetorical nod to that idea.

PRE-WAR ON TERROR AMERICA

A cold war is being conducted over the control of curriculum.

– Allan A. Glatthorn (2000, p. 15)

By 2000 the Cold War was, of course, over. The racial and gender politics of that War had structured U.S. curriculum reform (see Pinar, 2004, p. 65ff.), but by the turn-of-the-century a new form of war – terrorism – was on the horizon. The 1946 ASCD *Yearbook* expressed the post-World War II amalgamation of various strands of progressivism (see Pinar et al., 1995, p. 142ff.). In contrast, Allan Glatthorn's (2000) *The Principal as Curriculum Leader* captures America's rejection of progressivism;[12] his cold war comparison includes no macropolitical analysis, only bureaucratic quarrels over jurisdiction (see 2000, pp. 15, 21).

The most striking contrast between conceptions of the supervisor or curriculum leader in post-World War II and pre-War on Terror America is the virtual disappearance of progressive education.[13] The idea of organizing the curriculum around students' interests for the sake of the social reconstruction of the nation, the key to the progressive education movement, has disappeared in the school.[14] Now the school curriculum is organized around educational "outcomes," themselves synonymous with students' scores on standardized examinations, measuring, presumably, "generic skills" that are, also presumably, "transferable" to "any career"(see Glatthorn 2000, p. 7).[15]

The social engineering orientation of U.S. public education (see Pinar, 2006a, p. 110; Pinar et al., 1995, p. 91) has only intensified since the issuance of the first Coleman Report issued in the mid-1960s (see Pinar, 2006a, pp. 123-124). Now political conservatives insist that schooling, not government or the economy or even the church, is *the* social lever; they hold schools accountable not only for students' learning but for students' socio-economic fate, thereby displacing responsibility for social welfare from the government, and distracting the electorate from noticing that intensifying poverty in the U.S. has accrued from conservative policies. Now curriculum "alignment" is paramount (see Glatthorn, 2000, pp. 41, 86, 89), as it promises to improve student achievement – a euphemism for higher test scores. Illustrating the political emphasis on international test scores comparisons, Glatthorn reports that in those nations with "strong central control of the curriculum" there is

> greater consistency about what should be taught and what the teacher did teach, when compared with teachers in nations with greater local control. That variation in consistency is probably one of the factors accounting for international differences in achievement. (p. 4)

"Consistency" can be decoded as ideological control. Determined to move the nation far to the right, political conservatives' embrace of curriculum "alignment" is, then, unsurprising.[16]

Constructivism is the consolation prize; after all, many of those complicit with conservative school "deform" endorse a multiplicity of pedagogical styles (see Pinar, 2004, p. 213). For Glatthorn (2000), constructivism is one of those "trends" (p. 3) that, because it continues (p. 6, 123), warrants principals' attention. Its intrinsic merit is, evidently, beside the point. Glatthorn seems to accept without question the contemporary obsession with outcomes, devising guidelines for what he terms – employing empty business rhetoric – a "quality" (see pp. 11-12) or "mastery core" (p. 19) curriculum classroom teachers are then to "operationalize" (p. 19). For U.S. curriculum scholars, the key question remains conspicuously missing from this model: what knowledge is of most worth? It is precisely this intellectual, political, and subjective question conservatives wish to sidestep by focusing on "implementation" and "alignment." Lost is any consideration of the teacher's academic – intellectual – freedom. Without liberty we cannot teach (see Pinar, 2006b, p. xviii). We are left with the "management" of "learning" informed by others' ideological agendas.

Rather than forming the basis for the courses they teach, teachers' individuated knowledge of their subject matter qualifies today only as "enrichment." Glatthorn (2000) tells us that teachers can enrich the curriculum by "adding to the district curriculum special content that responds to their students' needs and enables them to use their own special knowledge" (p. 21) The patronizing tone of the final phrase is hardly helped by the substitution of the pseudopsychological concept "needs," in contemporary double-speak a decoy for those "skills" policy-makers and test-makers have decreed. Despite his suggestion – rendered almost as an afterthought – that curriculum leaders "consider the learners – their needs and interests" (p. 62), there seems no acknowledgment of differentiated generations with their own respective, and, indeed, distinctive challenges, a reality at least implied in the 1946 *Yearbook's* call to understand youth (1946, p. 8).

Even this professional "privilege" of adding "enrichment" to a standardized curriculum is hardly guaranteed,[17] as Glatthorn recommends that teachers make formal enrichment proposals to be reviewed by a central committee composed of teachers, school administrators, and parents. Committee members will review all enrichment proposals, asking:

- Do the proposed units enrich the curriculum?

- Are the proposed units likely to be approved by parents?
  (Glatthorn, 2000, p. 127)

Given the activism of right-wing parents in many U.S. districts, such reviews will ensure that nothing controversial will surface in the school curriculum, another contrast with the *Yearbook's* conception of curriculum supervision (see ASCD, 1946, p. 8).

By sharply separating curriculum from instruction (see Glatthorn, 2000, p. 24), the former becomes taken-for-granted, unquestioned content to be learned. Teaching is reduced to a means to deliver the curriculum, despite the multiple meanings of *teaching* (see p. 83). The eclipse of teachers' academic – intellectual – freedom is accomplished through the concept of curriculum leadership Glatthorn employs, namely, "the exercise of those functions that enable schools systems and their schools to achieve their goal of ensuring quality in what students learn" (p. 23, see also p. 58). Again, the business rhetoric is telling. Instead of schools organized as sites of practice and preparation for democratic living, we are stuck with schools as businesses preparing students for lives regulated by the corporate state.

Conclusion

> While it is defensible to assert that reality exists beyond texts, much of what we think of as real is – and can only be – apprehended through texts.
>
> – Noel Gough (1998, P. 97)

There is a danger in overstating the distinctions between the two texts. In Glatthorn's (2000) book there are echoes of Progressivism. For example, he is determined to act ethically (p. 154). In his discussion of implementation, he acknowledges arguments against monitoring teachers' implementation of the curriculum (see p. 94), among them the distrust of teachers that monitoring implies and the damages to school climate that it inflicts. He realizes that implementing the standard curriculum ignores student and school differences. Glatthorn acknowledges that linking the curriculum to student performance on standardized examinations

> forces the teacher to focus on test-like items, thus narrowing the curriculum and over-emphasizing direct instruction. Finally, excessive monitoring reduces the teacher to a mechanical implementer of what others have produced, thus deskilling teaching. (p. 94).

But these concerns – still a far cry from affirmations of teachers' academic freedom and the schools as places to prepare for democratic living – disappear in his "practical solution" (p. 95) to the implementation debate.

Glatthorn must be not be demonized nor the authors of the 1946 ASCD yearbook idealized. Perhaps all were reiterating the catechism of the day, "enriched" by their own minor additions and revisions. Even if that were the case, Progressivism, by its defining constructs, enables reformulation and reconstruction. It builds into the system not bureaucratic controls, but protections for disagreement, even controversy. It cautions against bureaucratic hierarchies rather than coordinates their smooth functioning. In the *Yearbook*, there is a relative intellectual and political independence built into the conception of educational leadership that is missing in Glatthorn's more contemporary conception. Finally, the curriculum to be supervised was one directed toward the world – specifically toward peace and democratization – through the subjective experience (i.e. interests) of students. In the contemporary version, the curriculum is directed toward performance on standardized examinations.

In drawing these distinctions between then and now, I disclaim any nostalgia for the past. But I do dispute any faith in progress, that the present, because it has followed a past time, is somehow better. Without question we are more technologically sophisticated than in 1946. No doubt the cultural lag between technology and society has been reduced during the sixty years following the *Yearbook's* publication. Nonetheless, the development of education leadership since 1946 has lead us into a season of great untruth, to invoke David G. Smith's (2006) phrase. Remembering the past compels us to tell the truth about the present.

NOTES

[1] The phrase is associated with the most populous Protestant sect in the U.S., the Southern Baptists, who at their 1998 national convention, emphasized the biblical justification for wives' submission to the authority of their husbands: (a) Ephesians 5:22-23a, 24b: "Wives, submit to your husbands as to the Lord. For the husband is the head of the wife . . . Wives should submit to their husbands in everything," (b) 1 Cor. 11:3: "The head of every man is Christ, and the head of the woman is the man," (c) 1 Cor .14:34-35: "Women should remain silent in the churches. They are not allowed to speak, but must be in submission as the Law says," (d) Tim. 2:12: "I do not permit a woman to teach or have authority over a man; she must be silent." Understanding U.S. teachers' political subjugation – in which even relative control of the curriculum, which includes *the means by which students' study of it is assessed*, has been legislated away – as deferred and displaced misogyny and racism renders the appropriation of this phrase appropriate (see Pinar, 2004, p. 46).

[2] Founded in 1943, the Association for Supervision and Curriculum Development (ASCD) is a nonprofit, nonpartisan organization that represents 175 000 educators from more than 135 countries and 58 affiliates: "Our members span the entire profession of educators-superintendents, supervisors, principals, teachers, professors of education, and school board members. . . . ASCD reflects the conscience and content of education." (ASCD, n.d.). The assertion that ASCD remains the "conscience" of education (despite its qualified criticism of *No Child Left Behind* on their website) would be contested by many U.S. professors of curriculum studies who deserted ASCD because, in their view, it abandoned its founding progressive mission in the early 1970s in favor of an opportunistic commercialism (see Pinar et al., 1995, pp. 208-211).

[3] In my view, Glatthorn's book is a representative, not definitive, statement of curriculum leadership today. Certainly it cannot be called the most reactionary statement circulating today. Indeed, there are echoes of progressivism in Glatthorn's book, rendering his sensitivity to reactionary trends more poignantly indicative of the "gracious submission" of teachers and of many education professors who attempt to work closely with them. I use the adjective *many* advisedly, as the work of James Henderson, for instance, underscores that not all those who work closely with school administrators and teachers succumb to the business model (see Henderson & Gornik, 2007).

[4] Today, technology is today employed to distract – rather than focus – the public's attention upon the problems of American democracy (see Pinar, 2004, p. 126). There is in the *Yearbook* one uncritical, indeed, anti-intellectual, comment regarding the educational potential of technology: "[The supervisor] knows that audio-visual aids [at least technology was relegated to "aids"] are important equipment for every school system. *They may be as important as books*" (ASCD, 1946, p. 25, emphasis mine). I remain skeptical that the age of the book is past or that, as a curriculum artifact or tool, the book has been supplanted by the Internet. (I prefer that those children conducting research take the advice of a professional librarian over what surfaces on a computer screen via an Internet search engine.) In 1946, because technology was now widely used in the military, its use in the schools should "accelerate"

(ASCD, 1946, p. 75). That the mission of the two institutions is rather different gets lost in this uncritical embrace of technology.

5 This conception of curriculum labor – with its Marxist echoes – has been reasserted recently (see Gaztambide-Fernandez and Sears, 2004).

6 The fatal political error German democrats had committed – allowing the Nazis to participate in the democratic process – remained painfully clear to postwar Progressive educators: "Propagandized and emotionalized mass thinking resulting from pressure group tactics should not be tolerated in American society" (ASCD, 1946, p. 8). Nor should they be tolerated today.

7 A subheading in the *Yearbook* proclaims "Curriculum Must Be Based on Child Needs"(1946, p. 73). Anticipating late twentieth-century autobiographical curriculum studies (see Pinar et al., 1995, pp. 515-566; Pinar, 2004, pp. 35-62), Marguerite Ransberger tells us that the supervisor appreciates that "integration takes place *within* the individual" (ASCD, 1946, p. 22, emphasis added) The ahistorical, indeed, apparently timeless character of developmentalism is tempered here with subjective and historical specificity. For a critique of developmentalism, see Baker (2001).

8 Progressive education has been rightly criticized as failing to include African Americans in their conceptions of general welfare, although on occasion both Jane Addams and John Dewey demonstrated their commitments to racial justice. Addams, for instance, joined with Ida B. Wells in fighting the segregation of Chicago public schools (see Pinar, 2001, 536); Dewey, for instance, spoke in 1909 at what was, in effect, the organizational meeting founding the NAACP (see Pinar 2001, 635). In the 1946 ASCD *Yearbook*, one of the "centers of learning," characterized as a "postwar concern," is "racial, religious, ethnic, social-economic relationships (intercultural education concerning minority groups, prejudice. Human relations)" (ASCD 1946, p. 15, see also p. 23). I cite this not to exonerate Progressive education, but to note that these statements of commitments were expressed as curriculum policy before *Brown v. Board of Education*, before the civil rights movements that followed, before racial social-justice became politically correct.

9 The political primacy – at least rhetorically – of the classroom teacher is made explicit in the Yearbook's chapter two, wherein Marguerite Ransberger (see ASCD, 1946, p. 22) reminds administrators that the curriculum is not theirs. Nor have they developed it "working alone in a secluded office." The teacher works with him [or her] exploring the latest material developed in other schools systems. They study, read, and think together." While I appreciate this democratic conception of "study" – reading and thinking together – I wonder why teachers and supervisors were not called to examine intellectual developments in university arts and science departments (see Pinar, 2006a)? Quite apart from the potential intellectual benefits, teachers and supervisors might have been able to respond more adequately to arts, humanities, and sciences faculties' scapegoating public education that gathered political momentum during the 1950s (see Pinar, 2004, p. 66). Nor is there any attention to academic knowledge in Glatthorn's (2000) scheme; instead, he devotes considerable attention to scheduling (see p. 65ff.). Scheduling, rather than academic

knowledge, is a "crucial aspect of school effectiveness and plays an important role inn delivering a quality curriculum" (p. 65).

[10] Blessedly, in the *Yearbook* there are relatively few references to evaluation. One finds an acknowledgment that evaluation should be "continuous," that it "should be used diagnostically" and, in an uncharacteristic use of business jargon, as a means for "improving school services" (ASCD, 1946, p. 74).

[11] No doubt postwar administrators were also concerned with career advancement, but the topic seems absent in the 1946 *Yearbook*. Perhaps the topic was considered in bad taste; certainly it was irrelevant to this progressive conception of administration as service. Soon enough, however, the profession of educational administration would need reminding, that "to administer is to minister to, to serve" (Huebner 1999, p. 385).

[12] An argument could be made that in the "conservative restoration" since 1968 the social efficiency wing of Progressivism has triumphed, but Diane Ravitch (2000, 86) rejects even that discredited (and from social reconstructionist and child-centered educational points of view, pseudoprogressive) tradition.

[13] Some readers will wonder if in comparing a professional association's yearbook with a solitary scholar's textbook I am not comparing "apples with oranges." I acknowledge these are distinctive genres, nor can I make any empirical claims based on the comparison. A yearbook may represent shared beliefs and attitudes (especially when two chapters are devoted to survey results) more than can a textbook composed by a solitary scholar. As will be evident, however, Professor Glatthorn is quite sensitive to shared beliefs and attitudes, specifically to the political realities faced by school administrators. While the two texts do represent different genres, they share an interest in speaking to broad audiences, requiring each to be attuned to the state of the schools. If not empirically reflective of their respective historical epochs or mentalities (see Tröhler, 2006, p. 91, n. 10.), each evokes historically distinctive conceptions of curriculum leadership.

[14] "The progressive education movement did not disappear in the 1950s," Diane Ravitch (2000) asserts that "the movement was at low ebb, but it sprang back to life in the early 1960s. More troubling, it sprang back to life with anti-intellectualism at the forefront" (p. 16) and, in doing so, contradicts the careful arguments of Lawrence Cremin (1961) The U.S. right-wing has never been fond of careful arguments (cf. global warming, evolutionary theory, stem-cell research, the religious inclinations of the Founding Fathers). If no fanatic herself, Ravitch nonetheless reiterates right-wing propaganda on this point.

[15] If and how skills that are learned in one setting transfer to other settings are questions that have preoccupied social and behavioral scientists in education for a century (see Pinar et al., 1995, p. 31; Ravitch, 2000, pp. 62-65, 68-69; Block, 2004, p. 178). Thorndike employed the concept to justify curriculum differentiation; Ravitch exploits it to support the contrary position.

[16] "Perhaps," Glatthorn (2000) suggests, "more diversity in curriculum will be found in the charter school movement, because charter schools are free of state curriculum control" (p. 6) This possibility encouraged me to endorse publicly-

funded independent schools (see Pinar, 2004, p. 227), provided there is relative academic – intellectual – freedom for teachers, specifically greater control of the curriculum they teach and the means by which student study of it is assessed.

17 Teachers' exercise of their intellectual freedom through the selection of materials to be taught and the means by which students' study of the subject is assessed is *not* a privilege, not even a matter of discretion; it is, in my view, one's professional *obligation* (see Pinar, 2004, p. 32). In Glatthorn's contradictory scheme, wherein the curriculum is both outcomes-based and open-ended (see Pinar, 2004, p. 50), teachers' individual creativity and individuated knowledge of the subject they teach is replaced by the "specialness of the school's curriculum," (Glatthorn, 2000,p. 47) a distinctiveness teachers are to describe in *three adjectives* (see Pinar, 2004, p. 47)! Never mind that this distinctiveness is ancillary and not very distinctive, as Glatthorn's (2000) illustrative adjectives – "developmentally appropriate, technologically sophisticated" (see p. 48) – make clear. "Perhaps the best advice about choosing a total program, he summarizes "is to check its 'track record'" (p. 60). In the U.S., democratic living and world peace as curricular aspirations have been eclipsed by competition for higher scores, providing bragging rights for politicians.

References

Association for Supervision and Curriculum Development. (n.d.). *About ASCD.* Retrieved on November 21, 2006 from http://www.ascd.org/portal/site/ascd/menuitem.f99ce1aeb9ea20a98d7ea23161a001ca/

Association for Supervision and Curriculum Development. (1946). *Leadership through supervision.* Washington, DC: ASCD.

Baker, Bernadette M. (2001). *In perpetual motion: Theories of power, educational history, and the child.* New York: Peter Lang.

Block, Alan A. (2004). *Talmud, curriculum, and the practical: Joseph Schwab and the Rabbis.* New York: Peter Lang.

Bruner, Edward. (1986). Ethnography as narrative. In V. W. Turner and E. M. Bruner (Eds.), *The anthropology of experience* (pp. 139-155). Urbana: University of Illinois Press.

Cremin, Lawrence A. (1961). *The transformation of the school: Progressivism in American education, 1876-1957.* New York: Alfred A. Knopf.

Gaztambide-Fernandez, Rubén A. and Sears, James T. (Eds.) (2004). *Curriculum work as a public moral enterprise* (pp. 119-126). Lanham, MD: Rowman & Littlefield.

Glatthorn, Allan A. (2000). *The principal as curriculum leader.* (2nd ed.) Thousand Oaks, CA: Corwin.

Gough, Noel. (1998). Reflections and diffractions: Functions of fiction in curriculum inquiry. In William F. Pinar (Ed.) *Curriculum: Toward new identities* (pp. 93-127). New York: Garland.

Henderson, James G. and Gornik, Rosemary (2007). *Transforming curriculum leadership.* (3rd ed.) Upper Saddle River, NJ: Pearson/Merrill Prentice Hall.

Huebner, Dwayne E. (1999). *The lure of the transcendent.* Mahwah, NJ: Lawrence Erlbaum.

Lesko, Nancy. (2001). *Act Your Age! A Cultural Construction of Adolescence.* New York: Routledge/Falmer.

Perlstein, Daniel. (2000). "There is no escape . . . from the ogre of indoctrination": George Counts and the civic dilemmas of democratic educators. In Larry Cuban and Dorothy Shipps (Eds.), *Reconstructing the common good in education: Coping with intractable dilemmas* (pp. 51-67). Stanford, CA: Stanford University Press.

Pinar, William F. (2001). *The gender of racial politics and violence in America: Lynching, prison rape, and the crisis of masculinity.* New York: Peter Lang.

Pinar, William F. (2004). *What is curriculum theory?* Mahwah, NJ: Lawrence Erlbaum.

Pinar, William F. (2006a). *The synoptic text today and other essays: Curriculum development after the reconceptualization.* New York: Peter Lang.

Pinar, William F. (2006b). Independence. In J. Milam, S. Springgay, K. Sloan, and B. S. Carpenter (Eds.), *Curriculum for a progressive, provocative, poetic and public pedagogy* (p. xi-xxiii). Troy, NY: Educator's International Press.

Pinar, William F., Reynolds, William M. Slattery, Patrick, and Taubman, Peter M. (1995). *Understanding curriculum.* New York: Peter Lang.

Ravitch, Diane. (2000). *Left back: A century of battles over school reform.* New York: Simon and Schuster.

Riley, Karen L. (Ed.) (2006). *Social reconstruction: People, politics, perspectives.* Greenwich, CT: Information Age Publishing.

Smith, David G. (2006). *Trying to teach in a season of great untruth: Globalization, empire, and the crises of pedagogy.* Rotterdam: Sense Publishers.

Tröhler, Daniel. (2006). The "Kingdom of God on Earth" and early Chicago pragmatism. *Educational Theory, 56*(1), 89-105.

Willis, Gary. (2006, November 16). A country ruled by faith. *New York Review of Books* LIII *18*, 8-12.

Zimmerman, Jonathan. (2002). *Whose America? Culture wars in the public schools.* Cambridge, MA: Harvard University Press.

SEVEN

CREATING HEALTHY LEARNING ORGANIZATIONS: A COMPLEX APPROACH TO A CRISIS OF PERCEPTION

Darren Stanley

In 1983, Fritjof Capra wrote The Turning Point, an important work which foreshadowed revolutions to come in a number of diverse areas, such as science, economics, and medicine, and the need for a shift in world views and values. Since that time, he also has written a number of other texts (Capra, 1996, 2002), extending his thoughts to a theoretical framework for understanding a wide range of highly interconnected phenomena of a nonlinear nature – living systems. Describing an assortment of problems ranging from "our health and livelihood, the quality of our environment and our social relationships, our economy, technology, and politics" (1983, p. 21), Capra suggests that the world finds itself in the middle of an intellectual, moral, and spiritual crisis previously unheard of in recorded human history. We are, in fact, bearing witness to a collection of problems that are all "different facets of one and the same crisis, and that this crisis is essentially a crisis of perception" (Capra, 1983, p. 15).

Manifestations of this crisis appear in education. But before any educational considerations will be explored, the nature of this "crisis of perception" must be examined. Although we live – and always have lived – in a highly interconnected world, a mechanistic view of the world, say, in the image of a clock composed of isolated and isolatable parts, persists in very untenable ways. Not only has this particular view of the world created troublesome conceptual problems for those who address a wide range of theoretical concerns and worries, but the matter has also created further difficulties for how humanity, generally speaking, perceives the world in a fragmented and fragmenting manner, void of relationships and interdependencies. Indeed, the problem seems to lie in our diminished ability to recognize and think about ecological patterns, complex living systems, and our relationships with others and this planet.

For this crisis to be transformed, our notions of wholeness, health, and healing need to be re-envisioned (Berry, 1995). Drawing upon contemporary notions of dynamical systems, this chapter presents a still emerging and on-going inquiry into some of the necessary conditions for a healthy educational system to thrive and survive. To this end, this chapter will explore the importance of nonlinearity, self-organization, fractals, and distributed leadership as key principles for healthy schools.

COMPLEXITY: PRINCIPLES, PROCESSES, AND PATTERNS

The twentieth-century has seen a rise in conceptual tools and theoretical perspectives for the purpose of describing, understanding, and creating the kinds of conditions for a wide range of phenomena that could be described as "paradigmatically complex" (Stanley, 2005b). Complexity, in short, is a concept invoked across a wide range of discourses, scholarly discussions and writings, and practical engagements with organizational or systemic structures. Scientists, scholars, and researchers from various disciplinary domains are embracing this emerging understanding of diverse phenomena, which is extending and shifting their worldview in order to include the holistic nature of life, ultimately prompting them to think about and understand certain questions and challenging problems differently. Complexity, it has been suggested, is forming a kind of transdisciplinary way of thinking about living systems across multiple scales of organization in a way that transcends many usually taken-for-granted boundaries (Davis & Sumara, 2006).

Historically, a number of different complexity-related theoretical frames – like catastrophe theory, chaos theory, self-organized criticality, and complex adaptive systems – have emerged to describe a class of phenomena encompassing a wide range of forms, scales of organization and organizational dynamics (Stanley, 2005a). To be sure, this collection of twentieth-century theoretical frames suggests an important shift in contemporary theories of dynamical systems toward a "science of complexity," and one prompted by a realization that there are dynamical phenomena appropriately described as *complex*, although there are also others that do not fit into such a class owing to other kind of attributes and dynamics (Waldrop, 1992). The notion of complex systems originally arose around the realization that there are different kinds of dynamic phenomena that call for different interpretive and descriptive frames. Warren Weaver, an early cyberneticist and information theorist, was one of the first prominent scientists to question and address on a formal level the differences in the dynamics of various phenomena. In his seminal paper, "Science and Complexity," Weaver (1948) outlined three different classes of phenomena that have attracted the interest of many other scientists since then.

Weaver's work signaled an important early distinction among three kinds of different dynamical patterns which he termed *simple, disorganized complexity* and *organized complexity*. Simple systems were thought of and discussed in terms of small numbers of independent parts or variables that determined the actions and patterns of a system,and included single-body projectiles, planetary orbits, and, generally speaking, mechanical systems where the parts and the interactions of those parts are well-defined.

Eventually, scientists and mathematicians encountered or created more complicated systems where the number of interacting parts or variables used to understand or model the system was larger than most simple systems. Mathematician Henri Poincaré, for instance, serves as an example of one individual who met up with the intractability of working with some apparently simple systems that fell outside the realm of computability, as when he considered the now famous *Three Body Problem*. In the late nineteenth-century, as individuals considered systems with increasingly larger numbers of interacting parts or variables, the need for special analytical tools became necessary. For example, new analytic tools – ones quite different from the tools of Newtonian mechanics – were introduced through the invention of statistical instruments and the use of probabilities which came into prominence during this time. As various systems became more complicated, individuals needed to rely more upon macrodescriptions of these systems when the analysis of large numbers of agents in interaction proved computationally impracticable and sometimes impossible. As Davis (2003) writes:

The move to probability and statistics, then, was in response to the realization that no flesh-based intelligence was sufficiently vast. It was commentary on the limits of humanity, not on the nature of the universe. There was no questioning of the laws of mechanics or their appropriate application, merely a resignation to the fact that increasingly complicated phenomena made for decreasingly reliable characterizations. (p. 41)

These kinds of dynamical phenomena were later described by Weaver as *disorganized systems*.

Moreover, this movement also coincided with the need for the standardization of various industrialized processes and products. Subsequently, statistical tools also were imported into domains like education and, in fact, remain quite familiar to individuals in the social sciences where such phenomena often continue to be analyzed as disorganized complexity in spite of not being such. These kinds of tools, however, are not really appropriate for living systems.

The problem is that there are other kinds of phenomena that stretch across a wide range of organizational structure, including physiological systems, various social collectivities, and cultural and ecological phenomena, that are not examples of disorganized complexity at all. They are, as Weaver originally described them, organized complexity. Such systems, like classrooms or the workplace, the nervous system or traffic jams, do not easily surrender to us the secrets of their very being, especially through the analytic tools that were initially designed to interpret chance events or statistical distributions of attributes of large aggregates (e.g., machine parts). In fact, the study of living systems marked a big break from the mechanistic mindset. This change came about upon realizing that such systems are volatile and unpredictable because they have a capacity to modify themselves or adapt.

Today, the terms simple and disorganized complexity are not so prominent, having been reduced to the concept of *complicated* systems, used in today's more contemporary discourses to refer to events involving individual or collective independent actions, which includes both simple and disorganized complex systems. Similarly, complexity is generally used in popular parlance, superseding Weaver's original concept of organized complexity (Waldrop, 1992).

Several key concepts lie at the heart of many studies of complex phenomena with writers, scholars, and researchers alluding to notions like nonlinearity, self-organization, self-similarity, scale invariance, emergence, fractals, variability, and so on. These are but a few concepts discussed in the complexity literature, which I can only present in brief here.

(NON)LINEARITY

The concept of linearity, for instance, surfaces in a number of different guises and distinct contexts where meanings of the idea differ slightly although the overall abstractions are quite similar. Two properties, in particular, are often invoked: the "property of proportionality" and the "property of independence" (West, 1985). A system or process is said to be linear, for instance, if the output of some operation is directly proportional to the input, and if the input is allowed to vary, then the output will also vary predictably by some constant of proportionality. That is, there can be no possibility for a small change in the initial conditions to prompt some dramatic effect. Generally, if several factors are implicated in some system or process, then it is said to be linear if the end result is proportional to each factor. Mathematically speaking, it follows that each constant of proportionality is independent from one another.

Most of the world, however, is not that straightforward, for in a world of complex patterns, a capacity to adapt to a changing world requires a nonlinear being; in fact, herein lays the importance of being nonlinear. The world, in fact, is a very kinky kind of place, filled with bumps and warps and twists and all measure of deviant details. In terms of nonlinearity, *recursion* tends to play a significant part in such forms and processes. Recursion, suggesting a kind of rewriting, takes some element (e.g., a number or computed value) and applies a rule to create a subsequent element in an on-going process. Snowflakes are wonderful canonical examples of a recursive process at work. Through the dust in the atmosphere, temperature gradients, moisture in the air and the molecular structure of water, snowflakes take formation in a recursive play of being and becoming. Recursive processes of a nonlinear kind, therefore, have a way of transforming what is given into something that is new. This happens when human beings, and especially children, play and are being creative. Dampening nonlinear processes, as when one works with linear approximations, tends to squash possibility and creative emergence.

SELF-ORGANIZATION

The concept of self-organization, which is not a new term *per se*, describes how a system may bring itself into being on its own with a minimum of external direction or assistance. Where self-organized patterns occur, the features of the self-organized whole cannot be deduced from the descriptions of the local interactions of the system. In other words, the behavioral complexity of self-organizing systems depends on the sum of its interactions and not its individuals or parts (Solé & Goodwin, 2000). That is, the type and variety of localized interactions have a great deal to do with the behavior of the emergent system.

In a large system, individuals within it have no sense of the global picture, let alone a sense of how to build such a collectively organized structure. Nevertheless, the agents in the system can and do interact with one another without some key organizing figure to bring forth some continuously generated forms. That is, a variety of widespread recognizable forms and universal patterns appear in the world – even though, for example, no two trees, two flocks, two rivers, two cities, two brains are ever the same – through processes of self-organization.

Self-organization is a term that is generally applied to a wide range of processes that give rise to patterns that emerge within physical and biological systems (Camazine, 2001). Frequently discussed examples – virtual and otherwise – tend to include ants and ant colonies, termites and wood chip mounds, and birds and flocks (Flake, 1998). Human beings also self-organize under particular conditions and for different reasons. For example, self-organization happens as people cross a crosswalk. In moments of crisis, for instance, thousands of people can self-organize to create what is needed in the moment to help those in need. Rheingold (2002) notes a particularly political example of self-organization: the use of cell phones and other technologies by demonstrators to converge upon a potential demonstration site with little preconceived planning.

Of course, not all processes or approaches to some given task are self-organizing in nature. Templates, recipes, lesson plans or blueprints, for instance, might suggest a kind of prescriptive approach to carrying out some task at hand where there is no self-organization required. But, to be clear, prescription is not necessarily a bad thing, especially where there is no need to self-organize. It is the situation that would seem to matter.

FRACTALS, SELF-SIMILARITY, AND SCALE INVARIANCE

The topic of fractals is a common one in many complexity-related discussions, offering a new aesthetic for artists and scientists (Spehar, Clifford, Newall, & Taylor, 2003). In fact, there is a particular beauty about them and perfection in their imperfections where images of cracks, fractures, and wrinkles are common identifying *signatures*. To be sure, the concept of a fractal continues to permeate into and throughout a growing collective understanding of the roughness and kinkiness of the world (Briggs, 1992).

In as much as human intrusions upon the world attempt to straighten and flatten out details, bumps, and deviations, much of the world and its features are not easily rendered into linear-like patterns nor do these forms avail themselves to the linear measurements of classical Euclidean forms. Certainly, many human-made structures are easy to measure and describe with all of the usual Euclidean metrics, however, as Benoit Mandelbrot (Quoted in Flake, 1998) tells us: "Clouds are not spheres, mountains are not cones, coastlines are not circles, and bark is not smooth, nor does lightening travel in a straight line" (p. 93). Fractal geometry is the geometry of life. Put differently, as James Gleick (1988) writes, fractal geometry "mirrors a universe that is rough, not rounded, scabrous, not smooth. It is a geometry of the pitted, pocked, and broken up, the twisted, tangled, and intertwined" (p. 94). In other words, the features of complex phenomena, as manifest through the geometry of fractal forms, are not so much blemishes and pitfalls to be overcome, but the *real thing* – living things, complex things. Where Euclidean geometry seems quite fitting for the fixed and given, fractal geometry serves the flexible and emergent (Davis & Sumara, 2000).

When one looks deeper into or pulls back just a bit from the fractal structure or process of some complex phenomenon, one can't help but notice the presence of many different scales of detail; in some case, a certain byzantine-like architecture of similar structures emerges with each level of magnification. Like a tree with its branches, smaller limbs and twigs, and the veins of its palmated-leaves, scales of organized and self-organizing structures that bear a resemblance to one another can be found across many different scales: the larger tree looks like a smaller limb, each with smaller limbs on them, and twigs on them. This kind of pattern has a degree of *self-similarity* where the same kind of pattern can be found across a number of different scales or levels. In addition, complex phenomena in general show *scale invariance*, which is the omnipresence of detail – of bumps, folds, graininess, and so on – across many scales of the phenomenon all-at-once.

Taken together, self-similarity and scale-invariance suggest that fractal patterns are always and already nested bodies of diverse forms. These bodies form the conceptual frame that underlies all systems and manifest in biological subsystems, the biological body, social collectivities, the political state, the world of evolved species, and the larger ecological body or ecosphere (Davis, Sumara, & Luce-Kapler, 2000). Complexity, however, not only allows one to see complex nested structures, but complex processes and interactions as well. Thus, studies of the processes and forms of complex bodies-in-action are providing researchers and scholars with augmented and enhanced collection of diverse (fractal) images and (living) metaphors to understand a wide range of complex phenomena.

COMPLEXITY PRINCIPLES AND HEALTHY ORGANIZATIONS

To be sure, the complexity sciences have opened up a formalized view for understanding certain phenomena that can be framed by different dynamical patterns and processes. That is, paradigmatic complexity has risen, to some degree, as a scientific discourse for the purposes of distinguishing the classes of simple and complicated phenomena from the class of complex forms. Conceptually, each phenomenon is shaped by particular assumptions, and certain tools and approaches appropriate to each class of phenomena have been developed over time through increasingly sophisticated technologies and tools. In the context of complex systems, diverse scale-free (fractal) patterns and processes, nonlinear interactions, and the principle aspects of emergence and self-organization are at the heart of many phenomena encompassing the very small and the very large. Understanding physiological heath in light of complexity science makes the concept of *health* useful in understanding and creating conditions for particular kinds of social organizations, including classrooms, schools, and communities.

Complex, living organizations manifest themselves in a wide range of possible forms and behaviors in health and sickness – even more so when they are healthy. Diverse fractal patterns and processes, connectivity, non-linear interactions, and emergence and self-organization are, generally speaking, aspects and features of healthy organizations. The contrapositive – that unhealthy organizations lack or are otherwise gravely reduced in their scale-free patterns, diversity in form and processes, nonlinear interactions, connectivity, and emergent possibilities – is an observable phenomenon fitting in an analogical manner for human interaction in a variety of different social domains.

Historically, the Western concept of the body suggested that the body functioned in an orderly fashion. In fact, much of conventional medical wisdom still suggests that disease and aging arise from the external stresses of the world around us which affect an otherwise orderly and machine-like body. This view of health as an orderly phenomenon has not always been shared. Traditional Chinese Medicine, for instance, still maintains that the body, as a dynamically stable form, is composed of a network of organs sustained through "human activities of storing and spreading, preserving and transforming, absorbing and eliminating, ascending and descending, activating and quieting" (Kaptchuk, 2000, p. 75). Chinese sensibilities hold that health is about balance and offers no notion of *illness,* which is a Western notion rooted in the measurable, quantifiable entities of a body out of order. Where the Chinese recognize patterns of harmony or disharmony, the tendency for the medical profession in the West is to think of bodily illness and disorder as something to be fixed so that particular somatic structures might continue to perform properly. In other words, if disease were associated with an imbalance of some sort, the required regimen, once the diagnosis was made, could be applied and directed toward restoring the health of the individual to a more balanced state.

More recently, the notion of balance in the body has been described in terms of *homeostasis,* a term originally described by Claude Bernard in 1878 where he suggested that the stability of an organization's structural interior milieu, i.e., the human body, was designed so that "concentrations and rates of processes tended toward a stable state, through multiple feedback mechanisms." (Bassingthwaighte, Liebovitch, & West, 1994, p. 327) Researchers, however, have questioned whether this is in fact the body's *modus operandi,* opting instead for a view of *homeodynamics* which allows for a more flexible view of how a system might operate in more complex ways under various perturbations even to the extent of inherent instability (Goldberger, Rigney, & West, 1990).

Ary Goldberger and his colleagues at Harvard Medical School have discovered some rather counterintuitive findings about the ways in which the human body functions. In fact, their unexpected findings suggest that various physiological systems have a capacity for erratic – that is, complex – behavior when human beings are young and healthy. Moreover, as human beings age or develop certain illnesses, particular systemic behaviors become increasingly regular and ordered. Goldberger has framed a number of physiological systems, connected as they are to one another, according to underlying dynamics and patterns along a spectrum of healthiness.

It would seem apparent that certain pathologies arise under particular conditions that might be described as unhealthy. Viewing physiological health within complexity science, therefore, seems to open up new possibilities for thinking about the sorts of conditions for healthy organizations of different kinds. Thus, one might now ask the question: How might schools be understood through the metaphorical lens of health as healthy learning organizations and what would it take to make them so?

CONNECTIONS TO HEALTHY SCHOOLS

In the broad context of education, therefore, the notion of healthy learning organizations opens up the possibility for some compelling and different stances and perspectives on a variety of aspects of education, including learning and its relation to the identity, practices, and knowledge of learners; classroom dynamics; the framing and understanding of school subjects; curriculum design; pre-service programs for new educators; the influences of community and physical space; and leadership, to name a few. For now, however, this chapter will consider only how matters in schools might otherwise "get done." That is, the concern here will be on the notion and concept of leadership.

The concept of leadership has a history of being associated, although not solely, with hierarchy, management, and control (Wheatley, 1999). As with the concept of leadership in other contexts, a pervasive problem affecting educational leadership is that its definition and evolution have long been associated with highly centralized administrative hierarchical command-and-control structures (Morrison, 2002). As such, the work of an educational leader needs some reconsideration so as to help foster healthier learning organizations. Developing a healthier sense of leadership, founded upon principles, perspectives, and values that recognize it as relative and circulative, rather than absolute and centralized, involves a sense of distributed or shared leadership whereby action is localized and distributed across organizations. Even more, as Pascale, Milleman, and Gioja (2000) suggest, complexity thinking and its attendant principles need to be "translated into practical designs for the purpose of revitalizing organizations" (p. 35). As such, there is the possibility for a "pragmatics of complex transformation" (Davis, 2003, p. 44).

As healthy human beings, we function in particular ways that are shared hallmarks for all other kinds of healthy organizations of all scales from the individual to the classroom to peer groups, and on from there to the entire school, the community in which a school is embedded, and even the larger ecology. A model for a healthy school, in light of complexity thinking will therefore be one that can thrive and adapt and will resemble most closely who and what we are as human beings. To harness this kind of complexity in schools, however, requires a knowledge that self-organization and emergence, shared aspects of healthy organizations, are the "twin engines in the evolution of all living things" (Pascale et al., 2000, p. 146). For a school to self-organize and emerge in and through creative possibility implies that leadership cannot be centralized at the top, governing the school *body*. Instead, it must be distributed across a flattened organization where leadership roles may circulate as needed by the individuals and various collectives, which give rise to the school itself. In other words, the school must function as a democracy through the collective wisdom to steer itself rather than by fiat. Such a notion is fitting of other collectivities where intelligence of the group is far greater than the intelligence of any one member of the collective (Surowiecki, 2004).

If the universe, then, is inherently participatory, the capacity for cocreative possibility and adapting on the fly can become much greater. As Margaret Wheatley (1999) tells us, "great things are possible when we increase participation" (p. 46); such promise or possibility is within the capacity and ability of healthy organizations. In fact, distributed leadership through self-organization leads to the possibility that the larger collective can adapt much better than any given individual in the larger collective to the on-going situations at hand. And, in fact, many different kinds of organizations self-organize quite well: cell assemblies, schools of fish, flocks of birds, grassroots movements, and so on. These kinds of things happen without the direction of a single agent, and decentralization of action is at the heart of how and why these phenomena work so well.

Of course, as living organizations, the social organizations of which we are a part are inherently relational: relationships are the currency of life (Lewin & Regine, 2001). Empirical research shows how people-centred environments and the inherent relationality of such places – developed through interdependence, open communication, cooperative settings, respect and need for diversity and self-organization – are important conditions for healthy organizations (Morrison, 2002). As has been suggested here and shown elsewhere (Goldberger, 1997; Goldberger Amaaral, Hausdorff, Ivanov, & Peng, 2002; Walleczek, 2000), this kind of currency also presents itself in the biological body. In this way, the connections to different *bodies* is appropriate here, especially since the concept of the body is also used to describe things like a body of knowledge and a body politic (Davis et al., 2000). Thus, one might imagine how the complexities of such bodies might inform social bodies like schools, and, more importantly, in ways in which they could function in healthy ways. The claim here is that the same kinds of patterns arise in all living organizations, no matter what scale. Depending on the health of the organization, we might discover a dynamic, diversified, adaptable, creative organization that is full of possibility through distributed leadership or a dull, homogenous, environment heading to a slow and stagnant death..

Thus, if a school is treated as a living organization, then no matter how it may be managed, the on-going results will resemble something healthy and alive or something close to death. Although the former suggests dynamism and the latter suggests stasis, no school is ever one or the other. It is most likely *both/and* – life is paradoxical. Like all living things, the shift between health and illness is a constant on-going emergence of patterns in an unending dance with the world. Clearly, organizational theorists and leaders are embracing more holistic ways of viewing organizations that acknowledge how living systems emerge, learn, adapt, and change. Therefore, to think and act in a way that resembles other living systems, leaders must deal with a leadership style that is fundamentally paradoxical: lead without leading. As suggested by the preceding line of thought, the way through this paradox is to engage in shared practices, that are distributed throughout healthy organizations.

While these practices may seem simple, they are actually quite hard. This kind of paradoxical leadership requires allowing things to emerge; dealing with the ambiguities, uncertainties, and redundancies; and allowing for experimentation and mistakes to happen. In addition, emotionally and physically present leadership is another part of this formula. Moreover, this kind of leadership style requires an empathic position, an ability to listen and respond, and a capacity to have faith and trust in processes that give rise to the organization (Lewin & Regine, 2001). What would a school look like that functioned in this way? Messy? Sure. Chaotic and uncontrolled? Seemingly so. But such places can exist and do exist. They are wonderfully, engaging, and playful places that are open to creative possibility. They are also, at heart, places of real democratic practices built upon relational and distributed forms of leadership and notions of autonomy and responsibility.

CONCLUSION

In summary, this chapter has drawn upon ideas from the emerging field of complexity science to frame the idea that healthy learning organizations resemble other healthy life forms and, as such, must function through distributed processes and forms of leadership. It would seem that a kind of paradoxical nature exists in the kind of leadership I have articualted in this piece. How can we lead in an organization that self-organizes itself for its own purpose? However, the answer lies in the way in which this notion of leadership is framed. If schools are inherently living systems that ought to function in healthy ways, then we would do well to follow the wisdom of the living world. By pointing to examples from life itself to reconceptualize modern notions of leadership in education and how schools might function otherwise, society just might be able to consider and enjoy some healthier alternatives to many of the current manifestations of the project of schooling.

References

Bassingthwaighte, J. B., Liebovitch, L. S., & West, B. J. (1994). *Fractal physiology*. New York: Oxford University Press.

Berry, W. (1995). Health is membership. In *Another turn of the crank: Essays* (pp. 86-109). Washington, DC: Counterpoint.

Briggs, J. (1992). *Fractals: The patterns of chaos; a new aesthetic of art, science, and nature.* New York: Simon and Schuster.

Camazine, S. (2001). *Self-organization in biological systems*. Princeton, NJ: Princeton University Press.

Capra, F. (1983). *The turning point: Science, society, and the rising culture.* Toronto: Bantam Books.

Capra, F. (1996). *The web of life: A new scientific understanding of living systems.* New York: Anchor Books.

Capra, F. (2002). *The hidden connections: Integrating the hidden connections among the biological, cognitive, and social dimensions of life.* New York: Doubleday.

Davis, B. (2003). Toward a pragmatics of complex transformation. *Journal of the Canadian Association for Curriculum Studies, 1*(1), 39-45.

Davis, B., & Sumara, D. J. (2000). Curriculum forms: On the assumed shapes of knowing and knowledge. *Journal of Curriculum Studies, 32*(6), 821-845.

Davis, B., & Sumara, D. J. (2006). *Complexity and education: Inquiries into learning, teaching, and research.* Mahwah, NJ: Lawrence Erlbaum.

Davis, B., Sumara, D. J., & Luce-Kapler, R. (2000). *Engaging minds: Learning and teaching in a complex world.* Mahwah, NJ: Lawrence Erlbaum.

Flake, G. W. (1998). *The computational beauty of nature: Computer explorations of fractals, chaos, complex systems, and adaptation.* Cambridge, MA: MIT Press.

Gleick, J. (1988). *Chaos: Making a new science.* New York: Penguin Books.

Goldberger, A. L. (1997). Fractal variability versus pathologic periodicity: Complexity loss and stereotypy in disease. *Perspectives in Biology and Medicine, 40*(4), 543-561.

Goldberger, A. L., Amaaral, L. A. N., Hausdorff, J. M., Ivanov, P. C., & Peng, C.-K. (2002). Fractal dynamics in physiology: Alterations with disease and aging. *Proceedings of the National Academy of Sciences (Online), 99*(1 (Suppl.)), 2466-2472.

Goldberger, A. L., Rigney, D. R., & West, B. J. (1990, Feb 1990). Chaos and fractals in human physiology. *Scientific American, 262*, 42-49.

Kaptchuk, T. J. (2000). *The web that has no weaver: Understanding chinese medicine* (Rev. ed.). Chicago: Contemporary Books.

Lewin, R., & Regine, B. (2001). *Weaving complexity and business. Engaging the soul at work.* New York: Texere.

Morrison, K. (2002). *School leadership and complexity theory.* London and New York: Routledge Falmer.

Pascale, R. T., Milleman, M., & Gioja, L. (2000). *Surfing the edge of chaos: The laws of nature and the new laws of business.* New York: Three Rivers Press.

Rheingold, H. (2002). *Smart mobs: The next social revolution.* Cambridge, MA: Perseus Pub.

Solé, R. V., & Goodwin, B. C. (2000). *Signs of life: How complexity pervades biology.* New York: Basic Books.

Spehar, B., Clifford, C. W. G., Newell, B. R., & Taylor, R. P. (2003). Universal aesthetic of fractals. *Computers and Graphics, 27*(5), 813-820.

Stanley, D. (2005a). Paradigmatic complexity: Emerging ideas and historical views of the complexity sciences. In W. Doll, M. J. Fleener & J. St. Julien (Eds.), *Chaos, complexity, curriculum and culture.* New York: Peter Lang Publishing.

Stanley, R. D. (2005b). *Toward a view of healthy learning organizations through complexity.* Unpublished Dissertation, University of Alberta, Edmonton, Alberta.

Surowiecki, J. (2004). *The wisdom of crowds: Why the many are smarter than the few and how collective wisdom shapes business, economies, societies, and nations.* New York: Doubleday.

Waldrop, M. M. (1992). *Complexity: The emerging science at the edge of order and chaos.* New York: Simon & Schuster.

Walleczek, J. (2000). *Self-organized biological dynamics & nonlinear control: Toward understanding complexity, chaos, and emergent function in living systems.* Cambridge, UK; New York: Cambridge University Press.

Weaver, W. (1948). Science and complexity. *American Scientist, 32,* 536-544.

West, B. J. (1985). *An essay on the importance of being nonlinear.* New York: Springer-Verlag.

Wheatley, M. J. (1999). *Leadership and the new science: Discovering order in a chaotic world* (2nd ed.). San Francisco, CA: Berrett-Koehler Publishers.

EIGHT

STORIES THAT MUST BE TOLD: RECLAIMING TEACHERS' *OTHERNESS* THROUGH CRITICAL AUTOBIOGRAPHICAL RESEARCH

Luigi Iannacci

The central problem is this: How can the oppressed, as divided, unauthentic beings, participate in developing the pedagogy of their liberation? Only as they discover themselves to be "hosts" of the oppressor can they contribute to the midwifery of their liberating pedagogy. As long as they live in the duality in which *to be* is *to be like*, and *to be like* is *to be like the oppressor*, this contribution is impossible.

– Paulo Freire, Pedagogy of the Oppressed (1995 ed. p. 30)

Freire's question and the challenge it presents has haunted me for some time. As a former ESL student whose linguistic and cultural self was devalued and compromised in school systems, I understand oppression and have had the opportunity to explore how I have both housed and hosted my oppressor (Iannacci, 1998). The recognition of this process and the pedagogies it has fostered in my own teaching have led me to attempt to share what I have learned in my journey toward the discovery of a liberating rather than poisonous pedagogy (Goldstein, 1998). This chapter will address and confront the ways in which coercive relations of power and years of *received knowing* (Belenky, Bond, & Weinstock, 1997) can be reproduced in teaching practices. The chapter will also provide an alternative that may help teachers discover the oppressors they house and end victim-becomes-victimizer cycles; cycles that perpetuate notions of *being* in teaching as synonymous with being like one's oppressor. To this end, I draw on my own experiences as a cultural and linguistic minority student as well as the responses of other teachers who were also minority students to my story to reveal the interrelated nature of personal experiences and the construction of professional identities (Galindo & Olguin, 1996). In doing so, I aim to further develop the notion that critical autobiographical research can offer one way for teachers who were formerly minority students to confront taken-for-granted narratives that have cast them as received knowers (Belenky et al., 1997). This shift allows teachers to begin a process of becoming something beyond what their past dictates. This chapter explores the potential for critical autobiographical research by teachers to interrogate power relations assumed to be right, fate-driven and natural for those who have been constructed as *other* to experience, in an effort to prevent such notions from being reinscribed in their teaching practices.

THE OTHER

Belenky, Bond, and Weinstock. (1997) describe the typically subordinate positions marginalized groups including language and culture minority groups occupy within society as *other*. These positions are understood by dominant groups to be the result of not being "endowed with intellectual power" (p. 8). Such presumptions are thought to be held by dominant groups because of an adherence to polarized thinking that mirrors *norm/non-norm*, *us/other* classification. Belenky et al. (1997) argue that "because dualisms seem to bring great clarity to the most ambiguous and elusive issues, people are particularly apt to use them to organize their thinking about morality, epistemology, and identity development – clearly among the most difficult and the most important subjects ordinary human beings try to ponder" (p.20). These impetuously constructed polarities help further the divide between the us and the other and function as hierarchies that distort social relationships as they satiate a perverse need for certainty and conformity.

Research conducted by The Berkeley Group (c.1950) indicated that personalities that held rigid, dichotomous, and categorical understandings about the world tended to demonstrate hostile and punitive feelings toward any and all groups seen as culturally different. This was embodied in what they deemed to be the authoritarian personality. The Berkeley Group found that "any sort of imaginative and ambiguous introspection, art, or discourse seemed to make highly prejudiced people feel uncomfortable. Things that could not be fitted into a simple binary framework were simply ignored or dismissed with disdain as 'soft-headed'" (Belenky et al., 1997, p. 43).

In its adherence and commitment to perpetuating the mythical *norm*, school systems are often instrumental in rewarding and helping to foster categorical and dichotomous understandings that move professionals toward embodying the authoritarian personality while ensuring that the other is punished for difference. Such narrow thinking has been linked to the influence the eugenics movement has had in education, epistemological racism, as well as fascistic and genocidal tendencies (Davis, 1997; Belenky et al., 1997). Despite these problematic and troubling links, a teacher's insider status is often dependent upon their familiarity with group norms of achievement and ability. Teacher education programs have been implicated in their attempt to socialize students toward norms, thus essentially invalidate the reasons why candidates from minority backgrounds are sought out in the first place (Grant & Secada, 1990, p. 407 in Galindo & Olguin, 1996, p. 29). Stooke (2005) argues that being able to describe "normal" achievement is regarded as a professional necessity, particularly for teachers of elementary students. How teachers understand their roles is then contingent upon their ability to detect, diagnose, and then direct those who do not demonstrate these defined norms toward "normal" achievement.

Belenky, Bond and Weinstock (1997) argue that these binaries, and the heavily dichotomized world they help to create, ensure that the other develops an unquestioning belief in the authority of the oppressor that keeps them distant from that position of normativity constructed as viable, intelligent, and worthy. As a result, those in marginalized positions become what has been termed *received knowers*.

> Received knowers see themselves as capable of receiving knowledge by listening to authorities, but not as able to give voice to their own ideas. Received knowers assume that any problem has only one right answer and that one learns to tell "right" from "wrong" by listening to authorities. (p.59)

Given Friere's initial question, it is especially perplexing that an "unquestioning conformity to authorities and the norms of one's community can be particularly problematic for people presumed to be Other" (p. 59). This unquestioned conformity sustains the oppressor, since victims of binary thinking accept and internalize the understandings that us/other constructions generate and subsequently replicate them in their own relationships. After years of negotiating and renegotiating their identities in order to gain access into academic institutions, teachers from minority backgrounds can begin to reproduce these internalized understandings in their own practices rather than rejecting them.

Galindo and Olguin's (1996) research demonstrates and describes this dilemma. They argue that a majority of today's bilingual teachers who come from minority backgrounds experienced the devaluing of their cultural selves in schools because the hidden and not-so-hidden curriculum did not recognize the cultural resources or history of their communities. They believe that given these policies toward minority students, an ironic situation confronts those same students who eventually became teachers. They found that "in some cases, minority students who became educators minimized, devalued, or negated their own cultural backgrounds and shifted their values to match those represented by the school" (p.29). Galindo and Olguin's work suggests that after years of being institutionalized to garner academic credentials, teachers from minority backgrounds unconsciously reproduce the same relations of power they were accustomed to as students. Subsequently, their primary focus becomes the *giving* of schooling to their students as it was *given* to them. Their pedagogies can reassert a commitment to institutional hegemony as opposed to recognizing, valuing, and accessing diversity by accessing the cultural and linguistic resources they may have at their disposal. They become the *teacher*, as defined as one who discerns and disseminates linguistically and culturally bound norms rather than one who fosters and facilitates diversity.

Such conceptualizations of *teacher* embody the authoritarian personality in that they adhere to normalized understandings of targeted development and language acquisition. These conceptions may be the result of the modeling that teachers from minority backgrounds were exposed to as students in climates that did not foster critical thinking and questioning. After years of being cast as received knowers trapped in us/other, oppressor/oppressed relationships constructed to destroy linguistic and cultural otherness, minority students who eventually become teachers themselves can inadvertently reproduce these very same relationships.

This process of reproduction was evident during an ESL course I taught that took place completely on-line and was considered an additional qualification that certified teachers could take to further their professional development. The course writer utilized my story, changing some details from its original form from my Master's thesis into the following case study:

CASE STUDY: LOU

BACKGROUND INFORMATION

Lou spoke little English when he entered kindergarten. He said to his teacher, "I don't know that much because I speak Portuguese." He made good progress through Kindergarten but began to experience difficulty in Grade One. There was no L1 support at school. He loves soccer and likes to talk about his grandparents who live down the street from him.

FAMILY INFLUENCES

Lou's family is supportive and values literacy and language learning. His parents have limited education but his father has a successful sub-contracting construction business. His parents value school and want Lou to succeed.

LANGUAGE DEVELOPMENT

Portuguese is spoken at home. Lou is placed in an ESL withdrawal program for a limited time (half hour every three days). He learned oral English quickly and has developed real strengths in the language of the playground.

ADDITIONAL INFORMATION

Questions are emerging about intellectual potential. Lou repeated first grade and was recommended for special education since there was little progress in literacy acquisition. He received special education through to grade five.

LOU'S RESPONSE TO SCHOOL

> He loves to listen to stories and is most fluent in English when telling family stories. Lou loves literature.

CONSIDER:

> What are the issues that you see emerging from the limited profile provided?
>
> What questions do you have about Lou's experience?
>
> How would you assist Lou in the regular program?

RESPONSE ANALYSIS

I have examined and analyzed reactions to my personal story by four teachers in the course who self-identified as coming from culturally and linguistically diverse backgrounds. The case study awakened their past school experiences. Some of them described the difficulties they faced acquiring a second language. One of the course participants disclosed feelings of withdrawal she experienced in school as well as her inappropriate identification and placement in special education. Some of the teachers made connections between their personal experiences as linguistic and cultural minority students and their chosen career paths as teachers as well as their subsequent interest in taking the course. Generally speaking, these teachers tended to empathize with Lou and fully recognized his situation.

However, when asked to raise issues or questions with regards to Lou's experience, they focused their attentions on how they might assist Lou in the classroom. They spoke of the importance of authentic literature experiences, the use of books on tape, teacher read-alouds, role-playing and drama, and using Lou's personal experiences to further his acquisition of English. The focus of their suggestions was exclusively technical in that it tended to reiterate current professional knowledge with respect to literacy instruction. Although many of the instructional strategies they mentioned are pedagogically sound and appropriate when used with and for ESL students, the emphasis placed on them limited dialogue within the course.

Despite the fact that many of the teachers had personal experiences with the acquisition of a second language and could directly relate to what it's like to be a cultural and linguistic minority student in an English-only environment, none of their suggestions advocated for the accessing of Lou's linguistic resources (i.e. his first language). What

I find telling about this absent dialogue is how the technical professional concerns of teachers (even those who have backgrounds that would imply otherwise) reinforced what can be described as a given. That is, that the monolingual classroom space must remain so. As such, conceptualizations of the work ESL teachers do reinforces the notion that their job is to *give* English to ESL students, therefore validating it's power and prestige over first languages. English remains the targeted and desired language. Mother tongues go unrecognized, perhaps even misunderstood as disadvantageous or interfering with ESL teachers' efforts to ensure that their students acquire English. The primary concern for ESL teachers remains the efficiency with which this goal becomes accomplished. This goal is set, reinforced and celebrated by hegemonic, assimilationist orientations perpetuated by school systems. These stances may be understood as indicative of the "shift of values" (Galindo and Olguin's, 1996, p. 29) teachers who come from minority backgrounds make to match those represented by schools.

It may be argued that the focus of the teacher respondents' aforementioned instructional suggestions simply speak to the practical nature of the teachers' concerns. I argue however, that such stances illustrate the notion that teachers' claims to professionalism are directly related to the insider status they perpetuate as they concern themselves with discerning, diagnosing, and directing students toward norms as opposed to recognizing, validating, accessing, and fostering diversity. The missing dialogue seems to reinforce the fact that teacher identities become very entwined in professional discourse at the expense of or in opposition to personal experiences and cultural and linguistic "insider knowledge" (Patton, 1998, p. 31). Teachers are no longer Italian or African-Canadian when they teach; they are *teachers* and as such the culture and language of the teaching profession becomes where they are centered, what they identify with and becomes *excessively* influential in how they perform. What dominates as they teach is the diffusion of the values and sensibilities ascribed in their professional knowledge and lives. They shift from reception to reproduction as they move from being minority students to teachers of cultural and linguistic minority students. In short, what they once received, they reproduce.

The totality of the depiction of teachers who come from minority backgrounds as hosts and performers of culturally devoid, professionally fuelled conceptions of *teacher* need to be interrogated. Livingstone (1987) argues that "teachers resent being stereotyped as bearers of middle-class culture or agents of social control" (p.251).

Galindo and Olguin (1996) identify various cultural resources – cross-cultural competence being one of them – that teachers from minority backgrounds may have at their disposal once they have reflected upon them via a process of writing their own autobiographies (p.32). The autobiographical process and its importance in helping me to reclaim my cultural and linguistic "other" self both professionally and personally will be discussed later in this chapter. First, I'd like to examine how the cross-cultural competence Galindo & Olguin (1996) speak of was demonstrated by the teachers I am discussing in their on-line responses to the case study despite the fact that they had not formally reflected upon their possession of this cultural resource.

Cross-cultural competence was demonstrated in how these teachers responded to some of their on-line colleagues' comments that seemed to question Lou's parents' commitment to and role in his academic life. The teacher respondents perceived their colleagues comments as directing blame toward Lou's parents for his lack of achievement and placement in Special Education. In stark contrast to these notions, the teachers from minority backgrounds tended to support Lou's parents by sharing their own parents' beliefs about the importance of school and highlighting the type of literacy provisions they received at home as children. They pointed out that their parents were instrumental in fostering literacy in ways that schools have not traditionally recognized. The prevalence of family stories and the overall richness of oral communication in their parents' homes were illustrations of this point. They mentioned how language barriers, financial difficulties, and cross-cultural differences in understandings of home-school relationships prevented their parents from performing culturally bound, middle-class understandings of parental literacy support. The respondents stressed both the emotional sustenance they received at home and the value their parents placed on literacy and education.

Reactions to their colleagues' comments conveyed the understanding that, although school conceptions of literacy support were not mirrored in their family situations, literacy was nonetheless being fostered and developed along with a respect for education. Without this insider knowledge (Patton, 1998), such communications would have potentially remained absent from the on-line discussion. The teachers' backgrounds therefore provided the impetus for such a discussion to become realized.

Unfortunately, the respondents' cross-cultural competence did not extend itself toward an understanding and advocacy for multiculturally literate classroom settings. Two of the teachers commented on the importance of home language maintenance since they felt that parents should continue to use their first language at home. These teachers also believed that parents needed to learn English in order to read to, and with, their children in two languages and code switch freely (alternate between their first language and English). Unfortunately, this fostering of multicultural literacy (Courts, 1997) was relegated solely to home activity. None of the teachers suggested that such practices be utilized in ESL instruction despite course content that made explicit and validated this practice. Instead, their discourse tended to reinforce the notion that ESL teaching is about the attainment of English without recognizing, valuing, or accessing first languages.

Also telling was one teacher's empathy with Lou's identification and placement in special education. The expression of empathy was followed by frustration in trying to get one of the ESL students in her class assessed in order to receive special education attention. Again, the role of teacher as discerner, diagnoser, and deliverer of *normed* understandings of development seemed to overshadow and silence the potential for teachers' cultural and linguistic *other* selves to be accessed as resources that may help to reconceptualize how they see themselves in the role of teacher and alter what they offer their students.

This shift of values from the personal and cultural to the institutional additionally ensured that the pathogolizing of ESL students in schools remained unquestioned. A political and critical understanding of the structures that reinforce deficit understandings with regards to language and culture also remain unvoiced. Problematizing the difference-as-deficit thinking imposed on students like Lou who go on to experience misidentification consistent with the over representation of minorities in special education (Bernhard et al., 1995; Patton, 1998), subsequently went unrecognized despite the personal experiences of teachers who had been victims of deficit models in school systems. In short, oppression continued to be reinscribed in and through the oppressed.

Perhaps some of the resentment teachers feel toward being stereotyped as "cultural tour guides" and "agents of social control" (Livingstone, 1987) has to do with the fact that many of the sensibilities explored thus far, are unconsciously internalized and manifestations of years of uncritically reflected upon knowledge reception. As such, the question posed by Freire that opened this chapter remains provocative and perplexing How can we make the unconscious, conscious? How do we shift what is understood and done unconsciously toward that which is consciously reflected upon? How do we become aware of, confront and exorcise the oppressors we house?

First, we must remember that "no one conscientizes anyone else" (Gadotti, 1994, p.166). However, if we consider Friere's notion of conscientization, we can begin to think about possibilities that may help minority teachers begin their journey toward that state. Bimbi (1994) outlines this process. She argues that a first step is to critically reflect upon circumstances in order to overcome them. Next, sharing the process in interaction and dialogue with communities is essential. Last, such community building ideally helps to establish the conditions for social transformation and societal change (in Gadotti, 1994, pp. 16-17). This final phase can "result in transformative praxis, a collectively organized act of education with emphasis on the subject" (Gadotti, 1994, p. 23). For minority teachers, this means a reevaluation of their professional selves, and a reawakening of their cultural and linguistic otherness. The researched return to who they were may allow them to see and value their students' connectedness to the cultural and linguistic communities they are apart of.

Critical autobiographical research can help teachers begin the first step of their journey toward conscientization. Galindo and Olguin (1996) believe that "teacher's life histories may be viewed as autobiographical funds of knowledge that provide information regarding cultural resources" (p.30). They argue that these resources "need to be reclaimed in order to counteract the many years during which the teachers may not have considered some of the resources as relevant or pertinent to their learning or teaching" (p. 30). Like the respondents in this study, some teachers may demonstrate cultural resources without having written critical autobiographical research. However Galindo & Olguin (1996) claim that there is a need to provide examples to teachers to demonstrate how they can reclaim cultural resources from their life histories (p. 30). Such examples can make explicit cultural values that are implicitly understood and, therefore, provide crucial information to nonminority teachers working with minority children (p. 40). They conceptualize this recuperative process as one that involves "educators making sense of their own socialization in terms of its meaning to them in their role as educators" in order to "counteract the many years of devaluing of cultural resources by institutions of formal education that might have caused some minority educators to negate or reject some of those resources" (pp. 30-31). This process serves a twofold purpose:

> (a) to draw attention to taken-for-granted cultural resources that may be important building blocks of personal teaching philosophies, and to work toward drafting one's understanding of those resources; and (b) to incorporate cultural resources in personal teaching philosophies in order to facilitate home-school connections and decrease the cultural alienation that minority students experience in school (p. 39).

Galindo and Olguin (1996) also claim that this process is essential for minority teachers to experience since they in fact "can present a more rigid transmission of dominant cultural values than that perpetuated by some non-minority teachers" (p. 40). This occurs because they "become convinced that minority students will not succeed unless they reject some of their cultural resources for the resources and values advocated by school culture" (p. 40). Galindo and Olguin argue that "the fact that these messages are presented by teachers from similar cultural backgrounds makes it especially troubling for minority students" (p. 40).

My personal experiences corroborate this notion and reinforce the importance and effectiveness of critical autobiographical teacher research in helping teachers toward conscientization. At this point I'd like to share what I found during the process of writing my critical autobiography. In examining the relevance of socialization in terms of my role as educator, I was able to begin the process of exorcising my housed oppressor, reclaiming my otherness and reconceptualizing my understandings of *teacher*.

One of the ways I did this was by recalling and critically analyzing discourse present within my practice. Through this exploration, dialectically problematic metaphors that were indicative of contradictory personas that I had taken on in my teaching became apparent. In examining these contrasting metaphors, I made some critical observations that revealed the influence my personal story had within my teaching. In examining these metaphors I came to realize that I ideally saw myself as a performer and, therefore, tried to foster an environment whereby my audience had power and influence in my performance. This was demonstrated in my description of the classroom as a theatre and my belief that all good teachers had to be aware of the importance of theatricality in ensuring that their students – the audience – remain interested. More importantly, students had to be of vital importance in determining what and how cirricula is performed.

It would appear that my belief in and use of the performer metaphor within my teaching ensured that I cultivated collaborative relations of power. However, in examining some of the other metaphoric language I used in my teaching, I came to realize that I also fostered coercive power relations that manifested in the use of what can best be described as nautical terms. In an effort to motivate and create class solidarity, I would refer to the classroom as a ship and declare that if everyone within it didn't do their job, then the ship would sink. As I reflected, I came to realize that if the classroom was a ship, then I of course saw myself as its captain. This would also explain why the *ship's captain* tended to emerge when issues of coverage, control and class management surfaced. The ship's captain figure and the metaphors he used were more aligned with what the school system valued and reinforced. The disparity between who I was and wanted to represent myself as within my teaching, and the personae that was created as a result of feeling the need to control the environment ensured that duplicitous and contrary teaching metaphors were developed and utilized in my teaching.

My working-class, ESL background ensured that when I exercised the need to cover, control, and coerce, I did so in good conscience. Since I taught in the same area I grew up in, I felt like I was facing a younger version of myself each day and, therefore, had the urge to *save* my students by providing them with what I felt they needed to succeed. I had strong feelings about working class ESL students and stunted upward mobility, for I had experienced this within my own elementary school career. Having *survived* this, I felt compelled to enable my students to *escape* the systemic inadequacies that disabled me. I felt extremely protective toward them and wanted them to have more than I had. Therefore, when the ship's captain personae surfaced and coverage, coercion, and control was exercised in the top-down fashion that the school system supported and fostered, I remained undeterred since I knew these conditions to be necessary in securing student success.

This had implications in terms of the power relations secured in the room. In those moments when the ship's captain emerged, I established a hierarchy of power that contrasted the collaborative power relations I worked hard to establish and learned to foster as I *performed* curriculum rather than transmitting it. When the ship's captain was in control, he knew what was best for everyone. They were all in his ship and he was determined to ensure that they reach the destination he had decided they needed to reach. In short, I ensured that the hierarchical, coercive relations of power I experienced in school went unquestioned and reproduced in my practice. I also felt justified in doing so because the system I represented in these moments viewed these relations as ideal since knowledge, control and authority remained in the hands of the teacher and, therefore, learning, in the systemic sense of the word, occurred. Students were being indoctrinated into the assimilative, middle class world that the school system reflects, supports, and fosters: a world I was excessively familiar with as a former ESL student.

Although rewarded and perversely vindicated, these particular moments also made me feel an uncomfortable sense of collaboration with this system without guilt since I still believed that my background meant that even though I was dispelling and coercing, I was doing so in a way that was beneficial for my students and would help secure their success within the school system. In terms of Lisa Delpit's (1995) work, I could be understood as reasserting the *culture of power* by setting conditions that allowed students to passively adopt its code as opposed to making its rules explicit while encouraging students to understand the value of the code they already possessed. Such stances ensure what Cummins (1991) has described as a subtractive rather than additive form of bilingualism and biculturalism.

CONCLUSION

The knowledge garnered through critical autobiographical work informed and continues to inform my practice. The process helped me begin to conceptualize a way of being in teaching that contradicted, confronted, and challenged what I had previously been led to believe was necessary in becoming a good teacher. Through the process of documenting and critically analyzing my story in relation to my role as teacher, I additionally came to understand how my cultural and linguistic resources could be accessed in order to foster a multiculturally literate classroom setting. I also began to alter the presence detrimental, coercive relations of power had in my own personal and professional life. Interrogation of my story provided me with an opportunity to use my previous subordinated status as an instrument for metamorphosis, therefore subverting its previous detrimental effects in the development of my pedagogy. I became empowered and liberated as I began to break the hold of the oppressor.

It must be noted that this process is not about blame and shame, but rather the deconstruction of what has been naturalized and taken for granted in education in order to avoid its continuance. By taking a critical look at our own stories as professionals and linking them to our practices, we may begin to destabilize and disempower the mythologies we have appropriated and reinforced. It is hoped that in doing so, we create new mythologies, storylines and ways of being in our profession that reflects our conscientization. In so doing, teachers from minority backgrounds may have a better chance of reconceptualizing their position as an agent of a system to one who has agency in a system.

It must also be noted that this process may be helpful for many teachers to experience regardless of their cultural and linguistic backgrounds since they were all students at on time and have encountered specific ideas of schooling and of *teacher*. Critical reflection of personal educational stories may serve as a great source of information that can lead teachers to a better understanding of themselves as people and as professionals. The process may help teachers ensure that the curriculums they perform are informed by power relations that serve liberating rather than oppressive pedagogies. This may in turn, enable the students they teach to critically consider their place within the world and subsequently promote reconceptualized understandings of that world.

References

Belenky, M.F., Bond, L.A., Weinstock, J.S. (1997). Otherness. In Belenky, M.F., Bond, L.A., Weinstock, J.S. (ed.), *A tradition that has no name: Nurturing the development of people, families, and communities.* (pp.3-66). New York: Basic Books.

Bernhard, K. et al. (1995). *Paths to equity. Cultural, linguistic and racial diversity in Canadian early childhood education.* Toronto: York Lanes Press.

Courts, P. (1997). *Multicultural literacies: Dialect, discourse, and diversity.* New York: Peter Lang Inc.

Cummins, J. (1991). Language development and academic learning. In Malave, L & Duquette, G. (Eds.), *Language, culture and cognition: A collection of studies in first and second language acquisition.* Philadelphia: Multilingual Matters.

Davis, L. (1997). Constructing normalcy. In L. Davis (ed.), *The disability studies reader* (pp.9-28). New York: Routledge.

Delpit, L. (1995). *Other peoples' children: Cultural conflict in the classroom.* New York: The New Press.

Freire, P. (1995). *Pedagogy of the oppressed.* New York: Continuum.

Gadotti, M. (1994). *Reading Paulo Freire: His life and work.* New York: S.U.N.Y Press.

Galindo, R. & Olguin, M. (1996). Reclaiming bilingual educators' cultural resources: An autobiographical approach. *Urban Education, 31*(1), 31-44.

Goldstein, L.S. (1998). More than gentle smiles and warm hugs: Applying the ethic of care to early childhood education. *Journal of Research in Childhood Education, 17*(2), 244-261.

Iannacci, L. (1998). *An autobiographical account of first language and culture replacement.* Unpublished master's thesis, University of Western Ontario, Ontario, Canada.

Livingstone, D. (1987). *Critical pedagogy and cultural power.* Toronto: Garamond Press.

Patton, J.M. (1998). The disproportionate representation of African Americans in special education: Looking behind the curtain for understanding and solutions. *The Journal of Special Education, 32*(1), 25-35.

Stooke, R. (2005). 'Many hands make light work' but 'too many cooks spoil the pot': Representing literacy teaching as a 'job for experts' undermines efforts to involve parents. *Journal of Curriculum Studies, 37*(1), 3-10.

NINE

FREEDOM OF ASSOCIATION – NOT JUST A *CASUAL* CONCERN: SOCIAL JUSTICE FOR SUBSTITUTE TEACHERS

Carmen Pickering

The growing casualization of Canada's workforce is an enduring and growing concern. Among other things, casual employment means less stability, greater uncertainty and more often than not, reduced income and benefits for an employee. A casual workforce is prevalent in many professions and sectors including education. Substitute teachers, occasional teachers, supply teachers and teachers-on-call encompass this casual contingent within the teaching profession and provide a vital support and function to the public education system. Consequently, these teachers should have the same rights and benefits afforded their full time, regularly employed counterparts – the ability to be represented by a teacher's union and subsequently, to be covered under a collective agreement. However, despite reasonable gains achieved in the teachers' employment context and in the labour movement in general, a number of jurisdictions across Canada continue to thwart casual teachers' efforts to do so. To refuse casual teachers this right is to deny teachers one of the primary tenets and principles of the labour movement: freedom of association and, thereby, obstructs a casual teacher's civil rights. In a modern, progressive society, this condition is simply unacceptable. Respect for human rights must be evident in every context: in the classroom, the communities and especially within the employment environment. How we treat each other is paramount.

This chapter will explore the topic of the casual workforce in the teaching profession in light of freedom of association. To that end, this chapter will illustrate the extent to which legislation and employer policy has treated casual teachers as a marginalized group within the teaching profession. Specifically, what is the extent of substitute teacher representation across Canada and what effect does provincial or territorial legislation have on whether substitutes are represented or not? In addition, a review of the union advantage in general will be provided, as well as an examination of whether the assumptions hold true for substitutes. As such, given a positive view of having substitutes in the bargaining unit or in their own bargaining unit, the challenges to associate freely will be highlighted using a recent Manitoba Teachers' Society case. To conclude, new strategies in overcoming the resistance to a casual's right of freedom of association in other sectors are offered to illustrate additional options available to achieve this fundamental civil right in public education.

Definitions

Casual Teacher

Within the teaching profession, substitutes, occasionals, supply and teachers-on-call comprise those teachers captured within the meaning of Human Resources and Social Development Canada's contingent workforce that are employed under nonstandard working conditions including such things as pay and hours of work. Intuitively, substitutes, occasionals, supply and teachers-on-call are those teachers employed on a day-to-day basis to replace a teacher who is temporarily absent. To the extent that substitutes are defined in provincial legislation, the descriptions are varied and often unique to the particular jurisdiction.

Freedom of Association

Enacted as Schedule B to the Canada Act 1982 (U.K.) 1982, c.11, the *Canadian Charter of Rights and Freedoms* provides under Section 2 that "everyone has the following fundamental freedoms," which includes the "freedom of association". Legal jurisprudence has summarized three elements of freedom of association as well as a critical fourth principle:

first, that s. 2(d) protects the freedom to establish, belong to and maintain an association; second, that s. 2(d) does not protect an activity solely on the ground that the activity is a foundational or essential purpose of an association; third, that s. 2(d) protects the exercise in association of the constitutional rights and freedoms of individuals; and fourth, that s. 2(d) protects the exercise in association of the lawful rights of individuals (*The Professional Institute of the Public Service of Canada v. Northwest Territories (Commissioner)*, 1990, p.40).

In other words, a substitute's right to belong to, participate in, and enjoy the benefits of membership in its teacher union without repercussion or fear of reprisal on legal or other grounds, are seemingly well entrenched in the legislation. However, the right is not absolute and frequently subject to challenge – as is the case of substitutes in a number of Canadian provincial jurisdictions. In addition, freedom *not to associate* is inferred.

INTERNATIONAL LABOUR ORGANIZATION

On July 9th, 1948, the General Conference of the International Labour Organization (ILO) adopted Convention 87: Freedom of Association and Protection of the Right to Organize. Convention 87 is recognized as "an important element in the protection of civil and political rights, namely the right to democracy" (Dunning, 1998, para. 4). Its connection to Human Rights is also well established: Convention 87 served as the platform for key elements of the United Nations Universal Declaration of Human Rights (Dunning, 1998).

The Convention on freedom of association promotes the recognition that workers have rights related to the establishment and the functioning of trade unions and the adoption by all ILO member States of laws or regulations that protect those rights. It includes

the right of workers' and employers' organizations to draw up their own constitutions and rules, to elect their own representatives. To formulate their own programmes, and to join federations, national and international; and to do this without interference by the public authorities (Dunning, 1998, para. 4).

All members of the ILO are required to formally accept the obligations of its Constitution, in which the principle of freedom of association is embodied. The ILOs Declaration of Philadelphia, signed in 1944, affirms its commitment to freedom of association: "The conference confirms the fundamental principles on which the Organization is based and, in particular, that . . . (b) freedom of expression and of association *are essential to sustained progress*" (ILO, 1944). Furthermore, the "Preamble" to the ILO Constitution also stresses recognition of the principle of freedom of association. By virtue of its membership in the ILO, Canada formally accepts the obligations of the ILO Constitution including the principle of freedom of association. Notably, with the support of all provincial and territorial governments, Canada ratified Convention 87 in March 1972 (Fudge, 2005).

Nonetheless, the freedom of association is not absolutely guaranteed by virtue of the *Charter* or by virtue of Canada's signing of C87. In 1987, The Supreme Court of Canada delivered its judgements in the *Labour Trilogy* – a collection of cases that answered the question as to whether the *Charter*'s guarantee of freedom of association would reflect the ILOs broad freedom of association principles. "The legal issue was whether the term 'freedom of association' as used in Section 2 of the *Charter* included the right to collective bargaining and the right to strike" (Fudge, 2005, p. 70). The Court took a much more limited view than that of the ILO and concluded that under the *Charter*, freedom of association did not include these rights and stated they "are not fundamental rights or freedoms. They are the creation of legislation"(Canadian Charter of Rights Decisions Digest, 2004, p.5). However, that premise was challenged by a successful legal ruling in 2001 that charged the Ontario government with violating the *Charter* by excluding agricultural workers from the *Ontario Labour Relations Act* (OLRA) and prompted passage of the *Agricultural Employees Protection Act* (AEPA) to allow farm workers to form associations but not unions (See *Dunmore v. Ontario (Attorney General)*, [2001] 3 S.C.R. 1016). Unfortunately, in a subsequent challenge of the AEPA on the grounds it continues to deny agriculture workers the right to collective bargain under the OLRA, the Court ruled the AEPA is not necessarily a contravention of the *Charter*. The result is under appeal by the United Food and Commercial Workers, who are representing the agriculture workers.

Substitute Representation

Legislative Impact

As the preceding highlights, moderately successful *Charter* challenges deem that freedom of association and all it may encompass is not a foregone conclusion, not least of which for casual workers including substitute teachers. Because of provincial or territorial legislation, New Brunswick, Prince Edward Island and the Yukon prevent substitute teachers from becoming members in the bargaining unit. All others include substitutes to varying degrees ranging from full inclusion and ongoing membership in the provincial bargaining unit (e.g. British Columbia) or in separate bargaining units (e.g. Ontario and Manitoba) to membership in the bargaining unit until the end of the school year or until they are no longer on the approved substitute roster of the school board (e.g. Alberta) or membership solely for the days taught (e.g. Nunavut).

In New Brunswick and the Yukon, how an *employee* is defined is what ultimately excludes substitute teachers. The New Brunswick *Public Service Labour Relations Act* defines an "'employee' as a person employed in the Public Service, other than . . .a person employed on a casual or temporary basis unless the person has been so employed for a continuous period of six months or more." In addition, substitute teachers are not recognized as employees under the definition captured by the Yukon's *Education Staff Relations Act*. "'Employee' means a person who is employed under the provision of this Act, or who is a member of the bargaining unit, but does not include . . . a person employed on a relief, casual, or substitute basis." Finally, the *Instructional Personnel Regulations* under Prince Edward Island's *School Act* explicitly prohibit substitute teachers from bargaining unit membership or coverage. Section 25 of this act acknowledges the Prince Edward Island Teachers' Federation 'shall be the authorized representative' of teachers but Section 2.(4) negates this representation for substitutes, "Other sections of these regulations *do not apply to substitutes* for teachers" (emphasis added).

THE UNION ADVANTAGE

BENEFITS FOR ALL WORKERS

In its comprehensive 2002 survey of more than 1 000 primary and secondary studies, the World Bank has confirmed the economic benefit conferred on unionized workers. Moreover, the Bank notes that comparative studies found little decrease in economic performance to negate the economic benefits for countries that enforce the right to collective bargaining and the right to freedom of association compared with those countries that do not protect these rights. (Tzannatos and Aidt, 2002). The report highlights the following worker and where appropriate, Canadian-worker specific benefits:

- Union members and other workers covered by collective agreements in industrial countries do, on average, get a wage mark up over their nonunionized (or uncovered) counterparts. The wage mark up is higher in the private sector than in the public sector.

- Unions compress the wage distribution. The wage differentials between skilled and unskilled workers and the private return to education are reduced when unions are present.

- Unions contribute to a reduction in the overall gender pay gap.

- Unions have been found to reduce the discrimination against indigenous people.

- Voluntary job turnover is lower and job tenure is longer.

- Lower working hours.

- Unionized workers tend to receive more training.

Reasonably, all teachers, their teacher associations, education administrators, and governmental bodies are hard pressed to ignore such compelling evidence. Indeed, allowing casual teachers to organize may provide benefits not only to the substitutes themselves, but also to society as a whole.

Statistics Canada's 1999 *Survey of Labour and Income Dynamics* also lends support to the union advantage, especially related to benefit coverage including extended medical, dental, life or disability insurance.

Workers in unionized jobs were almost twice as likely as their non-unionized counterparts to be covered in each of the three plans. For example 84% of unionized employees reported having an extended medical plan, compared with only 45% of non-unionized employees. The gap was even wider in terms of pension plan coverage, where 80% of unionized employees had such a plan, compared with only 27% of non-unionized employees (NUPGE News Release, 2002, para. 3).

BENEFITS FOR TEACHERS AND SUBSTITUTES

The benefit of union membership to teachers is borne out by the data, especially related to wage increases. Over a five year period, workers in the education sector received the same or higher average percentage increases than the average received by all industries in every year but one.

Effective Wage Increases in Collective Agreements

	2001	2002	2003	2004	2005
All Industries	3.3%	3.0%	2.6%	1.9%	2.4%
Education, Health, and Social Services	3.6%	3.2%	3.5%	1.6%	2.4%

Source: Statistic Canada, 2007, CANSIM, Table 278-0007

When one reviews the gains achieved for substitute teachers, the results are impressive and are not merely limited to wage benefits. Indeed, the responsibilities of these teachers for educating our children are no less than any other classroom teacher regardless of status. However, the disparity between the wages of those substitute teachers covered by a collective agreement and those not are compelling. Substitute teachers under a provincial and territorial teachers' collective agreement receive daily rates (effective September 1, 2006) reaching a high of $200.00 for educators covered by the Government of Northwest Territories teacher agreement, while teachers denied membership receive rates of $123.21, $140.00 and $176.59 in Prince Edward Island, New Brunswick and the Yukon, respectively. Certainly regional differences account for the large spread but grouping similar jurisdictions yields comparable results. Substitute teachers in

Newfoundland and Labrador fare significantly better than their New Brunswick and Prince Edward Island counterparts as do Nunavut and the Government of Northwest Territories substitute teachers compared to those in the Yukon.

DAILY RATES OF PAY (EFFECTIVE SEPTEMBER 1, 2006) IN SELECTED JURISDICTIONS

Jurisdiction	Daily Rate
Newfoundland & Labrador	$167.90
Nova Scotia	$140.00
New Brunswick	$140.00
Prince Edward Island	$123.21
Goverment of Northwest Territories	$200.00
Nunavut	$184.00
Yukon	$176.59

Source: Ibid.

Although competitive wage rates are a significant gain, for some substitute teachers union representation and benefits of membership extend beyond the negotiation of competitive wage rates. In a number of jurisdictions, substitute teachers are given or at least afforded the opportunity to obtain a number of benefits that their permanent teaching colleagues also receive. In order to continue to encourage and in some sense, reward the substitute teachers' ongoing service and commitment to their school and students, entitlement to benefits are one means by which education authorities can lessen the marginalization of this critical resource.

INSURANCE BENEFITS

Several jurisdictions offer substitutes a full opportunity to participate in their school board's group benefits plan which includes: accidental death and dismemberment, medical, dental, life insurance, short-term salary continuation, and liability. In Newfoundland and Labrador, substitutes contribute the full premium amounts and are then eligible to receive benefits in all plans but Liability, and may receive short-term salary only until the end of their contract period. In Nova Scotia, substitutes who work more than ten days in the school year and pay full premiums receive all benefits but short-term salary. In British Columbia, substitute teachers are eligible for all benefits but short-term salary provided they pay the full premiums and are not excluded due to the conditions in the health plans.

Regional differences account for varied opportunities to access group benefits in Alberta and Ontario. In Calgary, participation in the plan is a condition of employment while substitutes bear the full cost of the benefit plan premiums. They receive coverage under all categories but short-term salary and liability. Conversely, substitute teachers in Edmonton receive benefits solely related to workplace injury. The Board will reimburse medical expenses due to injury on the job and pay the substitute the per diem rate for a maximum of twenty consecutive teaching days immediately following the injury. For some substitute teachers covered by Elementary Teachers' Federation of Ontario agreements, benefits may be available for working a minimum number of days in the previous year and includes all but liability. Frequently, premiums are the responsibility of the teacher. In many instances, access to benefits at the teacher's expense applies to substitute teachers hired for a long-term occasional contract in Ontario School Boards.

Similarly, substitute teachers in Saskatchewan, Quebec, Manitoba, Government of Northwest Territories and Prince Edward Island have greater access to benefits upon a longer-term contract. In Quebec, benefits are available to replacement teachers on contract covering for an absence of at least three months while Manitoba substitutes on temporary contract for greater than 60 days or 120 days receive health and dental, and life, respectively. For Saskatchewan's substitutes, accidental death and dismemberment is available and voluntary upon hire while dental and life is available for teachers on contract for more than twenty days. Prince Edward Island substitute teachers on a term contract for three months are eligible for all benefits. Finally, substitutes on a term contract of a minimum of four months that are included in the Northwest Territories Teachers' Association bargaining unit for the Government of Northwest Territories have access to benefits after three months.

Not surprisingly, day-to-day substitutes in Prince Edward Island, New Brunswick and the Yukon are precluded access to benefits. Interestingly, although substitutes in Nunavut may be part of the bargaining unit, they are not eligible for group insurance benefits.

PENSION PLAN MEMBERSHIP

A majority of jurisdictions deem substitutes' participation in teachers' pension plans compulsory. This is the case in British Columbia, Saskatchewan, Ontario, Quebec, Nova Scotia, and to a lesser extent in Newfoundland and Labrador and the Government of Northwest Territories. In Newfoundland and Labrador, day-to-day substitutes make compulsory contributions to a Government Money-Purchase Plan while full membership in the pension plan is offered upon periods of teaching in excess of nineteen consecutive days. Substitutes covered by the Government of Northwest Territories collective agreement are required to participate if their teaching hours exceed 12 hours per week.

Voluntary pension plan membership is available to teachers in Alberta and Manitoba. In Manitoba, substitute teachers must participate if their earnings exceed one-quarter of yearly maximum pensionable earnings in two successive years.

Again, pension plan participation is not available to those substitutes excluded from membership in their respective bargaining units: New Brunswick and Prince Edward Island. However, Prince Edward Island demands compulsory pension plan membership for substitute teachers with twenty or more consecutive days in the same assignment. The Northwest Territories does not permit access to superannuation while in Nunavut, substitutes are not eligible for teachers' pension membership.

OTHER BENEFITS

Long-term contracts and a greater number of consecutive teaching days are the triggers to provide additional benefits to substitute teachers in all jurisdictions but the Yukon and Nunavut. Cumulative sick leave is available to substitutes in Newfoundland and Labrador for replacement teaching of twenty days or fifty days total substitute teaching, while in Prince Edward Island, Nova Scotia, and New Brunswick, substitute teachers receive cumulative sick leave after twenty consecutive teaching days in the same assignment. Teachers signed to a long-term occasional contract in Ontario receive credits per a certain number of teaching days or per month of teaching. Similarly, substitutes covered by the Government of Northwest Territories agreement receive sick leave credits per month worked provided they have worked more than ten days in that month. In British Columbia and some jurisdictions in Manitoba, substitute teachers are entitled to sick leave benefits from the sixth and ninth consecutive teaching day in a single assignment, respectively. Teachers' placement on a temporary or part-time contract in Quebec, Saskatchewan, and some Alberta regions determine eligibility to sick leave.

FREEDOM OF ASSOCIATION?

THE RECOGNITION CHALLENGE

Recent events in Manitoba highlight the obstacles that confront substitute teachers in exercising their freedom of association. In 2000, the provincial government enacted the *Public Schools Amendment and Consequential Amendments Act*, which brought teacher bargaining under the *Labour Relations Act* and necessitated issuing new bargaining certificates. At this juncture the employer group, Manitoba Association of School Trustees (MAST), objected to substitute teachers being part of the bargaining unit. Consequently, the Manitoba Teachers' Society (MTS) applied to the Labour Board for a determination that the definition of teacher included substitute teachers. In its 2003 decision, the Board decided that a *teacher* is a qualified teacher employed *under a written contract* and substitutes were not deemed employees for the purposes of the certificates issued. Therefore, the Board rejected the MTS position that substitutes were part of the bargaining unit and that there was a voluntary recognition by the employer of the substitutes bargaining rights: "The Board on review of the evidence presented is satisfied that the existence of pay rates and other incidental benefits does not in itself determine the substitutes have been given voluntary recognition" (*Manitoba Teachers' Society* in the Matter of the *Labour Relations Act*, 2003, para. 30). However, it recognized a further determination would be necessary "if and when an appropriate application for certification is before the Board" (*Manitoba Teachers' Society* in the Matter of the *Labour Relations Act*, 2003, para. 35).

The MTS filed an appeal of the decision and undertook to organize and obtain certification for a number of substitute teacher groups. Again, MAST filed an objection with the Labour Board and questioned the appropriateness of a bargaining unit comprised of casual replacement workers.

As it had done throughout previous submissions, the employer took the unbelievable position of asserting that substitutes did not fall within the definition of *teacher* and although it would be *difficult for schools to operate without them*, "teaching is not their primary role . . . substitutes are hired to supervise students and ensure their safety, with an expectation that the substitute will teach to the extent it is feasible to do so" (Taylor cited in *Manitoba Teachers' Society* in the Matter of the *Labour Relations Act*, 2004, p. 8). In the eyes of parents, children, and education colleagues, a view of substitutes as anything less than teachers is highly provocative. From their perspective, it is well understood that substitute teachers are of no lesser value in the education system and, as such, are fully regarded as teachers and held accountable to the same expectations, standards, and regulations as their full-time counterparts. Thus, in its submission, witnesses for MTS provided evidence that substitutes carry out the same responsibilities as regular teachers and exercise the same authority in the classroom. In addition, the MTS cited convincing jurisprudence to refute the employer's inappropriate position. In one case, the Canada Labour Relations Board held that "the fact remains that *casuals are employees* within the meaning of the *Code* and they do have the rights and protections bestowed upon employees by the statute" (*Canadian Imperial Bank of Commerce (Powell River Branch) v. British Columbia Government Employees' Union*, 1991, p.88 cited in *Manitoba Teachers' Society* in the Matter of the *Labour Relations Act*, 2004). In an earlier British Columbia ruling, the tribunal stated "A person who works for an employer on an irregular, casual basis . . . is no less an employee when working than the regular employee" (*Maple Ridge School District No. 42 v. Maple Ridge Teachers' Association*, 1987, p.5 cited in *Manitoba Teachers' Society* in the Matter of the *Labour Relations Act*, 2004).

The Board elected to first determine whether substitute teachers constitute an appropriate unit for collective bargaining and, on this issue, decided in the affirmative. Although allowing some merit to the employer's argument that intuitively casual teachers lack a strong employment connection, the Board observed that "substantial connection is not a determinative test, but rather one means of assessing whether the proposed unit is capable of supporting a viable collective bargaining relationship between the parties" (*Manitoba Teachers' Society* in the Matter of the *Labour Relations Act*, 2004, p. 21). Noting that the employer expressed apprehension but no cogent evidence of a problem, as well as relying on compelling Ontario evidence of successful substitute teacher collective bargaining, the Board found the proposed units would be appropriate for collective bargaining (*Manitoba Teachers' Society* in the Matter of the *Labour Relations Act*, 2004). In deciding on the issue of a bargaining unit for substitutes as its preliminary task and subsequently making its ruling, the Board affirmed freedom of association and collective bargaining rights for Manitoba's substitute teachers.

On all accounts, the ruling was a victory for the MTS and, not surprisingly, MAST appealed the result but in May 2005 the Manitoba Labour Relations Board upheld the previous decision. This outcome once again confirmed that substitute teachers are appropriate units for collective bargaining. However, resistance to including substitute teachers into collective bargaining continues despite two affirmative victories on the issue and the Minister of Education enacting an individual statutory contract specifically for substitute teachers that includes them in the existing bargaining units and provides coverage under the existing collective agreement. The employer continues to take the position that substitute teachers have no rights within their existing collective agreements unless there is a provision that expressly includes them. Consequently, only a small number of the certified substitute teacher bargaining units has successfully reached a negotiated agreement. Arguably, in Manitoba, as in New Brunswick, Prince Edward Island, and the Yukon, substitute teachers remain a disadvantaged group given that their rights to associate freely and bargain collectively continue to be denied.

THE WAY FORWARD

CHALLENGING STATUS QUO

If an employer such as that in Manitoba, or any employer, continues to refute and effectively negate the decisions of its Labour Board and that of its provincial Education Ministry related to the rights of casual workers, what possible avenue or argument is available to them in order that they achieve their fundamental civil rights as employees, not least of which is their right to freedom of association? Indeed, "it is the freedom of association which creates the possibility for citizens to win other freedoms" (Jordan cited in Fudge, 2005, p. 4).

Several unions have launched challenges to legislation that prevents their casual workers from joining unions in their provincial jurisdictions. In November 2005, the Ontario Public Service Employees Union (OPSEU) initiated a campaign advocating that part-time college staff have the opportunity to unionize. With the support of the Canadian Association of University Teachers, the OPSEU initiative demands that the government change the law that bars part-time college staff from unionizing. Consequently, in August 2007 the Ontario government announced that it will extend collective bargaining rights to part-time college workers. Legislation is anticipated in 2008. In New Brunswick, the New Brunswick Union of Public and Private Employees (NBU/NUPGE) have brought a suit against the provincial government on behalf its casual employees. In its statement, lawyers for NBU/NUPGE claim that the province is violating Section 2 (*d*) freedom of association and other sections of the *Charter* by preventing casual employees from joining a union.

LABOUR RIGHTS ARE HUMAN RIGHTS

In January 2006, the Canadian Teachers' Federation, the United Food and Commercial Workers International Union (UFCW), the National Union of Public and General Employees (NUPGE) and the Canadian Professional Police Association, joined forces to formally promote and protect collective bargaining in Canada. Recognizing that freedom of association and the right to organize and bargain collectively are under significant pressure, the groups have agreed to focus their cooperative efforts to enhance the ability of their combined organizations to prevent further erosion of these fundamental human rights. The *Mutual Aid and Assistance Pact* solidifies the signatories' commitment to collectively address issues of concern related to the protection of these fundamental rights. The agreement makes specific reference to initiatives in which the parties may engage in to further this objective.

Similarly, the NUPGE continues a national campaign alongside the UFCW based on the premise that "Labour Rights are Human Rights." The Unions initiative confirms the insidious erosion of the fundamental right of freedom of association in Canada through passage of 170 pieces of legislation that have denied or undermined these basic rights (Fudge, 2005) and urges the federal government to:

- Ensure all current and future federal labour legislation complies with the ILOs freedom of association principles

- Work with the provincial governments to ensure their respective labour laws also comply with the ILOs freedom of association principles

- Pressure the provincial governments of BC, Alberta, Ontario, Quebec and Newfoundland and Labrador to implement all current and outstanding ILO recommendations with respect to their various labour laws that have been found not to be in conformity with ILOs freedom of association principles (NUPGE, March 2, 2006).

A pivotal element of the campaign is the *Worker's Bill of Rights*, which stresses the right of workers to join a union and to bargain collectively. The document further asserts that the right is enshrined in a number of remote as well as relatively recent international documents that Canada is a signatory to including (but not limited to):

- The UN Universal Declaration of Human Rights (1948),

- ILO Convention No. 87 – Freedom of Association and Protection of the Right to Organize (1948), and

- ILO Declaration on Fundamental Principles and Rights at Work (1998) (NUPGE, March 2, 2006).

Similarly, the American Federation of Labour-Congress of Industrial Organizations including its affiliate the American Federation of Teachers (AFT) has strenuously advocated on behalf of workers for passage of the *Employee Free Choice Act* by Congress. The *Act* is a bipartisan bill that would allow all workers covered by the *National Labor Relations Act* to organize freely (American Federation of Teachers, 2005). In its 2005 Resolution, *Workers' Rights are Human Rights*, the AFT is taking action in response to hostile and "unprecedented, mean-spirited attacks on the rights and contractual benefits of thousands of employees" (McElroy, 2005/2006, p. 2).

The issues of freedom of association and worker rights are not without International attention. In mid-February 2006, the World Bank announced new lending principles that recognize labour rights. The

Bank's private sector lending arm, the International Finance Corporation (IFC), adopted a new loan performance standard on labour rights and working conditions. The policy requires all private companies that borrow from the IFC to abide by the core labour standards as defined by eight core Conventions of the ILO. The new regulations include a commitment to demand lenders respect fundamental labour rights as a condition of future IFC loan arrangements (NUPGE, 2006).

CONCLUSION

Despite the passage of Convention 87 – Freedom of Association and Protection of the Right to Organize almost sixty years ago and Canada's ratification of it nearly twenty-five years ago, this fundamental civil right and the foundation to labour and human rights has not achieved a level of acceptance reasonably expected in a progressive, modern society. The fact that Canada is named time and time again as a violator of this fundamental freedom is particularly shameful. "The labor movement was the principal force that transformed misery and despair into hope and progress. Those who would destroy or further limit the rights of organized labor . . . do a disservice to the cause of democracy" (Luther King, Jr. in AFL-CIO, 2005). In the public education system, the struggle for the freedom to associate and bargain collectively is more *present* than *past* for its substitute teachers.

Substitute teachers-and casual workers for that matter – in every provincial and territorial jurisdiction should be afforded the right of freedom of association. The denial of this basic principle denigrates an extremely worthwhile and valuable contributor to the employment sector. Legislation that prevents casual workers from joining their respective bargaining units by virtue of deeming them not employees is ill-advised, misinformed, and lacking vision. Substitutes *are* employees. Schools depend on their contributions and *it would be difficult to operate without them.*

Notwithstanding recent challenges in Manitoba, there is convincing evidence that providing substitutes with association and bargaining rights is a meaningful endeavor. Ontario has successfully organized separate bargaining units for its occasional teachers and "despite the obvious obstacles, on the facts, the result in Ontario has been viable collective bargaining" (*MTS et al. v. Manitoba Association of School Trustees*, 2004, p.22). British Columbia also provides an example where including substitutes is achievable. Here, substitutes are part of the provincial bargaining unit.

Collective voice affords numerous opportunities. The differences in wages and benefits between those substitutes covered by collective agreements and those who are not covered are compelling. Substitutes have achieved reasonable living wages in their daily rates of pay, access to teachers' pension plans, and a variety of health and welfare benefits beyond those of their nonbargaining unit counterparts. As professionals and colleagues, substitutes offer the same insight and wisdom on important and prevalent public education issues. For example, unified advocacy for greater inclusiveness, respect of diversity, and general improved learning conditions yields positive results for students and communities. As defenders of the public education system and advocates of the fundamental right of all students to access free public education, substitutes deserve no less than their fundamental Freedom to Associate. Substitutes are more than employees. Substitutes *are teachers.*

AUTHOR'S NOTE

A June 8th, 2007 Supreme Court of Canada decision may have paved the way for greater union representation for all casual workers including substitute teachers. By a margin of 6-1, the Court determined that the guarantee of freedom of association in Section 2(d) of the *Charter* protects the rights of Canadian workers to bargain collectively. In the view of the Court, collective bargaining is a fundamental aspect of Canadian society and "recognizing that workers have the right to bargain collectively as part of their freedom to associate reaffirms the value of dignity, personal autonomy, equality and democracy that are inherent in the *Charter*" (*Health Services and Support – Facilities Subsector Bargaining Assn v. British Columbia*, 2007, para. 3). The favourable ruling comes as a result of the British Columbia Health Employees' Union's challenge of the government's draconian 2002 legislation, the *Health and Social Services Delivery Improvement Act*, which essentially stripped contracts and removed collective agreement protections for hospital workers. Workers lost rights related to contracting out, and layoff and bumping rights. The Supreme Court suspended its judgement for twelve months to allow the government to bring the legislation in compliance with the *Charter*.

References

AFL-CIO. (2005). *Workers' rights are human rights: Teach-in on the freedom to form unions – AFL-CIO voice @ work campaign*. Retrieved January 16, 2006 from http://www.aflcio.org/joinaunion/voiceatwork/upload/teachins_d10.ppt

American Federation of Teachers. Workers' Rights are Human Rights, Resolution October 2005. Retrieved January 16, 2006 from http://www.aft.org/about/resolutions/2005/wkrs_rights.htm

Canadian Charter of Rights and Freedoms, Schedule B to the *Canada Act* 1982 (U.K.) 1982, c.11. Retrieved March 7, 2006 from http://laws.justice.gc.ca/en/charter/index.html

Canadian Charter of Rights Decisions Digest-Section 2(d). Retrieved November 18, 2005 from http://www.canlii.org/ca/com/chart/s-2-d.html

Convention No. 87 Freedom of Association and Protection of the Right to Organise convention of 1948. *International Labour Organization*. Retrieved March 7, 2006 from http://www.ilo.org/ilo-lex/cgilex/convde.pl?C087

Dunning, H. (1998). The origins of Convention No. 87 on freedom of association and the right to organize. *International Labour Review*, *137*(2), 149-158. Retrieved January 16, 2006 from ProQuest host database.

Dunmore v. Ontario (Attorney General). 2001 CanLII 94 (S.C.C.), [2001] 3 S.C.R. 1016. Retrieved November 14, 2005 from http://www.canlii.org/en/ca/scc/doc/2001/2001scc94/2001scc94.html

Education Staff Relations Act, Yukon, 2002, c. 62. Retrieved January 16, 2006 from http://www.gov.yk.ca/legislation/acts/edstre.pdf

Fudge, D. (2005). *Collective bargaining in Canada: Human right or Canadian illusion?* Nepean, ON: NUPGE and Rexdale, ON: UFCW.

International Labour Organization. (1944). *Annex to the Constitution: Declaration concerning the aims and purposes of the International Labour Organization*. Retrieved March 16, 2006 from http://www.ilo.org/public/english/about/iloconst.htm#annex

Instructional Personnel Regulations under Prince Edward Island's *School Act*, S. 147, R.S.P.E.I. 1988, Cap. S-2.1. Retrieved January 16, 2006 from http://www.gov.pe.ca/law/regulations/pdf/S&2-1-05.pdf

Health Services and Support – Facilities Subsector Bargaining Assn. v. British Columbia. 2007 SCC 27. Retrieved September 14, 2007 from http://scc/lexum.umontreal.ca/en/2007/2007/scc27/html

Manitoba Teachers' Society in the Matter of the Labour Relations Act. (2003). M.L.B.D. No. 13, Case Nos. 223/02/LRA-246/02/LRA. Retrieved March 8, 2006 from http://ql.quicklaw.com

Manitoba Teachers' Society in the Matter of the Labour Relations Act. (2004). M.L.B.D. Case Nos. 776/03/LRA, 777/03/LRA, 778/03/LRA & 149/04/LRA.

McElroy, Edward. (2005/2006). Workers' rights are human rights. *American Teacher*, December 2005/January 2006, p. 2.

National Union of Public and General Employees. (2005, March). *Canada's hidden human rights deficit: Freedom of association.* Retrieved November 14, 2005 from http://www.nupge.ca/news_2005/n24ma05a.htm.

National Union of Public and General Employees. (2006, January). *Four Canadian unions sign pact to protect collective bargaining.* Retrieved March 7, 2006 from http://www.nupge.ca/news_2006/n18ja06c.htm

National Union of Public and General Employees. (2006, March). *NUPGE calls on Canada's new government to restore rights.* Retrieved March 20, 2006 from http://www.nupge.ca/news_2006/n02ma06a.htm

National Union of Public and General Employees. (2005, October). *Public sector unions sue over rights for casual employees.* Retrieved October 3, 2005 from http://www.nupge.ca/news_2005/n02oc05a.htm

National Union of Public and General Employees. (2002, September). *Union members have far better benefits than others.* Retrieved March 20, 2006 from http://www.nupge.ca/news%5F2002/news%5Fsep02/n01se02b.htm

National Union of Public and General Employees. (2006, February). *World Bank takes step forward in recognizing labour rights.* Retrieved March 20, 2006 from http://www.nupge.ca/news_2006/n28fe06c.htm

The Professional Institute of the Public Service of Canada v. Northwest Territories (Commissioner), 1990 CanLII 72 (S.C.C.), [1990] 2 S.C.R. 367. Retrieved November 14, 2005 from www.lexum.umontreal.ca/csc-scc/en/pub/1990/vol2/html/1990scr2_0367.html

Public Service Labour Relations Act, New Brunswick, 1968, c.88, Third Schedule; 1983, c.4, s.19. Retrieved January 16, 2006 from http://www.gnb.ca/0062/PDF-acts/p-25.pdf

Statistics Canada . (2007). *Table 278-0007, Major wage settlements, by major industry division.* Retrieved September 14, 2007 from http://www40.statcan.ca/l01/cst01/labor14.htm?sdi=wage%20increases

Tzannatos, A. & Aidt, T. (2002). *Unions and collective bargaining: Economic effects in a global environment.* Washington: The World Bank.

TEN

FAREWELL, WELFARE STATE. GOOD MORNING, GLOBAL MARKET: POLICY PROCESSES IN RUSSIAN HIGHER EDUCATION

Tatiana Gounko

Since the 1990s, Russian higher education has experienced major changes that were first brought by perestroika and then by the need to align educational policies with the global developments in the field. The magnitude of the changes in Russia is often compared to those of the major Liberal reforms of the 1860s and the post-revolutionary radical restructuring of the whole educational system in the 1920s and 1930s in accordance with the new communist ideology (Deviatko, 2002).

During the first phase of the changes in higher education, the government rid the curriculum of the ideological ballast of the previous era, citing the need to make the education system more open, individual-centered, and humanized. Zajda (2005) stated that the ideas of democracy, humanization, and individuation became the three popular slogans of post-Soviet reforms. New approaches to education were reflected in the two laws adopted by the Yeltsin government in the 1990s, *Law on Education of the Russian Federation and Federal Law on Higher and Postgraduate Professional Education* (referred to subsequently as the *1992 Law* and the *1996 Law*). The thrust towards decentralization and the autonomy rights given to educational institutions were seen as a way to establish fundamentally different relations between the centre and regions and to make education relevant to the needs of the transition society. In the early 1990s, the Russian government continued to formulate its policies in accordance with socialist welfare policies. It guaranteed tuition free education in state higher education institutions to eligible students who successfully passed competitive entrance examinations, students' stipends, subsidized housing, and other support from the federal and local budgets.

Russian education reforms of the 1990s were designed as a necessary corrective to the inherited "deficiencies" of the previous ideological regime. The ideals of democracy and self-determination successfully challenged the hegemony of Marxism-Leninism in schooling, authority, and curricula control (Zajda, 2005). As Rust and Jacob (2005) pointed out, the new education reform rhetoric was not economics- or politics-driven. The focus was on the student's – the learner's – ability to make choices. Although educational reform is by its very nature a political process, the concepts on which the 1990s reform was based were lodged in the rhetoric prior to the political and economic realities of today's Russia.

Despite representing a significant shift in terms of dominant ideology, the adopted policies were consistent with those of the socialist welfare state, which considered education a public good as opposed to an individual good. Reflecting this view, the education policies of the 1990s consistently stressed the belief in the state's provision for education, and its continuing commitment to access and equality of opportunity for all Russian citizens.

The post-Soviet education laws laid the foundations for the implementation of sector-wide reforms in accordance with the new political and societal aspirations. However, the basic principles of the education reform coupled with the government's commitment to providing access to free education, including postsecondary, suggested that these reforms were essentially a modification of the previous Socialist welfare policies. The major shift occurred in the ideological substance of education policies and the emphasis on the humanization of education in general.

However, economic problems of the 1990s impeded the complete implementation of laws in general and higher education. With the continuing macroeconomic crisis, public funding for higher education was significantly reduced, whereas the private costs of higher education continued to rise. Russia has been on a wobbly path since the collapse of the economy in 1998 (Bucur & Eklof, 2003). Only recently, having recovered from the collapse, did the government turn its attention to education. This interest is associated with the strategic programs adopted by the Putin government since the year 2000.

HIGHER EDUCATION FOR THE GLOBAL ECONOMY

A turning point in Russia's political thinking came in 1999. It was the time when President Putin expressed his determination to implement liberal reforms in the country, which had been slowed down by the financial crisis during Yeltsin's presidency. The Minister of Economic Development and Commerce, German Gref, stated that the goal of the government was to create a market economy with "a social face," whose main foundation was provided by liberalization (Gref, 2000, p. 6). This goal implied a radical restructuring of the economy unprecedented in its scope, which would entail the "farthest possible withdrawal" of the state from the area of investment and would "shun any superfluous regulation of the market" (p. 6). Instead, the state would concentrate its efforts on legislative activities and the administration of justice with the aim of reinforcing the ability of state institutions to function properly. In the view promoted by the visionaries of the liberal reforms, only such an approach could rescue the Russian economy within the environment of global competition. A functioning market-economy could be created only if Russia's public-sector employees felt the pressure of competition from other countries, if entrepreneurs were subjected to pressure from investment funds, and if these funds were in turn under pressure from their own stakeholders and banks (Gref, 2000).

The reforms of the social sector that followed clearly reflected the views expressed by the Putin administration. Regarding educational reforms, Gref further noted that the government would be discontinuing the institutional financing of the state's higher education institutions: "In future, they [institutions] will receive the funds they require from students. Higher education institutions, therefore, also have to face up to competition. All of these, of course, are reforms of a far-reaching character" (Gref, 2000, p. 6).

The Putin government's education agenda expressed in the *National Doctrine for Education* and *Concept of Modernization of Russian Education* unified several major policy initiatives in general and higher education. The modernization program was meant to enhance efficiency, quality, and access to higher education by restructuring admission policies, establishing a new higher education financing framework ("money follows the student"), and harmonizing the education procedures and degrees in accordance with the Bologna Declaration.

The government's recent policies defined education as a major factor in the country's economic development during the transition into a truly democratic and lawful state with a market economy. As a result, education was becoming increasingly oriented toward the labor market and the nation's socio-economic growth requirements (Isakov, 2003). The state took responsibility for providing the necessary conditions for large-scale reforms of the education sector, which were expected to encourage higher education institutions to be not only more innovative, but also more responsive to the requirements of a globally competitive knowledge economy and labor market. The adopted government policies revealed changes in how the problems of education were currently defined and how they should be addressed in order to accomplish the government's liberal program for Russia.

Having abandoned their Socialist state ideology, Russian political leaders adopted a fairly new discourse within Russia of market and neo-liberalism. The most recent policy documents presented an example of such a shift in the educational discourse, which seemed to have moved into a new neo-liberal terrain, leaving its Soviet-era philosophy behind. For example, notions of *economic growth, competition, human capital, the democratic society, the market economy, effectiveness, efficiency, labor markets,* and *the knowledge-based economy,* commonly found in the World Bank's and the OECD's publications, were used throughout Russian policy documents. These notions are often combined with the political and public discourse of Russian political leaders. In this context, Marginson and Rhoades (2002) mentioned the striking commonalties among the higher education policies promoted by the World Bank in the developing world and the policies promoted by the European Union and other entities in the industrialized world.

Similarly, the purpose of Russia's current modernization of education is described in terms of its importance to the national economy and the ability of the country to compete in the globalized world economy. Education is considered a powerful force in ensuring consistent economic growth and the effectiveness and competitiveness of the national economy, all of which would be essential to the country's national security and wellbeing of its citizens. Higher education has to fulfill the need for highly trained specialists, who should be able to compete in the international labor markets and be mobile, entrepreneurial, dynamic, and responsible:

> The growth of country's competitiveness is the
> primary condition for strengthening the political and
> economic role of Russia and for improving on its
> population's quality of life. In the modern world, which
> is moving toward globalization, the ability to adapt to
> the conditions of the international competition
> becomes a major factor in successful and steady
> development. The main competitive advantage of a
> highly developed country stems from the ability to
> develop its human capital, which is defined mainly by
> its education system. (Ministry of Education and
> Science, 2005, p. 4)

In this excerpt, the increased competition is linked to the improved quality of life and economic and political stability. This connection corresponds to many of the ideas in the policies of the international agencies promoting neo-liberal approaches to economic and social problems (e.g., IMF, World Bank, OECD). The notions of the market economy, consumer and market demands, and capital, which were once associated with the capitalist societies, and therefore possessed negative connotations during the Soviet years, have been accepted and have found their place in Russia's political discourse, which spills over to other types of public discourses. According to McKenna (2004), the neo-liberal hegemony in Western culture is very close to absolute and it infuses discourses and social practices at all levels of public and social organization, no matter how appropriate, operating within the discursive constraints set by the IMF and the World Bank.

The policies adopted by the Putin government are based on a fundamentally different philosophical framework. These policies differ from the previous education legislation in both the substance of the reforms and the dominant discourse. One of the leitmotifs running through the policies adopted since 2000 is the instillation of market relations of competition in higher education as a means to increase its efficiency, accountability, quality, and control. The notion of "money follows the student" is an example of an application of market competition in higher education where universities are expected to compete with each other for the best students, who would bring with them money in the form of vouchers. Competition for government grants among institutions and academics is meant to increase flexibility, responsiveness to consumers, and rates of innovation. University-business links are heavily promoted through the national project

Education, a national initiative which encourages entrepreneurs' participation in higher education.

If the 1990s policies were viewed as the "end of ideology," the newly adopted discourse is consistently viewed as being neutral. However, the distinct discourse markers such as *market, competitiveness, flexibility, human capital, fiscal reduction, per capita funding,* and *consumers and providers* (the list goes on) clearly reflect the preferred philosophical position, that of neo-liberalism.

The adoption of the new policy discourse in education defined a shift in the government's approach to education policy, radically deviating from the reform trends of the 1990s. The present reform rhetoric is clearly market-economy driven. Rust and Jacob (2005) pointed out that contrary to the historical reform policies, which had concentrated on cultural integration and social welfare, free market values began to pervade educational reforms throughout the world in the past two decades. For example, Russian Prime Minister Fradkov (2004) stated that Russian higher education should contribute to increasing country's economic competitiveness. Thus, if the 1990s education reforms in Russia were precipitated by the society's historical transformation, the later education modernization was prompted by an entirely different agenda.

The introduction of market mechanisms and new models of educational financing constituting the core of education modernization policy points to a definite shift in the direction of government reforms. Notions of competitive economy, human capital, services, goods, economic returns as well as the application of an instrumental logic indicates the dominance of neo-liberal discourse that has recently replaced the previous Socialist welfare discourse.

TRANSLATING FROM *SOVIET* TO *NEO-LIBERAL*

According to Olssen, Codd and O'Neill (2004), policy documents express and reflect structural realities and perform certain functions of legitimation by establishing a political consensus. For example, Russian educational policies in the 1990s reflected the overall democratization course pursued by the state. Following the 1998 economic crisis, the neo-liberal policy framework started to gain prominence while the welfare state continued to diminish. The goals of the Russian education strategy were expressed in terms characteristic of the neo-liberal market ideology. Applying the human capital approach, Russian policy makers have redefined higher education as an individual good, as opposed to the previous Soviet view of education as a public good. This new vision justifies the principle of user fees in higher education, a principle which is becoming more prevalent in the current policies in Russia. The results of such policies are seen in every public university across Russia. Everywhere, the fee-paying students have replaced those enrolled with merit-based stipends. Previously, higher education was paid for by the federal budget, but now, fewer that half of all students receive state stipends, and tuition has become an "essential part of public institutions" (Bucur & Eklof, 2003, p. 403).

According to Shugurensky (2003), the scope and the depth of university restructuring throughout the world – with the adoption of similar ideologies and policies – could not be simply attributed to general disaffection with higher education. Restructuring is neither an inevitable nor an impersonal process but is, instead, the product of a double process of consensus and coercion carried out by concrete social actors. Considering that educational policies are a discourse of the state, they inevitably reflect its political stances and ideologies. They must be understood as "part and parcel of the political structure of society and as a form of political action" (Olssen et al., 2004, p. 71).

Since 2000, the Russian government has consistently stated that its financing of higher educational institutions would be based on the quality and the amount of educational services that the universities offer to their consumers. The official belief is that high quality and efficiency will be possible in education only by introducing the economic mechanisms based on the new principles of financing. Consequently, from this point of view, academic salaries should be based on teaching quality and results; the universities should be subjected to uniform evaluation and rating, and the role of business in education should be further expanded and strengthened. At the same time, higher education should become more flexible and responsive to the needs of the market.

Samoff (2003) argued that the market triumphalism, underpinned by the neo-liberal ideology, made the policy choice rather obvious, especially after the dissolution of the Socialist coalition and the collapse of the Soviet Union, which were interpreted as the definitive victory of capitalism over socialism and, by extension, the victory of the market over central planning. Within this framework, the privatization of education is an acceptable way to provide better educational financing.

In 2004, the government amended the 1992 *Law on Education* to allow unrestricted admission of fee-paying students to specializations such as Jurisprudence, Management, and State and Municipal Administration. As some government officials noted, this change was just the beginning of the privatization of higher education.

Russian liberal reformers constantly stress that free higher education is a notion of the past, and that Russia should restructure its system by using the Western experience. Russia's education minister confirmed that in the near future, the government would support only a limited number of students, primarily those from low-income families, geographically remote regions, or with disabilities (Fursenko, 2005). Thus, the institutionalization of the *user-pays* principle in Russian higher education has become inevitable.

FROM HOMO SOVIETICUS TO HOMO ECONOMICUS?

Considering Russia's fundamental philosophical, cultural, and economic differences from the West, educational researchers in Russia and abroad have cautioned for years against the blind application of Western models to Russian education. For example, Zajda (2005) noted that by in adopting the Western model of education, Russian policy makers have failed to understand the inherently contradictory nature of schooling in Western world. Accepting the Western model of education, Russia is moving away from its previously espoused egalitarianism to a more conservative and traditional schooling placing a far greater emphasis on the social reproduction, stratification, and hierarchy than on equality of educational opportunity: "Apart from the new hegemony in Russian education and society, there are now also visible signs of social divisions, defining the new and fast growing underclass and the rich" (p. 413).

The poverty of increasingly large segments of Russian society could be attributed to the 1990s economic crises as well as to the dismantling of the welfare safety nets, demanded by the promoters of "the great neo-liberal utopia" (Bourdieu, 1998, p. 1). Affected by "the continental drift" of neo-liberalism, the species once known to the world as *homo sovieticus*, is being transformed into *homo economicus*, the species supposedly better fit for survival in the global market economy.

TOWARD MARKET BOLSHEVISM

Today, the market ideology, which has replaced the former Socialist/Communist ideology, is becoming increasingly dogmatic. Some analysts have referred to the rigid application of the market ideology as "market bolshevism" (Reddaway & Glinski, 2001) because of its resemblance to the ruthless annihilation of the Tsarist order during the first decades of the Soviet regime. Under the banner of globalization and market competition, the government is dismantling its welfare policies, which were the foundation of the previous Soviet State. Although the Bolshevik revolutionary song about building a new world on the ruins of the old one is no longer a popular tune, its distant echo unmistakably underlies the government's approach to policy. As the market discourse came to dominate the policies and practices pursued by the Russian government, the long-standing social policies started to wither. The ideals of collectivity, social justice, and human rights are being exchanged for key economic concepts, including efficiency, productivity, competitiveness, and profit. Zajda (1999) argued that the neo-liberal ideology, which redefined education as the investment in human capital, has influenced the thinking of policy makers in Russia. Like many other nations, Russia has rejected a rational foundation for the modern welfare state, forsaken humanistic and rational ideals, and prefers instead a culture of personal gain rather than communal goals.

The 1990s were a decade of growing hegemonic neo-liberalism, which had been pushed by multilateral agencies and the most powerful states as the major global project for economic growth and development. Despite major setbacks in recent years (e.g., the East Asian financial crisis, economic polarization, and global resistance), the neo-liberal project has not been deeply challenged as the dominant economic doctrine for growth and distribution – "largely because of its ability to reconstruct its ability and tactics" (Bonal, 2003, p. 163). In many countries, including Russia, the effect of the conditions and recommendations imposed by the IMF and the World Bank has led to the dismantling of the welfare state. The "from the cradle to the grave" model of free social welfare of the Soviet Union has been steadily deteriorating during the past twenty years. The post-Soviet period saw a sharp decline in the overall quality of life of the majority of Russian citizens. The dramatic reduction in state subsidies for basic services, the hyperinflation of the early 1990s and the economic slump, the nonpayment of wages and the inadequate welfare system, and the collapse of the rouble in 1998 worsened the plight of the Russian citizens. In addition to these problems, some analysts (e.g., Markov, 2005; Reddaway & Glinski, 2001) cited the infamous "shock therapy," prescribed, in the early 1990s, by the IMF, whose control over the Russian economy is considered even more far-reaching than is admitted in public.

The long-lasting economic and fiscal crisis and subsequent stabilization and structural adjustment programs of the IMF and the World Bank hit public education hard. The proposed and imposed programs strongly encouraged the Russian government to reduce public expenditures on higher education and to diversify institutional revenues by introducing competitive funding mechanisms and by charging tuition fees. Some researchers (e.g., Ginsberg, Espinoza, Popa & Terano, 2005; Torres, 2003) considered the World Bank and the IMF the most prominent external sources of influence on higher education policies worldwide.

The urgency to restructure the welfare state policies in education was often framed in terms of successes and failures. Those countries that failed to restructure their education systems to meet the needs of the global economy were sure to become losers. Those who followed the prescribed steps would become the winners (World Bank, 1999).

> The stakes are high. The choice that countries make today about education could lead to sharply divergent outcomes in the decades ahead. Countries that respond astutely should experience extraordinary progress in education, with major social and economic benefits, including "catch-up" gains for the poor and marginalized. Countries that fail to recognize and respond risk stagnating and even slipping backwards, widening social and economic gaps and sowing seeds of unrest. (p. 1)

However, despite the advice of the global actors, the social and economic gap in Russia continues to grow. While large proportions of the population are in significant distress, Russia, according to *Forbes Magazine* of 2004, occupies the third place (behind the United States and Germany) on the list of the countries with the most dollar billionaires, that is, those who hold wealth in hard currency.

Currently, both Russian and Western observers share the view that some of the given advice and imposed *conditionalities* of the IMF, the World Bank and the OECD were inappropriate in the Russian context. Attacking the "impure" Communism-tainted institutional structures, the IMF and the World Bank conditions in fact contributed to the dismantling of the social safety net, which had already been compromised by the economic and fiscal crisis. Shortly, after the 1998 rouble collapse, the World Bank's Chief Economist, Joseph Stiglitz, wrote that standard Western advice wrongly took an ideological, fundamental, and root-and-branch approach to reform-mongering as opposed to an incremental, remedial, piecemeal, and adaptive approach (Stiglitz, 1999).

Instead of producing a gradual transition from a centrally planned, fully controlled economy that fostered institution building to fit the emerging market as a priority, the pursued policies weakened the state and exacerbated the plight of ordinary Russians. Since the 1990s, the leitmotifs of the IMF and the World Bank interventions and technical assistance have been austerity and budget cuts with little regard for the social consequences. Although the IMF's policy and advice focused on banking, finance, and fiscal areas rather than on structural and institutional reforms: its macroeconomic policies had significant implications for a much wider range of policies that the Fund wanted to admit. For example, Odling-Smee (2004) argued that the IMF's influence in Russia was modest; the Fund had only a limited impact on overall fiscal policy and the major structural reforms. However, the institution played a major role in "transferring knowledge about macroeconomic policymaking and implementation" (p. 50). Whatever the degree of influence in Russia's past reforms the Fund is ready to accept, even today, after recognizing the adverse affect of the budget cuts on the social safety net, the IMF still insists on the government's commitment to reducing its spending in favor of "balancing the books."

In education, the proposed market-oriented approach also led to unintended consequences. The universities in Russia have clearly suffered from painful financial downsizing, including the erosion of real faculty compensation, the demise of entire departments and degree programs, and the superimposition of entrepreneurial activities involving both faculty and facilities (Johnston, Aurora, & Experton, 1998). Perhaps one of the most devastating consequences for institutions was "the abolition of Russian academia as a full-time job" (Neave, 2006). Low salaries and a lack of adequate funding forced many academics to look for additional sources of income, usually outside universities, and significantly increased the brain drain to other professions and countries.

Commenting on the consequences of the educational reform, Smolin (2003) stated that the international organizations – specifically the World Bank and the OECD – that started out by teaching Russian policy makers how to carry out reforms in education were now reproaching them because the level of inequality in education had gone beyond all acceptable limits. During the modernization of education, quality higher education has become a privilege of wealthier families, while the majority have to do with a second-rate education ("Putin's Triumph," 2004).

Kukhtevich et al. (2002) argued that no matter how promising and attractive Western educational models are, the actual effect of their adoption is always determined by the extent to which people are ready to accept them. For more than seventy years of the Soviet Union's existence, the official political discourse emphasized proletariat hegemony and egalitarianism. The dominant ideology and discourse were those of socialism/communism, which was the foundation of economic and social policies in the USSR. Within the socialist normative framework, humans have the potential to live cooperatively and equally, and economic and political systems should be structured accordingly to encourage communalism and equality (Gibbins & Youngman, 1996). The socio-economic and ideological positions of the Soviet Union were reflected in the extensive welfare programs available to people, which are being dismantled largely due to the adopted structural adjustment policies and the neo-liberal ideology emanating from the international funding agencies. According to Marginson and Rhoades (2002), the World Bank's policies were premised on the existence of sufficient private wealth to enable higher education institutions to generate their own revenues. However, such private wealth does not exist in contemporary Russia. In 2005, the Gross Domestic Product (GDP) per person in Russia was estimated at $ 4,330 (US) (c.f. $ 41,530 [US] in the United States) ("The World in 2005," 2005, p. 89).

For more than seven decades, a strong emphasis was placed on providing free public higher education, which was a part of the social contract defining the relationships between the state and the citizens. International agencies continue to push the government to decrease public support despite the country's historical commitment to free public higher education. At the same time, universities are obliged to transform instantaneously from fully funded budgetary state organizations into entrepreneurial-type educational institutions (Beliakov, Lugachov & Markov, 1998, p. 20).

As the public universities increasingly become framed by free market practices, the traditional sense of the public good linked to the collectivist values is shifting to more individualist interests (Rhoads, Torres & Brewster, 2005). However, the neo-liberal assumptions concerning the nature of the individual, as an economically self-interested subject, rational optimizer, and the best judge of his or her own interests may not necessarily fit the profile of Russian citizens (Olssen et al., 2004; Olssen & Peters, 2005). Consequently, the policies premised on the neo-liberal philosophy may not be fully compatible with the social practice and values espoused by Russian society. Kempner and Jurema (2002) argued that that neo-liberal and globalization policies are not culturally neutral, nor are the economic and social assumptions on which they are based necessarily associated with the social and political realities of the countries on which such ideas are imposed.

Considering that tuition fees in many popular universities and for some specializations exceed the combined annual income of most families (the national average wage in Russia is estimated at around $200 [US] per month [Bacon & Wyman, 2006]) and that the number of budget-funded institutions is constantly decreasing, the access to higher education may become even more dependent on family wealth. In order for the citizens to exercise their rights and choice in higher education, a befitting infrastructure that will allow them to do so should be put in place. If the Russian government insists on the introduction of the market mechanisms in higher education through charging tuition fees, it should also implement concrete policies that would ensure access to higher education for everybody regardless of his or her socio-economic background.

Although the government stressed its commitment to provide wide access to high-quality education in defining the priorities of educational modernization, recent initiatives have raised serious concerns among educators in regards to this commitment. For example, the Chairman of the Duma's Committee on Education, Ivan Melnikov (2000), stated that the current reform aimed to commercialize education rather than guarantee access and equality of opportunity. Moving away from tuition-free higher education was cited as one of the obstacles to ensuring access to higher education. The analysis of the Russian policy documents also indicates the absence of a clearly defined plan on how to meet the financial needs of prospective students.   While the establishment of some form of student loan or credit systems was mentioned in the 1992 *Law on Education*, comprehensive measures are yet to be seen.

At the same time, the government canceled the previously established limit on the admission of fee-paying students in the programs of jurisprudence, economics, and management. Considering that graduates with these specializations usually form the economic and political elite in the country, social stratification will likely continue to deepen. Young people from middle- and low-income families will have no chance of becoming a part of the economic and political elite (Smolin, 2003). This conclusion is consistent with the literature on the increasingly self-reproductive tendencies in Russian higher education. Researchers (Boiko, 2004; Buzgalin, 2001; Smolentseva, 1999) described the social make-up of university students as being asymmetrical to the social structure of society with a very narrow social base of replenishment. If in the mid-1990s, as many as 60 % of students came from families of professionals with university degrees, in the new millennium the number of students whose parents have high income and social status is expected to increase further.

THE ETERNAL QUESTION – WHAT SHOULD BE DONE?

As the depth and pace of the university restructuring is contingent on the political economy and the historic traditions of each nation-state and each individual institution (Shugurensky, 2003), one of the most important tasks for the government is to match its educational policies with the existing politico-economic and social situation. For example, the appropriate legal and economic base should support the introduction of the market mechanisms in higher education. Can government guarantee equal access to higher education without establishing the necessary infrastructure? In designing education policies, the government should consider both the real financial capabilities and broad societal opinion of the population, especially when trying to impose progress and modernization from above. The government should also recognize that the proposed, and often imposed, models of the international agencies may not necessarily be compatible with the society's cultural values and historic traditions. As a recent study by the Russian and American sociologists suggested, young Russian people continued to espouse egalitarian values, traditionally characteristic of Russians' national political positions (Dobrynina & Kukhtevich, 2002, p. 43).

Thus, those trying to invent and construct a new economic and social order in Russia should ensure that a fit between the real situation and the adopted policies exists. At this point, one can observe a considerable mismatch between the government policy discourse and the socio-economic reality in Russia, which may result in devastating consequences, including physical and symbolic loss of the country's "human capital."

References

Beliakov, S., Lugachov, M., & Markov, A. (1998). *Financial and institutional change in Russian higher education*. Edinburgh, UK: Center for Economic Reform and Transformation. Retrieved from http://www.hw.ac.uk/ecoWWW/cert/certhp.htm.

Boiko, L. (2004). Transformation of the functions of higher education, and the social positions of college students. *Russian Education and Society, 46*(8), 54-65.

Bonal, X. (2003). The neoliberal educational agenda and the legitimation crisis: Old and new state strategies. *British Journal of Sociology of Education, 24*(2), 159-175.

Bourdieu, P. (1998). The essence of neoliberalism. *La Monde*, December 1998, Retrieved March 18, 2005, from http://ww.analitica.com/biblioteca/bourdieu/neoliberalism.asp

Bucur, M., & Eklof, B. (2003). Russia and Eastern Europe. In R.F. Arnove & C.R. Torres (Eds.) *Comparative education. The dialectic of the global and the local* (2nd ed.). (pp. 384-408). Oxford: Rowman & Littlefield.

Buzgalin, A. (2001). The myth of educational reform. *Prism, 7*(4), 1-5. Retrieved June 23, 2003 from http://russia.jamestown.org/pubs/view/pri_007_004_004.htm

Deviatko, I. F. (2002). Changing profile of the Russian higher education: A sociologist view on educational reform in progress. In H.C. Cardiel & R.R. Gomes (Eds.) *Reformas en los Sistemas Nacionales de Educacion Superior* (Serie Universidad Contemporanea). (pp. 79-107). A Coruña, ESP: Risen-Netbiblo.

Dobrynina, V., & Kuhktevich, T. (2002). The cultural worlds of young Russians. *Russian Education and Society, 44*(5), 32-44.

Gibbins, R., & Youngman, L. (1996). *Mindscapes. Political ideologies towards 21st century*. Toronto: McGraw-Hill Ryerson Limited.

Ginsberg, M., Espinoza, O., Popa, S., & Terano, M. (2005). Globalization and higher education in Chile and Romania: the roles of the International Monetary Fund, World Bank, and World Trade Organization. In J. Zajda (Ed.) *International handbook on globalization, education and policy research. Global pedagogies and policies.* (pp. 221-234). Dordrecht, HOL: Springer.

Gref, G. (2000). *Social market economy – a model for Russia in the age of globalisation?* Paper presented at 15th Sinclair House debate Capitalism without morals? Ethical principles of a global economy, November 17-18, 2000.

Fradkov, M. (2004). *Systema rossiiskogo obrazovania*. [The system of Russian education]. RIA Novosti. Retrieved October 10, 2004, from http://www.ege.ru/news2.html.

Fursenko, A. (2005). *O kachstve obrazovaniya i vostrebovannosti ego resultatov.* [On the quality of education and demands]. Vestnik Obrazovaniya (On-line). Retrieved February 2, 2005, from at http://vestnik.edu.ru/min0205.html

Isakov, Y.N. (2003). Russia's revised national education policy reflects ICPD international education agenda. *UN Chronicles, 2,* 49-50.

Johnstone, D.B., Aurora, A., & Experton, W. (1998). *The financing and management of higher education: The status report on worldwide reforms.* Washington: the World Bank.

Kempner, K. & Jurema, A.L. (2002) 'The global politics of education: Brazil and the World Bank', *Higher Education, 43,* 331-354.

Kukhtevich, T., Bolotin, I., Vasenina, I., Gegel, L., Dobrynina, V., Krukhmaleva, O., Lapsheva, O., Mamedeili, R., Moskvicheva, L., Smolentseva, A., Sorokina, N., Faustova, E., & Shchepkina, E. (2002). The Moscow State University student: Vector of changes. *Russian Education and Society, 44*(2), 18-36.

Marginson, S., & Rhoades, G. (2002). Beyond national states, markets, and systems of higher education: A glonacal agency heuristic. *Higher Education, 43,* 281-309.

Markov, S. (2005). Vazhneishaya politicheskaya reforma strany. [The main Political reform of the country]. *GlobalRus,* 27/05, 3-7. Retrieved May 5, 2005 from http://www.globalrus.doc/03/html

Melnikov, I. (2000). *Budut gen'gi – dadim.* [If there is money – we will give]. Retrieved March 30, 2001, from http://www.cinfo.ru/OB.

McKenna, B. (2004). Critical discourse studies; Where to from here? *Critical Discourse Studies, 1*(1), 9-39.

Ministry of Education and Science. (2005). *Federal'naya tselevaya programma razvitiya obrazovaniya na 2006-2010 gody* [Federal program for the development of education for 2006-2010]. Retrieved May 1, 2006, from http://mon.gov.ru/edu-politic/priority/2048.

Neave, G. (2006). Redefining social contract. *Higher Education Policy, 19,* 269-286.

Odling-Smee, J. (2004). *IMF Working Paper. The IMF and Russia in the 1990s.* Washington, D.C.: International Monetary Fund.

Olssen, M., Codd, J., & O'Neill, A.-M. (2004). *Education policy: Globalization, citizenship and democracy.* London: Sage Publications Ltd.

Olssen, M., & Peters, M. (2005). Neoliberalism, higher education and knowledge economy: From the free market to knowledge capitalism. *Journal of Education Policy, 20*(3), 313-345.

Putin's Triumph. (2004, May 13). *Zavtra* [Tomorrow], p. 1.

Reddaway, P., & Glinski, D. (2001). *The tragedy of Russia's reforms.* Washington, D.C.; United States Institute of Peace Press.

Rhoads, R. A., Torres, C.A, & Brewster, A. (2005). Neoliberalism, globalization, and Latin American higher education: The challenge to national universities. In J. Zajda (Ed.). *International handbook on globalization, education and policy research. Global pedagogies and policies.* (pp. 131-145). Dordrecht, HOL: Springer.

Rust, V., & Jacob, W. (2005). Globalization and educational policy shifts. In J. Zajda (Ed.). *International handbook on globalization, education and policy research. Global pedagogies and policies.* (pp. 235-252). Dordrecht, HOL: Springer.

Samoff, J. (2003). Internationalizing international influence. In R.F. Arnove & C.A., Torres (Eds.). *Comparative education: The dialectic of the global and local.* (pp. 52-91). Oxford: Rowman and Littlefield.

Shugurensky, D. (2003). Higher education restructuring in the era of globalization towards a heteronomous model? In R.F. Arnove & C. A, Torres (Eds.). *Comparative education: The dialectic of the global and local.* (pp. 292-312). Oxford: Rowman and Littlefield.

Smolentseva, A. (1999). Current trends in Russian higher education. *International Higher Education, 16*(7), 1-2.

Smolin, O. (2003). Legislative regulation of the economics of education as an ideological problem. *Russian Education and Society, 45*(10), 6-20.

Stiglitz, J. (1999). Wither reform?: Ten years of transition. Washington, D.C.: The World Bank.

Torres, C. A. (2003). Comparative education. In R.F. Arnove & C.A., Torres (Eds.). *Comparative education: The dialectic of the global and local.* (pp. 446-461). Oxford: Rowman and Littlefield.

World Bank. (1999). Education sector strategy. Washington, D.C.: Author.

The World in 2005. (2005). The world in figures: Countries. *The Economist.*

Zajda, J. (1999). Adult education and lifelong learning: New developments in Russia. *Comparative Education, 35*(2), 151-161.

Zajda, J. (Ed.). (2005). *International handbook on globalization, education and policy research. Global pedagogies and policies.* Dordrecht, HOL: Springer.

Ecological and Socio-Cultural Approaches

ELEVEN

FOUR DOUBLE BINDS THAT LIMIT
THE DEVELOPMENT OF AN ECO-JUSTICE PEDAGOGY

C. A. Bowers

In previous writings, I have highlighted the cultural implications of the ecological crisis by juxtaposing the rising trend line of population growth and worldwide levels of consumption with the declining trend line in the viability of natural systems: such as marine ecosystems, forest cover, species diversity, aquifers, and river systems. Perhaps a more useful way, one that clarifies why the diverging trend lines argument has been largely ignored by educators, is the concept of the double bind. The nature of a double bind, as I am using the concept, is summed up in Einstein's observation that problems cannot be solved within the mindset that created them.

The explanatory power of the concept of the double bind became clearer to me when I read Kirkpatrick Sale's description of the kind of individual that the industrial system of production could most easily control as a worker and consumer. Sale summarized in the following way what the Industrial Revolution had to destroy in order to create the new individualism:

> All that 'community' implies – self-sufficiency, mutual aid, morality in the marketplace, stubborn tradition, regulation by custom, organic knowledge instead of mechanistic science – had to be steadily and systematically disrupted and displaced. All the practices that kept the individual from being a consumer had to be done way with so that the cogs and wheels of an

unfettered machine called the 'economy' could operate without interference, influenced merely by the invisible hands and inevitable balances and all the rest of that benevolent free-market system... (1995, p. 38)

What has gone largely unnoticed is the similarity between the mindset that is changing the chemistry of the Earth's ecosystems by promoting consumerism as the ultimate expression of success and happiness and the mindset of the autonomous, critically reflective individual advocated by such prominent and diverse thinkers as Robert M. Hutchins, John Dewey, Paulo Freire, and their followers. To state Einstein's insight into the nature of the double bind in a way that clarifies the connection between education and the ecological crisis: the ideal of the emancipatory tradition in educational theory is based on the same deep cultural assumptions that gave conceptual direction and moral legitimation to the Industrial Revolution. These assumptions included representing the ideal individual as self-directing and thus free of the network of community traditions, change as linear and progressive, humans as separate from Nature and the need to use these assumptions as the basis for judging the stage of development of other cultures. The early promoters of the industrial system of production and consumption made these assumptions the basis of the Classical Liberal explanation of how markets operate and the individual's basic motivation to pursue self-interest. Ironically, while contemporary educational proponents of an emancipatory education have criticized the exploitative and colonizing nature of the Industrial Revolution, they have never questioned the deep cultural assumptions they share with the tradition that connects William Cartwright, Henry Ford, and Bill Gates. I know that some readers will point out that Dewey's view of the social nature of intelligence should exempt him from this criticism, thus I will address their concerns shortly.

Before addressing how the basic insights contained in the quotation from Sale's book, *Rebels Against the Future: The Luddites and Their War on the Industrial Revolution*, can be used to articulate the nature of an eco-justice pedagogy, I want to examine briefly four approaches to educational reform mistakenly seen as providing solutions to today's problems. The primary focus of my analysis will be on how these reform proposals and practices reinforce the basic cultural assumptions that underlie the technology-dependent, consumer lifestyle now being globalized. To put it another way, I will be examining how the intergenerational knowledge within communities that reduces dependency upon consumerism is being undermined by what are claimed to be emancipatory educational reforms.

DOUBLE BIND IN HIGHER EDUCATION

Universities are responsible for determining what constitutes high- and low-status knowledge by virtue of what is omitted from the curriculum. What is generally not recognized is that high-status knowledge is based on the assumptions that co-evolved with the Industrial Revolution – thus the emphasis on viewing intelligence as the attribute of the individual, the relentless pursuit of new ideas and technologies, the need to encode knowledge in print and other systems of abstract representation that marginalize context and other cultural ways of knowing, and the need to view language as a conduit that supports the myth that objective knowledge can be communicated between individuals. In addition, high-status knowledge privileges reliance on abstract theory, empirical evidence, and the use of an elaborated language code to establish what has authority. It further promotes the development of new technologies to control and exploit nature; increasingly, high-status knowledge is being justified on the grounds that it contributes to the ability to turn knowledge and relationships into commodities, and that it enables individuals to achieve higher levels of consumption. There is also the messianic expectation that a university education will enable individuals to apply their technical, problem-solving knowledge anywhere in the world. In short, universities are major contributors to the myth that technology and other expert forms of knowledge free humans from all limitations.

Marginalized and distorted by a university education are the forms of knowledge that are the basis of living a less consumer-dependent lifestyle. These include (a) understanding the metaphorical nature of language and thus the way in which language reproduces the meta-cognitive schemata derived from the mythopoetic narratives of a culture; (b) the ways in which we are embedded, reenact, empowered, and restricted by traditions; (c) the importance of local context in the development and utilization of technologies; (d) the role of intergenerational knowledge in providing skills and patterns of moral reciprocity that are the basis of relatively more self-reliant families and communities; (e) the importance of face-to-face interaction to the civic life of the community and to its systems of mutual support.

If we compare what universities marginalize and distort with Sale's list of what the industrial system had to destroy in order to create the type of individual who would value personal mobility and consumerism over place, community, and self-sufficiency, the connections between high-status knowledge and the hyperconsumerism now undermining the viability of natural systems become clearer. Similarly, an examination of the characteristics of low-status knowledge, which vary from culture to culture and do not always meet our standards of social justice, will be seen to have a smaller ecological footprint. The double bind is thus further exacerbated by the reality that the institution primarily responsible for legitimating the knowledge that is the basis of everyday life continues to undermine communities that have a more sustainable ecological footprint.

Double Binds in the Use of Computers

Contrary to popular belief, computers are not a culturally neutral technology. While they enable us to do many things, and to do them more effectively, they also reinforce the same deep cultural assumptions that were the basis of an earlier phase of the Industrial Revolution. Indeed, the western educated elites in most of the world's cultures are rushing to embrace computers and thus to enter the digital phase of the Industrial Revolution, but few are asking about what is being lost through the use of this technology. That computers commodify both thought and communication should be obvious to any person or institution that must continually purchase the latest system in order to stay online. What is more difficult to recognize is how computers reinforce the conceptual patterns and moral relativism of high-status knowledge – where explicit and decontextualized knowledge is privileged over the tacit and contextual; where language is represented as a conduit, thus reducing awareness that different languages encode different cultural epistemologies; and where individuals experience the western sense of temporality that makes the past and future dependent upon the subjective judgment of individuals who experience a false sense of autonomy when sitting in front of the computer screen. Anthropocentrism, equating change with progress, and the view that technology is culturally neutral are also reinforced by the experience of self in cyberspace.

Computers contribute to the ecological crisis and the loss of cultural diversity by globalizing the corporate agenda of transforming nonconsumer-centered cultures into modern societies where individuals, in being freed from intergenerational knowledge and responsibilities, become dependent upon the industrial mode of production and consumption. Computers facilitate the existence of cyberspace communities centered on shared interests, but they cannot replace the critically important aspects of face-to-face communities. They cannot, for example, replace mentoring relationships, and they cannot reproduce the stories told face-to-face that form identities and pass on the values of the family and community. Nor can they be used as a substitute for embodied experiences that bond people to a physical environment in ways where there is a sense of connectedness to a greater whole. And they cannot provide virtual substitutes for participating in ceremonies, and for the moral accountability that accompanies most face-to-face interactions.

While computers are being used to model changes in ecosystems and to create less environmentally destructive technologies, computer proponents and futuristic thinkers continue to take for granted the cultural assumptions that equate experimenting with the symbolic foundations of the world's cultures, and now experimenting with genetic basis of life itself, with progress. They are also reviving the late nineteenth-century myth that represented progress as the outcome of natural selection and, thus, of an evolutionary process. Instead of addressing the double bind inherent in the use of computers, proponents are now writing with unqualified optimism about entering the "postbiological phase of evolution," to quote Han Moravec (1988, pp. 4-5). Gregory Stock's claim that we are witnessing the merging of humans and machines into a global superorganism (to cite the subtitle of his 1993 book, Metaman), has now been surpassed by Ray Kurzweil's prediction that not only will computers take on human personalities but will also have spiritual experiences (1999, pp. 152-153). These predictions are being made by highly, yet narrowly educated people who do not understand where their areas of actual expertise end and where ideology based on an ecologically problematic set of cultural assumptions takes over. It is also important to note that their pronouncements have both a racist and colonizing ring to them.

One additional point needs to be made about why the double bind inherent in the cultural-mediating characteristics of computers has largely gone unrecognized by the guardians of high-status knowledge. The embrace of computers within the academic community, which is leading to the further commodification of the educational process, can be accounted for in terms of the difficulty people have in recognizing their own taken-for-granted assumptions. As computers reinforce the same cultural assumptions that underlie most academic disciplines, faculty treat them as an indispensable tool for conducting research, transmitting information to students., and communication with colleagues in distant places.

DOUBLE BIND IN EMANCIPATORY EDUCATIONAL THEORIES

The challenge today is to use criteria dictated by the rapid changes in the Earth's ecosystems as the basis for assessing the ideas of emancipatory educational theorists such as John Dewey and Paulo Freire and their many followers. What must be asked of these emancipatory educational theorists include the following: Do their proposals for reform perpetuate the western tradition of anthropocentric thinking? Do they equate change with progress? Do they assume that each generation should overturn the traditions of previous generations and that critical reflection is the only legitimate source of knowledge? While there are minor differences between how Dewey and Freire interpret the nature of critical reflection, they both agree that other sources of knowledge and values must be rejected, which leads to a host of other concerns that I shall examine more closely.

Freire's philosophical anthropology, which he articulates in *Pedagogy of the Oppressed* (1974), represents individuals as realizing the fullest potential of their human nature when they speak a "true word" which transforms the world (p. 75). As he put it, "To exist, humanly, is to <u>name</u> the world, to change it. Once named, the world in its turn reappears to the namers as a problem and requires of them a new naming" (p. 76). What separates Freire's view of the self-determining individual from the autonomous individual required by the Industrial Revolution is Freire's emphasis on the individual's capacity for critical reflection. Before we accept this as a fundamental and defining difference, however, we need to keep in mind that the early industrialists, as well as the entrepreneurs of Silicon Valley, were driven to create new products that overturned the traditions of daily life. In effect, they were, and continue to be, motivated by the same assumption that underlies Freire's proposal "to understand life, not necessarily as the daily repetition of things, but as the effort to create and recreate, and thus as an effort to rebel as well" (1985, p. 199). While industrialists embraced this view of replacing traditions with new products that would enhance profits, and Freire also embraced it as an Enlightenment thinker, their ideas lead to the same colonizing relationship with cultures that do not share their formulaic way of equating change with progress.

At first glance Dewey's ideas would appear to differ radically from the assumptions that lead to thinking of individual autonomy as the primary goal of education. He continually states that intelligence is social and that its effectiveness in solving problems is enlarged to the degree it becomes a participatory activity within the community. Even the obvious criticism of the anthropocentric nature of his ideas is being challenged by philosophers who claim "that Dewey's naturalism is capable of supporting Leopold's land ethic" (Hickman, 1996, p. 66). While there is much in Dewey's thoughts that remains relevant today, I find that, on the whole, he does not overcome the sources of the double bind inherent in a cultural approach to progress that degrades the environment we all depend upon.

My concerns go beyond Dewey's emphasis on the use of the scientific method of inquiry as the only valid approach to knowledge (or to resolving problematic situations, to use a phrase he would be more comfortable with). They even go beyond his instrumental approach to determining which values should guide action, and his view of education as the ongoing process of reconstructing experience. The more problematic part of Dewey's thinking, which increases my concern about the above, can be traced to his failure to follow his own recommendations about grounding inquiry within the context of ongoing experience. As most of his followers share the same assumptions upon which his worldview rests, they have not noticed that Dewey's contacts with the cultural groups flooding into Chicago and New York during his most productive academic years did not lead him to modify his own ideas in ways that took account of the positive aspects of the diverse range of cultural epistemologies and the forms of community they sustained. I find it especially telling that the lectures he gave in 1919 at the Imperial University of Japan, which became the basis of *Reconstruction in Philosophy*, were arguments for adopting a western way of thinking. For example, his statement that "change becomes significant of new possibilities and ends to be attained; it becomes prophetic of a better future. Change is associated with progress rather than with lapse and fall" (1957 edition, p. 116) must have sounded foreign and even deeply arrogant to most of the Japanese in his audience.

A careful examination of the deep cultural assumptions (root metaphors) underlying Dewey's epistemology – anthropocentrism, the progressive nature of change (i.e., the reconstruction of experience), and that there is one method of intelligence that should be universalized – yields another disturbing limitation in his thinking-and in the thinking of his current followers. This limitation is rooted in his failure to understand how the metaphorical nature of language encodes earlier ways of thinking and carries forward these cognitive maps as a taken-for-granted part of thinking and acting ("problem solving," as Dewey would put it). In short, his emphasis on explaining how the method of intelligence could be freed from the limitations of a spectator view of knowledge and from the absolutes of earlier times did not take account of how language influences thought and moral behavior – a key relationship that his contemporary Edward Sapir was writing about in the late 1920s. Dewey's failure to understand how language reproduces a culture's epistemology led him to make the astonishing naïve recommendation in *Knowing and the Known* to empty words of previous meanings that might inhibit ongoing observations (Dewey & Bentley, 1949, p. 49). His misunderstanding of the constitutive role of language also accounts for his reductionist view of tradition.

While Dewey appears to be arguing for schools to teach a mode of inquiry that strengthens the capacity of communities to engage in participatory decision making, he is in fact promoting a form of community that would require different cultural groups to give up their traditions – including the mythopoetic narratives that are the basis of their self identity and moral values. Other traditions that would be displaced by learning to apply his method of intelligence to community problem solving include the varied intergenerational ways in which cultural groups encode and share knowledge – which even in his day represented alternatives to meeting daily needs through consumerism. The double bind in Dewey's thinking is that his vision of educating people to live in more democratic communities, and of learning how to apply the scientific method of inquiry to daily problems, also involves colonizing other cultural groups. Indeed, if Dewey's ideas were to become the basis of education in the broadest sense of the term, they would lead to a monoculture that would have many of the characteristics required by an industrial system bent on transforming noncommodified traditions into new markets. While Dewey was a critic of capitalism, his emphasis on the need to continually reconstruct experience is echoed today in corporate slogans about the the "significance of new possibilities" and the progressive nature of experimental thinking. Both are hallmarks of his epistemology. A case can even be made that Dewey shares with today's corporate culture the view that traditions represent impediments to progress. That is, both Dewey and the current ethos of corporations ignore the complex role that traditions play in the daily life of individuals, and in the patterns of moral reciprocity and support that are at the core of viable communities. Dewey's proclivity of equating traditions with habits, which he describes as "routine ways of acting or degenerate into ways of action to which we are enslaved just in the degree intelligence is disconnected from them" (1916, p. 58) represents a serious limitation. It is a limitation, as I will subsequently explain, that prevents his ideas from being used to address eco-justice issues.

Double Bind in Science Education

Environmental education, it would seem, is free of the double binds that characterize high-status knowledge, computers, and emancipatory theories of education. Unfortunately, this is not the case. In order to understand how environmental education in public schools, as well as science-based environmental studies courses at the university level, reinforce the more ecologically problematic aspects of the western mindset even as they contribute to restoring local habitats and identifying sources of environmental abuse, we have to understand the Janus face of science. That is, we have to understand how science contributed to the Industrial Revolution, including how science is now making it possible to industrialize and market the genetic reengineering of life processes. We also need to understand the influence of culture, particularly western cultural assumptions, on how scientists think – particularly how they frame and justify their research, as well as the futuristic extrapolations they make from it.

As an epistemology, science has contributed to a more accurate understanding of natural processes, and to the development of many useful technologies. But scientists are continually going beyond the limits of their epistemology to make claims based on cultural assumptions they largely take for granted. This failure to understand differences in cultural ways of knowing has recently been carried to the extreme where culture itself is being explained as having a genetic basis and thus under the control of natural selection (Dawkins, 1976; Wilson, 1998a). A list of cultural assumptions taken for granted by most scientists turns out to be nearly identical with the assumptions upon which the Industrial Revolution was based: an anthropocentric view of Nature, equating new understandings and technologies with progress, representing intelligence as an attribute of the autonomous individual – and now the electrochemical processes in the brain, a conduit view of language, and the expectation that Third World cultures will adopt the western model of development and mindset.

The failure among scientists to understand the complex nature of culture, and its diverse forms of expression, is particularly apparent in the claims now being made by leading scientists. E. O. Wilson (1998b), for example, claims that moral values are genetically hardwired. He further claims that as soon as the cultures of the world understand recent discoveries in evolutionary biology they will abandon the superstitions upon which their religions are based and embrace science as the basis of a new universal religion (1998a, pp. 255-265). The assertion by Carl Sagan (1997) that science is the only legitimate source of knowledge (p 30) and the prediction by Lee Silver, a molecular biologist at Princeton University, that biotechnology is on the verge of creating a separate GenRich class of humans who will control future symbolic developments and will evolve into a separate species are equally troubling (1997, pp. 4-7). These scientists are not on the fringe but are representative of what has become the most high-status fields of scientific inquiry – and the most integrated into corporate culture.

The widespread ignorance about the nature of the world's cultures, as well as the cultural changes that must be made if we are to have a sustainable future, carries over to environmental education and environmental studies. This has led to reinforcing in the thinking of the next generation of a management approach to the environment and a continuing disregard of the cultural beliefs and practices that have an adverse impact on the environment. It has also contributed to disregarding the importance of including in environmental education and studies an understanding of sustainable cultural traditions and how they are being undermined by new technologies and the extrapolations of scientific findings.

The double bind in the western approach to science, that is, how it has contributed to the ecological crisis even as it contributes to reversing the degraded state of natural systems, can be seen in the following description of a popular environmental education software program.

According its the designers, SimLife prepares the next generation to be more ecologically informed citizens by learning to think about the environment in the following way:

> SimLife is the first genetic engineering game available for personal computers. It lets players manipulate the very fabric of existence, giving life to creatures that defy the wildest imaginations. Players create exotic plants and animals of various shapes, sizes, and temperaments, turn them loose into a custom-designed environment in which only the best-adapted species survive! With SimLife the budding mad scientist can people the landscape with mutagens (agents that cause mutation and, indirectly, evolution). Or change the individual genetics of one creature and see what effects its offspring have on the long-term survival of its species and on the ecosystem as a whole (1995, p. 1).

A culturally specific set of assumptions frame the decisions that students are to make, as well as how they are to understand their relationship with natural systems. Yet, I seriously doubt that many environmental educators would be aware of them. As these assumptions are also the basis of thinking in the sciences that underlie developments in biotechnology, it is also doubtful that many scientists would recognize these assumptions as ecologically problematic, or make the connection between these assumptions and the conceptual foundations of the Industrial Revolution.

The double bind can be seen in other aspects of environmental education, such as the increasing reliance upon a *constructivist* theory of learning and the efforts on the part of some environmental educators to embed their curriculum within the ideological framework of an emancipatory theory of education. To reiterate a key point: both constructivist and emancipatory theories of learning are based on the same family of ideas and values that undermine community, cultural diversity, and ecological sustainability.

How Language Reproduces
Earlier Forms of Cultural Intelligence

Destroying the natural systems we are dependent upon and globalizing a mindset and consumer-dependent lifestyle that diminishes the quality of relationships could be attributed to a lack of intelligence – and even to such characteristics as greed, hubris, and the pursuit of self-interest. I think this would be the wrong conclusion to draw. These problems are not due to a lack of intelligence or good intentions. Each of the areas of education that I have identified as caught in a double bind has had leaders who were working to improve the human condition. The problem, or at least one dimension of it, is that they unknowingly have relied upon earlier patterns of thinking, that is, they based their thinking on meta-cognitive schemata learned in the process of language acquisition both as children and as they progressed through graduate school. To put this another way, the metaphorical nature of language – the root metaphors that frame the process of analogic thinking that, in turn, are encoded in the iconic metaphors that are such a taken-for-granted part of thought and communication that they go largely unnoticed – reproduces earlier patterns of thinking – even as new understandings are being achieved. I could use patriarchy, individualism, progress, anthropocentrism, and, now, evolution to demonstrate how these deep and unconsciously held root metaphors have influenced thought and the creation of material culture over hundreds, even thousands, of years. Instead, I will use the example of mechanism, which is a root metaphor that is especially prominent in the thinking of scientists. The use of this root metaphor can be traced back over four hundred years of scientific discovery and has influenced other areas of cultural development such as political theory, architecture, agriculture, medicine, and education.

Johannes Kepler (1571-1630), for example wrote that "my aim is to show that the celestial machine is to be likened not to a divine organism but to a clockwork" (Merchant, 1980, pp. 128-129). Marvin Minsky, an early leader in the field of artificial intelligence, utilizes the same root metaphor to explain how our "conscious thoughts use signal-signs to steer the engines in our mind, controlling countless processes of which we're never much aware" (1985, p. 56). In addition to describing the body as a "survival machine," Richard Dawkins states that "brains may be regarded as analogous in function to computers. They are analogous in that both types of machines generate complex patterns of output, after analysis of complex patterns of input, and after reference to stored information" (1976, p. 52). The prevalence of the machine root metaphor can be seen in the scientific writings of Antonio R. Damasio (1994), Francis Crick (1994), and E. O. Wilson (1998), to name just a few of the more prominent scientists. The root metaphor of mechanism can also be seen the university classroom explanation of the cell where the mitochondrion is labeled as the "powerhouse," the Golgi apparatus as the "storage plant," and the lysosome as the "recycling center."

The metaphorical nature of language, as well as the metanarratives of different cultures that are the source of their root metaphors, need to be understood if we are to address the double binds that are putting our future into question. There is also the need to understand the cultural beliefs and practices both within the dominant culture as well as within minority cultures that contribute to community and to a less consumer-dependent lifestyle. As I have written elsewhere about why educational reforms based on an understanding of how earlier ways of thinking are reproduced in the languaging processes in the classroom (Bowers & Flinders, 1990; Bowers 1993a, 1993b, 1995, 1997, 2000, 2001), I will focus now on how an eco-justuce oriented curriculum contributes to regenerating community-based alternatives to a work- and consumer-centered lifestyle that is harming the environment, increasing the health risks of marginalized cultural groups, and becoming the latest model for western colonialism.

EDUCATIONAL IMPLICATIONS OF ECO-JUSTICE

First, it is necessary to identify three aspects of eco-justuce that have particular relevance to educational reform. It is also necessary to explain why the phrase eco-justuce rather than social justice is being used here. Social justice issues of class, race, and gender are often understood in terms of providing equal opportunity within an individualistic, work- and consumer-dependent society. While various forms of discrimination remain unresolved, I think it makes more sense to frame these issues, as well as a number of other issues ignored in the social justice discourse in terms of the root metaphor of an ecology rather than in terms of the root metaphor of the autonomous, self-directing individual.

The original Greek word *oikos*, which Ernst Haekel turned into *Ooecologie* (later shortened to *ecology*) referred to the family household and its daily maintenance. As a root metaphor – cognitive schemata – it foregrounds the relational and interdependent nature of existence, both within human and natural communities. It thus provides a far more accurate way of understanding the nature of human communities than the metaphor of individualism, which, as Sale's quotation brings out, suggests that the fullest expression of our individuality can be achieved only as we separate ourselves from the interdependent networks of a community. Ecology is also the most accurate metaphor for highlighting how human ecology (communities) influence, and are influenced by, natural ecosystems. This brief overview of the origins and explanatory power of ecology as a root metaphor is directly related to the current discourse on how educators can address social justice issues. In effect, I am proposing that the unresolved issues of class, race, and gender be addressed within a conceptual and moral framework that takes account of the multiple ecologies – both cultural and natural – we are dependent upon, and which are being undermined in ways that can no longer be hidden by the technologies and mythic thinking associated with high-status knowledge. The rate and scale of changes in the environment, such as the melting of the polar icecaps and the disappearance of a significant percentage of the earth's species of plants and animals, brings into question the myth that science and technology will ensure the continuation of human progress.

The three aspects of eco-justice that have the most direct implications for educators include: (a) the right of economically and politically marginalized groups to live and work in environments that are free of toxic contamination; (b) the need to recover the noncommodified aspects of community, including the right of minority cultures to renew what remains of their noncommodified traditions rather than be pressured to assimilate fully into the dominant culture of consumerism, technological dependency, and self-centered individualism; (c) the right of unborn generations to live in a viable environment that can sustain morally coherent, community-centered lives. Providing the conceptual basis for addressing the vast differences in the distribution of wealth – within American society and between the North and South – should also be part of an eco-justice pedagogy. Unless the curriculum also addresses the need to help students within mainstream culture learn about community-centered alternatives to hyperconsumerism that reduce the environmentally destructive cycle, little progress can be made in the other areas of eco-justice.

An eco-justuce orientated curriculum that takes seriously differences in cultural ways of knowing and approaches to community cannot be based on the root metaphors that supported the Industrial Revolution, and the digital phase we are now entering. Thinking of ourselves as autonomous individuals, change as inherently progressive in nature, a human-centered relationship with nature, mechanism as a model for understanding life forming and sustaining processes, and so forth have always misrepresented how we are embedded in, reenact, and transform the complex symbolic systems we call culture. Of the many misrepresentations that can be attributed to these root metaphors is the idea that as rational, self-determining individuals we can separate ourselves from traditions. Representing tradition as undermining individual empowerment and impeding scientific and technological innovations has been as essential to the spread of the industrial system of production and consumption as it has been fundamentally erroneous.

Contrary to current thinking, an eco-justice pedagogy that contributes to renewing community and educating responsible ecological citizens is dependent upon a more complex and accurate understanding of tradition. Thus, before any meaningful discussion of what constitutes an eco-justuce pedagogy can take place, the following characteristics of tradition need to be understood: (a) that all the patterns, practices, and technologies that are sustained over four generations or cohorts are examples of a tradition; (b) that some traditions were wrongly constituted in the first place and represent cruel and unjust treatment of others; (c) that some traditions change too slowly, while others undergo change and disappear entirely before we are fully aware of their value to our lives; (d) that lost traditions cannot be reestablished, while attenuated traditions can be renewed; (e) that traditions change from within, and from the external influences; (f) that ideas, technologies, and practices that appear new actually represent a further refinement of traditions that extend well into the past; (g) that many new forms of expression never become traditions because they are not sustained by people over the four generations it takes to adopt a taken-for-granted attitude toward them; and (h) that there are many aspects of high-status knowledge that can best be described, to use Edward Shills' phrase, as "antitradition traditions" (1981, pp. 235-239). There are many implications of this more complex view of tradition, which is made even more complex when we recognize the vast range of differences between cultures, even as they come under the influence of the West. But the most obvious implication, which has been ignored by emancipatory educational theorists, is that specific traditions rather than a generalized view of tradition should be singled out for reform. To reject all traditions, as Freire does in his recommendation that each generation must rename the world, and in his statement that equates traditions with the "alienating daily routine that repeats itself," (1985, p. 199) indicates a basic misunderstanding of his own taken-for-granted patterns as well as the patterns other people depend upon.

Both critical reflection and the political infrastructure that too often resists changes that would eliminate eco-racism are examples of tradition. Critical reflection has a particularly long history and has been articulated in many different ways – and has led to genuine benefits as well as failures that resulted from good intentions. The tradition of critical reflection has a key role to play in an eco-justice oriented curriculum; however, it must be balanced by helping students understand that some traditions are sources of empowerment, basic to a civil society, and represent alternatives to the environmentally destructive pathways that globalization has put us on. As these traditions are understood within the context of a multicultural world, students are more likely to recognize the many different ways knowledge and values are encoded and renewed over generations, including those that have contributed to racist- and sexist-based traditions. They are also more likely to recognize that their relationships within the processes of intergenerational renewal should not always be described as a "banking" process of learning, to quote Freire again (1972, p. 101), and that there are some processes of intergenerational learning where critical reflection becomes isolating, reductionist, and even destructive. These relationships and activities include mentoring in a wide range of skills, participation in family and community ceremonies, musical and arts centered activities, storytelling, games, everyday conversations, and other activities and relationships where learning, community, and intergenerational renewal come together as alternatives to a consumer-dependent existence. One further observation is in order before sketching the outlines of an eco-justice oriented curriculum. That is, it is important to keep in mind that while a recommendation may appear relevant to one set of eco-justice issues, such as helping to renew the noncommodified traditions within minority cultures, it will also have implications for the other two main foci of an eco-justice pedagogy: eco-racism and the rights of future generations. As in all ecological systems, changes occurring in one part of the system lead to changes in other parts.

RECOMMENDATION ONE

If we take account of the amount of environmental destruction that accompanies the spread of the consumer-dependent lifestyle, as well as its adverse impact on communities, it becomes clearer that educational efforts to promote recycling and the knowledge of local ecosystems do not address the core problem. The reductionist thinking that equates being a responsible environmental citizen with recycling may actually have the unintended effect of reinforcing the belief that they can continue or even raise their level of consumption. The media also plays a destructive role by connecting images of the success and happiness with consumerism, while also reinforcing the myth that science and technology will ensure that environmental disasters will not have a lasting impact. Parents who model for their children the relentless pursuit of materialist values also contribute to the problem. Simply stated, most students have encountered so many cultural messages that reinforce consumerism that they do not know what the alternatives are.

The starting point for learning the community-centered alternatives to consumerism is to address the taken-for-granted status of the student's daily life. This will have different foci, depending upon the students' economic and ethnic situation. But even for students coming from impoverished backgrounds, and especially for students from the middle class, documenting the many ways the students' personal relationships and activities involve consumerism will provide a framework for understanding the degree of personal dependency on a market place mentality that has no self-limiting principle to guide it. It also provides a curricular point of departure for examining where products come from and where they go as waste. Where were the basic resources extracted? How far were the resources transported before reaching the manufacturing stage? What were the wages and living conditions of the workers who assembled the products? What were the media costs associated with selling the products? Which consumer products are genuinely beneficial and which are acquired for reasons of status and conformity to what is fashionable? Where are the wastes disposed? Who is adversely affected? What are the health problems connected with toxic contamination? These questions will bring out the network of destructive relationships that many students will recognize themselves as being caught up in.

This part of an eco-justice curriculum should also enable students to recognize the noncommodified alternatives within mainstream culture and within minority cultural groups that have not been totally assimilated. This area of curriculum reform requires taking seriously what universities have relegated to the status of low-status knowledge. Just as making explicit the daily patterns of consumer-dependent relationships and activities is an important starting place for examining other taken-for-granted aspects of the students' embeddedness in the global system of production, consumption, and environmental destruction, making explicit the noncommodified activities and relationships that go largely unnoticed within the students' community is essential to recognizing the activities and relationships they can participate in. To put this another way, the curriculum should provide students with an understanding of the noncommodified resources of their neighborhood, including the networks of support and intergenerational learning that bond people together as a community. Who are the mentors in the neighborhood, and what skills and previously unrecognized interests and talents will emerge from the mentoring relationship? What other face-to-face activities are being carried on in the neighborhood that have not been recognized because they are not represented in the chat room or discovered by surfing the internet or have not been discovered because of the way Nintendo and other computer games narrow the students' awareness to the dimensions of the screen? These noncommodified activities might range from gardening, local theatre, musical groups, poetry and chess clubs, various dance groups, community-organized sports, volunteer work, and so forth.

Learning about the patterns of minority cultures that are not totally overwhelmed by assimilation pressures should also be part of an eco-justuce curriculum. Understanding the ability of these cultural groups to retain a sense of identity as well as the traditions of intergenerational responsibility and mutual aid – which may range from the connections between food, ceremony, and community to healing practices and performing arts – have two educational benefits. First, it provides students from the dominant culture with a more complex understanding of how the various expressions of community, as well as the importance of intergenerational relationships, contribute to a deeper sense of connectedness and personal identity. Consumerism is too often used to fill the void that accompanies the lack of connectedness with others – as though identity and connectedness can be acquired in the depersonalized marketplace. The double bind is that it leads to further isolation from community building relationships.

The second benefit from studying the noncommodified traditions of cultural groups still centered on face-to-face, intergenerational knowledge, and networks of mutual aid is that it overcomes stereotypical thinking of them as backward. While not all minority cultural groups meet today's standards of social justice, students can still learn a great deal from them about how to live less materialistic lives. A case can even be made that many of the patterns of interdependency within their communities and with the natural environment will suggest approaches that can be taken within mainstream culture of how to live when the myth of unlimited resources is finally recognized as unsustainable. But again, it needs to be emphasized that learning from them the art of living less consumer-dependent lives has to be balanced with overcoming the poverty that many members of these cultures experience on a daily basis – in meeting basic levels of health care, diet, housing, and education. Unless learning what they have to teach us about moral reciprocity and intergenerational responsibility (which is different than borrowing from them), is accompanied by basic reforms in the distribution of wealth, this part of an eco-justuce curriculum will represent yet another form of appropriation.

RECOMMENDATION TWO

An eco-justuce centered curriculum should engage students in the examination of two characteristics of the dominant culture that are at the center of the double bind, where technology-based approaches to progress undermine what remains of self-sufficient communities and cultural groups. The first has to do with the mythic view of language perpetuated by the keepers of high-status knowledge. The sender/receiver model of communication, what Michael Reddy calls the "conduit view of language" (1979), supports a number of other key myths: that data and knowledge are objective; that intelligence is an activity and attribute of the autonomous individual, now considered the electrochemical process occurring in the individual's brain; and that the rational process, including critical reflection and scientific approaches to inquiry, transcend cultural ways of knowing. That is, the sender/receiver view of communication reinforces the idea that supposedly objective knowledge can be taken as the standard of how to think and live by the members of all cultures – and, failing this, it can be imposed upon them in the name of progress.

Students need to learn how the metaphorical nature of language carries forward earlier ways of thinking, thus influencing present understandings in ways not often recognized. They also need to learn how the *languaging* processes in everyday life influence what they understand as real and important, and how their personal identities are influenced not only by the languaging of others but also by the values and ways of thinking encoded and communicated through the material expressions of the culture. Learning that words have a history and carry forward earlier culturally specific assumptions – which may be the source of destructive relationships, or may, in other cases, contain wisdom refined over generations – is critical to making informed decisions about the cultural forces that threaten our future ecological survival. That is, learning to put the layers of metaphorical thinking in historical and cross-cultural perspective is as essential to participating in a democratic society as it is to recognizing how language is being used to legitimate new forms of colonization.

This brings us to the second characteristic of the dominant culture that students need to understand. What now exerts the most influence in shaping our lives and ecological future is the least studied in terms of its cultural roots and current influence. The educational process should provide students with a knowledge of the history of science and technology. This would include examining their genuine contributions as well as their adverse influence on the diverse cultural traditions of self-sufficiency. Students should also be able to recognize when scientists and technologists are proposing changes in areas of cultural life where they have no special expertise or democratic mandate. The patenting of genes, the efforts to translate scientific knowledge into technologies that create further dependencies upon drugs and experts, the cloning of animals and the goal of extending this technology to humans, the promise of extending life hundreds of years, and so forth represent decisions that should be debated by an informed public. Democratizing decisions now being made by scientists and technologists, corporations, and venture capitalists is one of the most essential and difficult challenges we now face. When students encounter a continual listing of scientific achievements, and promises of even greater breakthroughs, with no mention of unanticipated consequences that people are still struggling to deal with, there is a sense that science and technology are so integral to sustaining human progress that no need exists to bring them under democratic control. Similarly, an eco-justuce curriculum needs to include the study of technology as a cultural phenomena. This would go a long way toward overturning the myth that it is both culturally neutral – that is, a tool – and the expression of progress. Students need to understand the difference between traditional (indigenous) and modern technologies, how modern technologies influence thought patterns and language, what skills are undermined by different technologies, how modern technology is ideologically embedded in the corporate agenda of globalization, how technologies both separate and connect people. The influences of technology on communities should also be considered, with cultural differences being part of the discussion. The primary purpose in studying what is the most dominant aspect of contemporary life is to provide the conceptual understandings necessary for people to make decisions about which technologies add to the quality of life, support cultural diversity, and have the least adverse impact on natural systems. That the development of new technologies is largely driven by the relentless quest to create new markets, with little regard for its human and environmental consequences, make it especially imperative that our educational institutions provide a curriculum that engages students in an in-depth examination of technology.

In her book *The Poisonwood Bible*, Barbara Klingsolver (1999) observes that "we construct our lives around basic misunderstandings" (p. 532). She goes on to say that "illusions mistaken for truth are the pavement under our feet" (p. 532). As ecological systems become increasingly stressed, it becomes clearer that our materialistic and individually centered approach to progress is an illusion that must be seen, regardless of how pain, for what it is. Giving up this illusion, however, does not mean we must return to the past (which would be impossible), or borrow from cultures that have taken a less environmentally destructive path. Rather, it means taking up the task of evaluating which of our traditions contribute to cultural diversity and living less consumer-dependent lives. The major reference point for assessing this renewal and reform process is the viability of natural systems. Modern consciousness is so focused on the future, and the relentless pursuit of realizing even more conveniences, happiness, and power to control the environment that it has lost sight of a fundamental fact of cultural existence: namely, that all aspects of human life involve a mix of short-lived fashions, innovations that may survive as new traditions, and individualized and group interpretations of how to reenact and extend the traditions of our cultural group. This generalization takes account of such areas as new scientific discoveries and technologies, art forms that proclaim themselves to be against all traditions, and messianic ideologies that are too often mistakenly seen as going beyond the constraints of tradition when they are, in fact, extensions of multiple traditions. The focus of educational reform should be centered on sorting out the illusions from the life-enhancing traditions. This will lead to a more viable democracy and a greater sense of eco-justice than what is achieved by basing educational reform on the need to discover new ideas, technologies, and forms of individual expression that are, as the illusion holds, free of ecological accountability.

References

Bowers, C. A. (1993a). *Education, cultural myths, and the ecological crisis.* Albany, NY: State University of New York Press.

Bowers, C. A. (1993b). *Critical essays on education, modernity, and the recovery of the ecological imperative.* New York: Teachers College Press.

Bowers, C. A. (1995). *Educating for an ecologically sustainable culture: Rethinking moral education, creativity, intelligence, and other modern orthodoxies.* Albany, NY: State University of New York Press.

Bowers, C. A. (1997). *The culture of denial: Why the environmental movement needs a strategy for reforming universities and public schools.* Albany, NY: State University of New York Press.

Bowers, C. A. (2000). *Let them eat data: How computers affect education, cultural diversity, and the prospects of ecological sustainability.* Athens, Georgia: University of Georgia Press.

Bowers, C. A. (2001). *Educating for eco-justice and community.* Athens, GA: University of Georgia Press.

Bowers, C. A., & Flinders, D. (1990). *Responsive Teaching: An ecological approach to classroom patterns of language, culture, and thought.* New York: Teachers College Press.

Damasio, A.R. (1994). *Descartes' error: Emotion, reason, and the human brain.* New York: G. P. Putnam's Sons.

Dawkins, R. (1976). *The selfish gene.* New York: Oxford University Press.

Dewey, J. (1916). *Democracy and education.* New York: Macmillan.

Dewey, J. (1957). *Reconstruction in philosophy.* Boston: Beacon Press.

Dewey, J., & Bentley, A. (1949). *Knowing and the known.* Boston: Beacon Press.

Freire, P. (1972). *Pedagogy of the oppressed.* Harmondsworth: Penguin.

Freire, P. (1974). *Pedagogy of the oppressed.* New York: Herder and Herder.

Freire, P. (1985). *The politics of education: Power, culture, and liberation.* South Hadley, MA: Bergin & Garvey.

Hickman, L.A. (1996). Nature as culture: John Dewey's pragmatic naturalism. In A. Light & E. Katz (Eds.), *Environmental pragmatism.* London: Routledge.

Kingsolver, B. (1999). *The Poisonwood Bible.* New York: Harper Perennial.

Kurzweil, R. (1999). *The age of spiritual machines: When computers exceed human intelligence.* New York: Viking Press.

Merchant, C. (1980). *The death of nature: Women, ecology, and the scientific revolution.* New York: Harper & Row.

Minsky, M. (1985). *Society of mind.* New York: Simon & Schuster.

Moravec, H. (1988). *Mind children: The future of robot and human intelligence.* Cambridge: Harvard University Press.

Reddy, M. J. (1977). The conduit metaphor – A case of frame conflict in our language about language. In A. Ortony (Ed.), *Metaphor and thought*. Cambridge, UK: Cambridge University Press.

Sagan, C. (1997). *The demon-haunted world: Science as a candle in the dark*. London: Headline Book Publishing.

Sale, K. (1995). *Rebels against the future: The Luddites and their war on the industrial revolution*. Reading, MA: Addison-Wesley.

Shills, E. (1981). *Tradition*. Chicago: The University of Chicago Press.

Silver, L. (1997). *Remaking eden: How cloning and beyond will change the human family*. New York: Avon Books.

SimLife. (1995). Orinda, CA: Maxis.

Stock, G. (1993). *Metaman: The merging of humans and machines into a global superorganism*. Toronto: Doubleday Canada.

Wilson, E.O. (1998a). *Consilience: The unity of knowledge*. New York: Alfred A. Knopf.

Wilson, E.O. (1988b). The biological basis of morality. *The Atlantic Monthly, 281*(4), 53-70.

TWELVE

ENVIRONMENTAL EDUCATIONAL LEADERSHIP AND ITS ORIGINS

Kelly Young

The origins of environmental education in North America can be traced to the Brownie, Girl Guide, and Scouting youth movements, which are deeply rooted in the imperial practices of Baden-Powell's paramilitary scheme, as well as in Seton's Woodcraft Indians, as an extension of an appropriation of Indigenous Knowledge (IK) and Traditional Ecological Knowledge (TEK) and practices (Baden-Powell, 1909; Jeal, 2001; MacDonald, 1993; Seton, 1912; Wadland, 1978; Young, 2006). Since IK formed the basis for the pre- and post-contact environmental education movement in North America, this literature review focuses on a profile of recently published work about IK and TEK in environmental education that includes a more recent body of literature on eco-justice education.

Literature concerning First Nations storytelling and its importance in environmental education was surveyed together with the academic and applied literature that pertains to the inclusion of IK and TEK in environmental education. For the purpose of this literature review, IK and TEK refer to Earth-based peoples' traditional knowledge in the form of sustainable environmental knowledge and practices that have been sought across the world in order to inform environmental issues and environmental education (Cajete, 1994; McGregor, 2004).

In order to get a current representation of the nature of the academic literature, a search was conducted in the *Educational Resources Information Centre* (ERIC) database for academic articles spanning a thirty-year retrospective. Other databases that were searched included the *Social Sciences* database and *Sociological Abstracts*, the *Natural Sciences* database, *Books In Print* (R.R. Bowker Company, New York) and *Sociological Abstracts* (Sociological Abstracts, Inc.). My search considered these topics: Indigenous Knowledge and environmental education, Traditional Ecological Knowledge and environmental education, Indigenous Knowledge, and Traditional Ecological Knowledge. The search generated 139 titles of works related to IK and TEK in environmental education. In most of the works, environmental education is not the first concern. By limiting the works to only those in which IK and TEK in environmental education are the primary focus of the work, a total of 56 titles were identified. Several of the articles are listed in two or more databases. I also reviewed the *Canadian Journal of Environmental Education* (CJEE), as well as *The Journal of Environmental Education* (JEE) and *Environmental Education Research* (EER) specifically for special theme issues related to IK and TEK in environmental education.

The works can be separated into two broad categories: (a) ecosystems, agriculture and natural resources management and training informed by IK and TEK and (b) curriculum development and place-based experiential education informed by IK and TEK. McGregor (2004) believes that within the scope of IK and TEK in environmental education

> there is a major dichotomy in the realm of TEK that needs to be understood: there is the Aboriginal view of TEK, which reflects an Indigenous understanding of relationships to Creation, and there is the dominant Eurocentric view of TEK, which reflects colonial attitudes toward Aboriginal people and their knowledge. In my view, to understand where TEK comes from one must start with Indigenous people and our own understanding of the world. (p. 386)

At least part of what makes TEK and IK different from non-indigenous environmental education is that these non-indigenous forms develop from university educated and, hence, literate practices while Indigenous environmental education is constituted by a set of practices embedded in the natural world. These indigenous practices reflect in their structure, both the order of the cosmos and a profound appreciation of the phases of the development of the human nervous system, while also accounting for human entry into the spirit world. Indigenous environmental education, besides being deeply experiential in traditional territories, is also constituted by an oral tradition perpetuated by the experiential depth, producing a good fit between spoken and lived legacies in traditional territories.

McGregor's (2004) assertion that there are two approaches to TEK informed my reading of the literature through the recognition that both Western and Indigenous worldviews appear in the databases surveyed. McGregor also outlines the ways in which TEK has emerged on a global level from a recognition of Indigenous Peoples' development of sustainable environmental knowledge and practices, as evidenced through the 1987 *Brundtland Report,* or the *Report of the World Commission on Environment and Development,* the 1992 United Nations Conference on Environment and Development and the Convention on Biodiversity (CBD). The majority of the literature reveals that TEK and IK in environmental education are being appropriated and applied within Western science in so far as they inform or fit a broadly defined Eurocentric viewpoint. Krimmerer (2002) provides a few examples of how TEK and IK inform emerging sciences:

> TEK is increasingly being sought by academics, agency scientists, and policy makers as a potential source of ideas for emerging models of ecosystem management, conservation biology, and ecological restoration. It has been recognized as complementary and equivalent to scientific knowledge. (p. 432)

A part of the literature deals with TEK and IK's recognition in western scientific research. Another part of the literature deals with TEK and IK in environmental education that is being taken up in terms of the ways in which TEK and IK can inform education from Kindergarten to Doctoral studies. McKinley (2005) writes:

> Indigenous writers have argued the importance of connecting school science education to the students' cultural background (Cajete 1995, Kawagley 1995, Kawagley and Barnhardt 1999, McKinley 1997). This argument can be divided into two strategies. First is making science 'relevant' to the student, which usually involves teaching in culturally relevant contexts or everyday science. The second strategy is aimed at improving indigenous students' learning through more appropriate teaching approaches and models, often

called culturally responsive teaching or culturally based pedagogy (See Bishop and Glynn 1994, Ladson-Billings 1995). (p. 230)

Conversely, Battiste and Henderson (2000) are concerned about the inclusion of IK and TEK as part of the curriculum because of the domination of western science in the integration of IK and TEK. The overview of literature below reveals that the field of IK and TEK in environmental education is dominated by a Eurocentric worldview, which generally seeks only IK and TEK that are compatible with the presumptions of western science

THEMES IN THE LITERATURE: WESTERN SCIENCE INFORMED THROUGH AN INTEGRATION OF IK AND TEK

Overall, there is a high degree of concentration on issues of integration of IK and TEK within Western Science. These themes include environment management (natural resources management and training), agricultural management, and sustainable development (environment restoration, preservation, and assessment).

Environment Management (Natural Resources Management and Training): Emerging models of ecosystem management, conservation biology and ecological restoration (Kimmerer, 2002); Restoration of the land (Sellers, McDonald, & Wilson, 2001); A study on the benefits of incorporating cross-cultural perspectives into environmental science and natural resources training (Kimmerer, 1998); TEK and management research (Whiteman, 2004); Sacred ecology and TEK (Berkes, 1999).

Agricultural Management: Agricultural practices of Indigenous Peoples in Peru, Papua New Guinea, and Thailand (Brookfield & Padoch, 1994); A study of modernized agriculture in underdeveloped countries through women's environmental activism for sustainable agriculture (Angeles & Tarbotton, 2001); The role of IK in the development of environmentally sound agriculture systems (Schafer, 1993); Maintenance and adaptation of TEK (Danby, Hik, Slocombe, & Williams, 2003).

Sustainable Development (Environment Restoration, Preservation and Assessment): A study of discourses of sustainable development (Bannerji, 2003); Endangered languages and biocultural diversity (Maffi, 2002); Environmental education and indigenous knowledge as a basis for local planning among the Rendille nomads in Northern Kenya (Oba, 1992); The role of indigenous knowledge in resource management and environmental assessment (Roue & Nakashima, 2002); On ethnoeconomics (Cavalcanti, 2002); Indigenous environmental studies in the area of sustainable Indigenous communities (Alfred, 1999; Laduke, 1999; Mohawk, 2000; Osborne, 1991; Shiva, 1993, 2000; Wade, 1996).

CURRICULUM DEVELOPMENT AND PLACE-BASED EXPERIENTIAL EDUCATION INFORMED BY IK AND TEK

A part of the literature focuses on TEK and IK in Kindergarten to Doctoral educational contexts. The themes include storytelling and First Nations traditions, cultural restoration, education ecology and culture, higher education, curriculum program and development, science education, ecological literacy, and spiritual approaches to environmental education.

Storytelling and First Nations Traditions: A Saulteaux Elder's view of Native education (Akan, 1993); On First Nation's longhouses (Archibald, 2001); A viewpoint from a Western Apache on the Western Apache (Basso, 1996); Yukon Native Elders (Cruikshank, 1981, 1990b); Cree Native Elders (Lightning, 1993; Wilson, 1993); Childhood development and ecology of imagination (Cobb, 1959; Egan, 1986); Learning by story and nature (Berry, 1991; Cajete, 1994; Dooling & Jordan-Smith, 1989; Kane, 1995; Postman, 1989; Shepard, 1977; Sheridan, 1991, 1994; Turner, 1985, 1990); Work on the modern environmental movement and First Nations environmental wisdom (Suzuki, 1997; Suzuki & Knudtson, 1992); A recent work encourages the integration of storytelling into environmental and outdoor education and promotes imagination and an environmental ethic (Plotkin & Sheridan, 1995); A study of the primeval nature and mythic consciousness of storytelling (Sheridan, 2001); The relationship between traditional territory and imagination (Sheridan & Longboat, 2006).

Maria Montessori's nontraditional approach to education is an example of a European attempt to inform education through a holistic approach to learning. The Montessori method has no active affiliation with IK and TEK, but it may have a better fit than in normative teacher education. On the origins of the Montessori method (Walter, 2004); On the experience of nature as part of daily curriculum (Hildebrandt Cichucki, 2004); On nature observation (Loughran, 2001); Studies comparing traditional models with Montessori approaches to education (Cossentino, 2005, 2006; Giovannini, 2000; Greene, 2005; Rathunde & Csikszentmihalyi, 2005a, 2005b).

Articles exploring storytelling and narrative inquiry as a vehicle for environmental education (Cheney, 2002; Fawcett, 2002; Fontes, 2002; Hart, 2002; Johnston, 2002; Lotz-Sisitka, 2002; Moore, 2002); Articles on the practice of environmental education that include a critique of conventional schooling practices by advocating for outdoor education among other things (Curthoys & Cuthbertson, 2002; Nicol, 2002; Sheridan, 2002; Warkentin, 2002).

Cultural Restoration: There is a collection of studies on First Nations perspectives on sustainable Indigenous communities and practices (Akan, 1993; Archibald, 2001; Armstrong, 1992; Basso, 1996; Cajete, 1994; Cruikshank, 1990a; Orr, 1992, 1994; Shiva, 1993; Suzuki, 1997; Suzuki & Knudtson, 1992); A study of the role of TEK in maintaining the diversity of human social and cultural systems as well as the environment (Chase, 1993); A study of efforts at cultural maintenance of environmental knowledge through storytelling and observational learning of the Seri people of Sonora Mexico (Nabhan & Rosenberg, 1997).

Education Ecology and Culture: A research study involves Vermont teachers and university students that are introduced to concepts of education, ecology, and culture in Oaxaca, Mexico (Teran & Esteva, 2000); A study of high school experiential education engaged in with Dene Elders is a study of a ten-day summer camp (Andrews, 2002); A study of a fish recovery program involving high school students (Galindo & Barta, 2001); Ways of learning among the Yupiaq people of Alaska (Kawagley, 1999); The use of IK and TEK in Maori science education (McKinley, 2005); A representation of an academic take on Indigenous traditions and ecology (Cole, 1998); Linkages between social-ecological resilience and adaptive learning (Davidson-Hunt & Berkes, 2003); Translating aboriginal cultures through land and language (Cole, 2002); Anticolonial strategies for sustaining IK (Simpson, 2004); Cultural approaches to environmental education (Agyeman, 2002); Weaving education, culture, and the environment (Wilson, 1998, 2002).

Higher Education: Studies included research on the institutionalization of IK and environmental education in Southern Africa (Van Damme & Neluvhalani, 2004); Research on Western science and TEK in higher education in southwestern United States (Brandt, 2004); A study of some of the philosophical and epistemological tensions in TEK-based environmental education (Reid, Tearney, & Dillon, 2004); A collection of essays on the importance of an ecological approach to education that focuses on cultural traditions and natural environments, which includes Wagner's paper on "Ecology and Basic Education among the Indigenous Peoples of Canada" (Hautecoeur, 2002); Theorizing about the reinvention and reframing of university education through a universe story (O'Sullivan, 2002) originally articulated by Berry and Swimme (1992).

Curriculum and Program Development: A study of a blend of traditional knowledge of ecology and Euro-American scientific principles in the development of a curriculum for the University of California for American Indian natural resource workers (Harris & Cox, 1997); A report on the development of a doctoral program that focuses on integrating Earth-based knowledge with Western Science (Simonelli, 1994); A national study of environmental education in pre-service teacher preparation (Heimlich, Braus, Olivolo, McKeown-Ice, & Barringer-Smith, 2004).

Science Education: Studies of TEK and multicultural science and pedagogy (Snively & Corsiglia, 2001; Svennbeck, 2001); Comparing tradition ecological knowledge in a study of water quality through a university exchange study abroad program (Calhoon, Wildcat, Annett, Peirotti, & Griswold, 2003); Transformative learning in the context of Hawaiian TEK (Feinstein, 2004); Epistemology of Western science and TEK through ethnobotany (Brandt, 2004); A study of Seri people, their customs and traditions, in terms of local knowledge (Nabhan & Rosenberg, 1997); Components of successful Indigenous environmental education science programs at the postsecondary level (Simpson, 2002); Youth experiences in science in nonformal settings (Ponzio & Marzolla, 2002); A model for indigenous science education (Cajete, 1999).

Ecological Literacy: There is a small but growing body of research in the area of ecological literacy. Studies include research on the development of ecological literacy (Abram, 1996; Bateson 1972; Berry, 1995; Bowers, 2001, 2002, 2003, 2005, 2006; Bowers & Apffel-Marglin, 2004; Bowers & Flinders, 1990; Gruenewald, 2003a, 2003b, 2003c; Kirkpatrick, 1985; Leopold, 1987; Martusewicz, 2001, 2005a, 2005b; Martusewicz & Edmundson, 2004; Orr, 1992, 1994; Shiva, 1993; Snyder, 1990; Young 2005). Eco-justice educational research has been linked to such research approaches as ecofeminism (Plumwood, 1994; Warren,

2000, 1997). Eco-justice education is an approach that analyzes the increasing destruction of the world's diverse ecosystems, languages, and cultures by the globalizing and ethnocentric forces of Western consumer culture. A central idea in eco-justice education is that of the *commons*, defined as all the shared resources and relationships that support life in the community, including the land, the water, the air, the language, the traditions, the decision-making processes, the day-to-day practices and so on (Bowers, 2004).

Spiritual Approaches to Nature: The broader realm of environmental education as a body of literature can be traced back to the 1970s. Little is published prior to this time. IK and TEK in environmental education is a relatively recent phenomenon in the literature with the exception of related themes in environmental education whereby spiritual approaches to nature are a focus (Kohl & Benedok, 1991; Vahey, 1992; Whitcombe, 1991). Another related theme is environmental education relative to Native North America. Several articles deal with the use of stories, the practice of storytelling, and the correspondence between story and landscape as a basis for epistemological practices throughout North America. Moreover, these studies consider environmental education relative to North America Indigenous practices in terms of methodological use of stories, in general, and the use of North American stories of land, in particular, derived from literary texts that are in turn situated in stories that produce IK and TEK (Bruchac & Caduto, 1988, 1991; Caduto, 1983; DeFaveri, 1992; Fraser, 1983; Horwood, 1989; King, 2003; Nabhan, 1997; Quinn, 1993; Sharpes, 1974).

CONCLUDING REMARKS

Since the 1970s, the literature on environmental educational research has been primarily concerned with education outside of a relation with Indigenous cultural authorities and IK. affirms that environmental education has, for the most part, continued to divert from Woodcraft's original intentions starting with the IK practices in Baden-Powell's imperial training to present day non-existent environmental education curriculum in Ontario specifically. Environmental education, then, has grown out of science education's refusal to engage the spiritual due to the commitment in the scientific community to secularity. In response to the lack of literature, Sheridan (1994) suggests that: "there does not seem to be much concern with any kind of spiritual connection with nature in non-Native traditions" (p. 37). Furthermore he contends that a discourse has been established in environmental education that is "implicitly technical and institutional rather than inherently cultural," and resonantly and methodologically embedded in traditional territories in the literature on environmental education (Sheridan, 1994, p. 37).

There are several examples of place-based experiential education that provide opportunities for IK's holistic view to enact itself as a sustainable model for environmental educational leadership (Cajete, 1994; Henley, 1989; Longboat, 2006; Seton, 1912). The literature suggests that a growing number of educators are looking to IK, TEK, and eco-justice education for alternative approaches to environmental education. Outside of Cajete's (1994) text, which provides Indigenous education perspectives on teaching and learning, and Henley's (1989) project, almost all of the research is based outside of North America.

This literature review focused on a body of research in the field of environmental education informed by IK and TEK that specifically engages notions of ecological and traditional environmental sustainability. This literature review has demonstrated that most of environmental education is conceived in traditions and paradigms of alienated models and can only cease to *power out*, a term Lightning (1993) uses to refer to a crisis of environmental degradation whereby natural ecosystems no longer sustain life. Thus, these models bring us no closer to an appropriate environmental educational model for North America, which involves an integrated model (Sheridan, 1994). However, the evidence from the literature also suggests that cultural transformation is possible and necessary within an integrated model. Environmental imperatives require that we put environmental education back on track through environmental educational leadership and practice that revives its origins.

References

Abram, D. (1996). *The spell of the sensuous: Perception in a more-than-human world*. New York: Pantheon Books.

Agyeman, J. (2002). Cultural environmental education: From First Nation to frustration. *Canadian Journal of Environmental Education, 7*(1), 5-12.

Akan, L. (1993). Pimosatamowin Sikaw Kakeequaywin: Walking and talking, A Saulteux Elder's view of Native education. *Canadian Journal of Native Education, 19*(2), 189-214.

Alfred, T. (1999). *Peace, power, righteousness: An Indigenous manifesto*. Don Mills, ON: Oxford University Press.

Andrews, T. (2002). The land is like a book. *The Ontario Journal of Outdoor Education, 14*(1), 18-20.

Angeles, L., C., & Tarbotton, R. (2001). Local transformation through global connection: Women's assets and environmental activism for sustainable agriculture in Ladakh, India. *Women's Studies Quarterly, 29*(1-2), 99-115.

Archibald, J.-A. (2001). *The First Nations Longhouse: Our home away from home*. Vancouver, BC: First Nations House of Learning.

Armstrong, J. (1992). *Give back: First Nations perspectives on cultural practice*. North Vancouver, BC: Gallerie Publications.

Baden-Powell, R. (1909). *Scouting for boys: A handbook for instruction in good citizenship through woodcraft*. Ottawa: National Council of Boy Scouts of Canada.

Bannerji, S. B. (2003). Who sustains whose development? Sustainable development and the reinvention of nature. *Organization Studies, 24*(1), 143-180.

Basso, K. (1996). *Wisdom sits in places: Landscape and language among the western Apache*. Alburquerque, NM: University of New Mexico Press.

Bateson, G. (1972). *Steps to an ecological mind: Collected essays in anthropology, psychiatry, evolution, and epistemology*. San Francisco: Chandler Pub. Co.

Battiste, M., & Henderson, J. (2000). *Protecting Indigenous knowledge and heritage: A global challenge*. Saskatoon, SK: Purich Publishing.

Berkes, F. (1999). *Sacred ecology: Traditional ecological knowledge and resource management*. Philadelphia, PA: Taylor & Francis.

Berry, T., & Swimme, B. (1992). *The universe story: From the primordial flaring forth to the ecozoic era: A celebration of the unfolding cosmos*. San Francisco: CA: Harper.

Berry, W. (1991). Out of your car, off your horse. *Atlantic Monthly*, February, 61-63.

Berry, W. (1995). *Another turn of the crank*. Washington, DC: Counterpoints.

Bowers, C. A. (2001). *Educating for eco-justice and community*. Athens, GA: The University of Georgia Press.

Bowers, C. A. (2002). Toward an eco-justice pedagogy. *Environmental Education Research, 8*(1), 21-34.

Bowers, C. A. (2003). *Mindful conservatism: Rethinking the ideological and educational basis of an ecologically sustainable future*. Lanham, MD: Rowman & Littlefield.

Bowers, C. A. (2004). EcoJustice Dictionary. Retrieved July 31st, 2007, from http://www.ecojusticeeducation.org

Bowers, C. A. (2005). *The false promises of constructivist theories of learning: A global and ecological critique (complicated conversation).* New York: Peter Lang Publishing.

Bowers, C. A. (2006). *Revitalizing the commons: Cultural and educational sites of resistance and affirmation.* Landam, MD: Lexington Books.

Bowers, C. A. & Apffel-Marglin, F. (2004). *Re-thinking Freire: Globalization and the environmental crisis.* Mahwah, NH: Lawrence Erlbaum Associates.

Bowers, C. A., & Flinders, D. J. (1990). *Responsive teaching: An ecological approach to classroom patterns of language, culture and thought.* New York: Teachers College Press.

Brandt, C. (2004). A thirst for justice in the arid southwest: The role of epistemology and place in higher education. *Educational Studies Journal of the American Educational Studies Association, 36*(1), 93-107.

Brookfield, H., & Padoch, C. (1994). Appreciating agrodiversity: A look at the dynamism and diversity of Indigenous farming practices. *Environment, 36*(5), 6-11, 37-45.

Bruchac, J., & Caduto, M. (1988). *Keepers of the earth: Native American stories and environmental activities for children and keepers of the earth (Teacher's Guide).* Golden, CO: Fulcrum Publishing.

Bruchac, J., & Caduto, M. (1991). *Keepers of the animals: Native American stories and wildlife activities for children and teacher's guide.* Golden, Co: Fulcrum Publishing.

Caduto, M. (1983). Toward a comprehensive strategy for environmental values education. *Journal of Environmental Education, 14*(4), 12-18.

Cajete, G. (1994). *Look to the mountain: An ecology of Indigenous education.* Skyland, NC: Kivaki Press.

Cajete, G. (1999). *Igniting the sparkle: An indigenous science education model.* Skyland, NC: Kivaki Press.

Calhoon, J. A., Wildcat, D., Annett, C., Pierotti, R., Griswold, W. (2003). Creating meaningful study abroad programs for American Indian postsecondary students. *Journal of American Indian Education, 42*(1), 46-57.

Cavalcanti, C. (2002). Economic thinking: Traditional ecological knowledge and ethnoeconomics. *Current Sociology/La Sociologie Contemporaine, 50*(1), 39-55.

Chase, A. (1993). Traditional ecological knowledge: Wisdom for sustainable development. *The Australian Journal of Anthropology, 4*(3), 245-247.

Cheney, J. (2002). The moral epistemology of First Nations stories. *Canadian Journal of Environmental Education, 7*(2), 88-100.

Cobb, E. (1959). The ecology of imagination in childhood. *Daedalus: Journal of the American Academy of Arts and Sciences, 88*(Summer), 537-548.

Cole, P. (1998). An academic take on "Indigenous traditions and ecology." *Canadian Journal of Environmental Education, 3,* 100-115.

Cole, P. (2002). Land and language: Translating aboriginal cultures. *Canadian Journal of Environmental Education, 7*(1), 67-85.

Cossentino, J. (2005). Ritualizing expertise: A non-Montessorian view of the Montessori method. *American Journal of Education, 111*(2), 211-233.

Cossentino, J. (2006). Big work: Goodness, vocation, and engagement in the Montessori method. *Curriculum Inquiry, 36*(1), 63-92.

Cruikshank, J. (1981). Legend and landscape: Convergence of oral and scientific traditions in the Yukon Territory. *Arctic Anthropology, xviii*(2), 67-93.

Cruikshank, J. (1990a). Getting words right: Perspectives on naming and places in Athapaskan oral history. *Arctic Anthropology, 27*(1), 52-65.

Cruikshank, J. (1990b). *Life lived like a story: Life stories of three Yukon Native Elders.* Vancouver, BC: University of British Columbia Press.

Curthoys, L. P., & Cuthbertson, B. (2002). Listening to the landscape. *Canadian Journal of Environmental Education, 7*(2), 224-240.

Danby, R. K., Hik, D. S., Slocombe, D. S., & Williams, A. (2003). Science and the St. Elias: An evolving framework for sustainability in North America's highest mountains. *Geographical Journal, 169*(3), 191-204.

Davidson-Hunt, I., & Berkes, F. (2003). Learning as you journey: Anishinaabe perceptions of social-ecological environments and adaptive learning. *Conservation Ecology, 8*(1), 1-21.

DeFaveri, I. (1992). Developing ecological literacy for citizen action. *Ecological Record, 73*(2), 37-41.

Dooling, D. M., & Jordan-Smith, P. (Eds.). (1989). *I become part of it. Sacred dimension in Native American life.* San Francisco: HarperCollins.

Egan, K. (1986). *Literacy, society, and schooling: A reader.* Cambridge, MA: Cambridge University Press.

Fawcett, L. (2002). Children's wild animal stories. *Canadian Journal of Environmental Education, 7*(2), 125-139.

Feinstein, B. (2004). Learning and transformation in the context of Hawaiian traditional ecological knowledge. *Adult Education Quarterly, 54*(2), 105-120.

Fontes, P. J. (2002). The stories (woman) teachers tell. *Canadian Journal of Environmental Education, 7*(2), 256-268.

Fraser, T. (1983). *A Dogrib history.* Yellowknife, NWT: Northwest Territories Department of Education.

Galindo, E., & Barta, J. (2001). Indian summer: A "hands-on, feet-wet" approach to science education. *Winds of Change, 16*(4), 54-56.

Giovannini, J. (2000). The Montessori method. *Architecture, 89*(6), 116-121.

Greene, P. (2005). Dear Maria Montessori. *Kappa Delta Pi Record, 41*(4), 164-167.

Gruenewald, D. (2003a). At home with the other: Reclaiming the ecological roots of development and literacy. *The Journal of Environmental Education, 35*(1), 33-43.

Gruenewald, D. (2003b). The best of both worlds: A critical pedagogy of place. *Educational Researcher, 32*, 3-12.

Gruenewald, D. (2003c). Foundations of place: A multidisciplinary framework for place-conscious education. *American Educational Research Journal, 40*, 619-654.

Harris, R. R., & Cox, R. (1997). Curriculum on ecology and natural resources management for Indian natural resource workers. *American Indian Culture and Research Journal, 21*(2), 33-48.

Hart, P. (2002). Narrative knowing, and emerging methodologies in environmental education research. *Canadian Journal of Environmental Education, 7*(2), 140-165.

Hautecoeur, J.-P. (Ed.). (2002). *Ecological education in everyday life.* Hamburg, Germany: United Nations Educational, Scientific, and Cultural Organization Institute for Education.

Heimlich, J., Braus, J., Olivolo, B., McKeown-Ice, R., & Barringer-Smith, L. (2004). Environmental education and preservice teacher preparation: A national study. *The Journal of Environmental Education, 35*(2), 17-48.

Henley, T. (1989). *Project rediscovery: Ancient pathways-new directions.* Vancouver, BC: Western Canada Wilderness Association.

Hildebrandt Cichucki, P. (2004, Winter). Keeping in touch with nature. *Montessori Life, 16*, 14.

Horwood, B. (1989). Introducing spiritual dimensions of outdoor education. *The Ontario Journal of Outdoor Education, 1*(2), 5-9.

Jeal, T. (2001). *Baden-Powell: Founder of the boy scouts.* New Haven, CT: Yale University Press.

Johnston, R. (2002). Wild Berwyn or Coy Nature Reserve. *Canadian Journal of Environmental Education, 7*(2), 166-178.

Kane, S. (1995). *Wisdom of the mythtellers.* Peterborough, ON: Broadview Press.

Kawagley, A. O. (1999). Alaska Native education: History and adaptation in the new millennium. *Journal of American Indian Education, 39*(1), 31-51.

Kimmerer, R. (1998). Intellectual diversity: Bringing the Native perspective into natural resources education. *Winds of Change, 13*(3), 14-18.

Kimmerer, R. (2002). Weaving traditional ecological knowledge into biological education: A call to action. *Bioscience, 52*(5), 432-439.

King, T. (2003). *The truth about stories: A native narrative.* Toronto: House of Anansi Press.

Kirkpatrick, S. (1985). *Dwellers in the land.* San Francisco: Sierra Club.

Kohl, A., & Benedok, A. (1991). *Environmental education and training in Hungary.* Geneva, Switzerland: Training Discussion Paper No. 23.

Laduke, W. (1999). *All our relations: Native struggles for land and life – selection.* Cambridge, MA: South End Press.

Leopold. A. (1987). *A Sand County almanac, and sketches here and there.* New York: Oxford University Press.

Lightning, W. (1993). Compassionate mind: Implications of a text written by Elder Louis Sunchild. *Canadian Journal of Native Education, 19*(2), 215-253.

Longboat, D. (2006). *Kawenoke the Haudenosaunee archipelago: The Nature and necessity of biocultural restoration and revitalization.* Unpublished doctoral dissertation, York University, Toronto, ON.

Lotz-Sisitka, H. (2002). Weaving cloths. *Canadian Journal of Environmental Education, 7*(2), 101-124.

Loughran, S. (2001). An artist among young artists: A lesson for teachers. *Childhood Education, 77*(4), 204-208.

MacDonald, R. (1993). *Sons of the empire: The frontier and the Boy Scout movement, 1880-1918.* Toronto: University of Toronto Press.

Maffi, L. (2002). Endangered languages, endangered knowledge. *International Social Science Journal, 54*(3), 385-393.

Martusewicz, R. (2001). Earth, ethics, education. In R. Martusewicz (Ed.), *Seeking passage: Post-structuralism, pedagogy, ethics.* New York: Teachers College Press

Martusewicz, R. (2005a). Eros in the commons: Educating the eco-ethical consciousness in a poetics of place. *Ethics, Place & Environment, 8*(3), 331-348.

Martusewicz, R. (2005b). On acknowledging differences that make a difference: My two cents. *Educational Studies Journal of the American Educational Studies Association, 37*(2), 215-224.

Martusewicz, R. & Edmundson, J. (2004). Social foundations as pedagogies of responsibility and eco-ethical commitment. In D. Butin (Ed.), *Teaching context: A primer for the social foundations of education.* Mahwah, NJ: Lawrence Erlbaum Publishers.

McGregor, D. (2004). Coming full circle: Indigenous knowledge, environment and our future. *American Indian Quarterly, 28*(3-4), 385-410.

McKinley, E. (2005). Locating the global: Culture, language and science education for indigenous students. *International Journal of Science Education, 27*(2), 227-241.

Mohawk, J. (2000). *Utopian legacies: A history of conquest and oppression in the Western world.* Santa Fe, NM: Clear Light Publishers.

Moore, J. (2002). Lessons from environmental education. *Canadian Journal of Environmental Education, 7*(2), 179-192.

Nabhan, G. (1997). *Cultures of habitat: On nature, culture, and story.* Washington, D.C.: Counterpoint Press.

Nabhan, G., & Rosenberg, J. (1997). Where ancient stories guide children home. *Natural History, 106*(9), 54-61.

Nicol, R. (2002). Outdoor environmental education in the United Kingdom. *Canadian Journal of Environmental Education, 7*(2), 193-206.

O'Sullivan, E. (2002). What kind of education should you experience at university? *Canadian Journal of Environmental Education, 7*(2), 54-72.

Oba, G. (1992). Environmental education for sustainable development among the Nomadic Peoples: The UNESCO-IPAL experience in Northern Kenya. *Nomadic Peoples, 30*, 53-73.

Orr, D. (1992). *Ecological literacy: Education and the transition to a postmodern world.* Albany, NY: State University of New York Press.

Orr, D. (1994). *Earth in mind: On education environment and the human prospect.* Washington, D. C.: Island Press.

Osborne, K. (1991). *Teaching for democratic citizenship.* Toronto: Our Schools/Our Selves Education Foundation.

Plotkin, R., & Sheridan, J. (1995). History and personal narratives in outdoor education. Pathways: *The Ontario Journal of Outdoor Education, 7*(5), 10-13.

Plumwood, V. (1994). *Feminism and the mastery of nature.* London: Routledge.

Ponzio, R., & Marzolla, M. A. (2002). Snails trails and science tales. *Canadian Journal of Environmental Education, 7*(2), 269-281.

Postman, N. (1989). Learning by story. *Atlantic Monthly*, December, 119-124.

Quinn, W. (1993). Native American hunting traditions as a basis for outdoor education. *Journal of Outdoor Education, 26*, 12-18.

Rathunde, K., & Csikszentmihalyi, M. (2005a). Middle school students' motivation and quality of experience: A comparison of montessori and traditional school environments. *American Journal of Education, 111*(3), 341-371.

Rathunde, K., & Csikszentmihalyi, M. (2005b). The social context of middle school: Teachers, friends, and activities in Montessori and traditional school environments. *The Elementary School Journal, 106*(1), 59-70.

Reid, A., Tearney, K., & Dillon, J. (2004). Valuing and utilizing traditional ecological knowledge: Tensions in the context of education and the environment. *Environment Education Research, 10*(2), 237-254.

Roue, M., & Nakashima, D. (2002). Knowledge and foresight: The predictive capacity of traditional knowledge applied to environmental assessment. *International Social Science Journal, 54*(3), 337-347.

Schafer, J. (1993). Introducing agronomy students to concepts of Indigenous and cultural knowledge. *Journal of Natural Resources and Life Sciences Education, 22*(1), 22-30.

Sellers, P., McDonald, R. C., & Wilson, A. (2001). Healing the land: CIER helps First Nation's project and restore the environment. *Winds of Change, 16*(2), 36-39.

Seton, E. T. (1912). *The book of woodcraft and Indian lore.* London: Constable & Co.

Sharpes, D. (1974). *A new curriculum design for Native American schools.* Oglala, South Dakota: American Indian Resource Associates.

Shepard, P. (1977). Place in American culture. *North American Review, Fall*, 22-32.

Sheridan, J. (1991). The silence before drowning in alphabet soup. *Canadian Journal of Native Education, 18*(1), 23-31.

Sheridan, J. (1994). *Alienation and integration: Environmental education in Turtle Island.* Unpublished doctoral dissertation, University of Alberta, Edmonton, AB.

Sheridan, J. (2001). Mythic ecology. *Canadian Journal of Environmental Education, 6,* 197-207.

Sheridan, J. (2002). My name is Walker. *Canadian Journal of Environmental Education, 7*(2), 193-206.

Sheridan, J., & Longboat, D. (2006). The Haudenosaunee imagination and the ecology of the sacred. *Space and Culture, 9*(4), 365-381.

Shiva, V. (1993). *Monocultures of the mind: Perspectives on biodiversity and biotechnology.* Penang, Malaysia: Third World Network.

Shiva, V. (2000). *Indigenous knowledges in global contexts: Multiple readings of our world.* Toronto: University of Toronto Press.

Simonelli, R. (1994). Traditional knowledge leads to a Ph.D.: Doctoral program designed around Native heritage. *Winds of Change, 9*(4), 43-48.

Simpson, L. (2002). Indigenous environmental education for cultural survival. *Canadian Journal of Environmental Education, 7*(1), 13-25.

Simpson, L. (2004). Anticolonial strategies for the recovery and maintenance of Indigenous Knowledge. *American Indian Quarterly, 28*(3-4), 373-384.

Snively, G., & Corsiglia, J. (2001). Discovering indigenous science: Implications for science education. *Science Education, 85*(1), 6-34.

Snyder, G. (1990). *The practice of the wild.* New York: North Point Press.

Suzuki, D. (1997). *The sacred balance: A vision of life on earth.* Vancouver, British Columbia: Greystone Books.

Suzuki, D., & Knudtson, P. (1992). *Wisdom of the elders.* Toronto: Stoddart Publishing.

Svennbeck, M. (2001). Rethinking the discussions about science education n a multicultural world: Some alternative questions as a new point of departure. *Science Education, 85*(1), 80-81.

Teran, G. A., & Esteva, G. (2000). Education, ecology and culture: Stories from the margins. *Progressive Perspectives, 3*(1), 6.

Turner, F. (1985). Cultivating the American garden: Toward a secular view of nature. *Harper's Magazine, August,* 45-52.

Turner, F. (1990). The self-effacing art: Restoration as imitation of nature. In W. R. e. a. Jordan (Ed.), *Restoration ecology,* (pp. 47-50). Cambridge: Cambridge University Press.

Vahey, T. (1992). The Profanity of "Why?" *Pathways: The Ontario Journal of Outdoor Education, 4*(6), 12-15.

Van Damme, L. S. M., & Neluvhalani, E. F. (2004). Indigenous knowledge in environmental education processes: Perspectives on a growing research arena. *Environmental Education Research, 10*(3), 353-370.

Wade, D. (1996). *One river: Explorations and discoveries in the American rain forest.* New York: Simon & Schuster.

Wadland, J. (1978). *Ernest Thomas Seton: Man in nature and the progressive era 1880-1915.* New York: Arno Press.

Walter, S. (2004). The Montessori method: The origins of an educational innovation. *Library Journal, 129*(11), 79-80.

Warkentin, T. (2002). It's not just what you say, but how you say it. *Canadian Journal of Environmental Education, 7*(2), 241-255.

Warren, K. J. (Ed.). (1997). *EcoFeminism: Women, culture and nature.* Bloomington: Indiana University Press.

Warren, K. J. (2000). *EcoFeminist philosophy: A western perspective on what it is and why it matters.* New York: Rowman and Littlefield.

Whitcombe, M. (1991). Healing the earth within us. *Pathways: The Ontario Journal of Outdoor Education, 3*(3), 5-7.

Whiteman, G. (2004). Why are we talking inside? Reflecting on traditional ecological knowledge (TEK) and management research. *Journal of Management Inquiry, 13*(3), 261-277.

Wilson, E. O. (1998). *Consilience: The unity of knowledge.* New York: Knopf.

Wilson, E. O. (2002). *The future of life.* New York: Knopf.

Wilson, S. (1993). *An Indigenous American's interpretation of the relationship between Indigenous peoples and people of European descent.* Paper presented at the World Indigenous People's Conference on Education. Wollongong, AUS.

Young, K. (2005). Developing ecological literacy as a habit of mind in teacher education. *The EcoJustice Review: Educating for the Commons, 1*(1), 1-7.

Young, K. (2006). *Girls of the empire: The origins of environmental education and the contest for Brownies and Girl Guides.* Unpublished doctoral dissertation, York University, Toronto, ON.

Thirteen

Translating Eco-Poetic Stories and Literacies: Environmental Educational Leadership

Andrejs Kulnieks

Ezermala sapņi

Sapņos dziedāju, dziesmās ar
    draugiem
atstādams miegu pirms saulīte aust
rušinot kvēlošās ogles, atverot
    aizkarus
starp sarkanu-oranždzeltenu
    debess un uguni

pusnomodā atplūst stāsti
ko darbos es rakstīšu
domās pie senčiem pastaigājos
kas aizsaulē solīsus sper

skats vilno pār ūdens spoguli
saule auž laiku
udeņi atmiņas daudzgadiem nestos
makoņu veidoļus krāšņos

pie akmens sienām es tuvojos
caur dūmiem meźvistiņa iemana
    mani
iedrāźas pilnsparā diźajā stumbrā
nemanot pate kur iet

meźś norība śai mirklī skaļi
pats nezin kas radīja to
radusas norises apvidū
pasaule runā un stāsta

Lakeshore dreams

Dreams sing songs storied with
    friends
plants stretch towards dawn
rekindle coals, draw curtains
between orange-red sky and
    fire-place glow

slowly movement percolates stories
places and words dance
ancestral lifestyles uncovered in tales
from footsteps beyond the sun

waves ripple liquid mirror
luminiferous sunrise weaves time
memory emanates water respires
clouds shape shift in sky

I tread lightly near rock walls
through smoke clouds pheasant
    senses and sees
flies full force into the trunk of a tree
life path chosen, mistaken

forest echoes this moment
unknowing who created
course terrain destines thoughts
landscapes communicate

caur zariem tumśa spīd acs
pēkšni cilpu met tā
skatotics manī tā paźūd
svārstigā neliclā alā

black eye glows through branches
body sweeps unseen circle
disappears watching me
ungulfed beyond cavernous walls

caur akmeņiem redzu spalviņas
bildējot aizeju prom
spārni tad sitas pret akmeņiem
satrauksme parvēršas nesaprašanā

feathers become rock silhouettes
unfocused on film
wings pound rock in distance
chaos and silence in motion

gaiss drēgns plūst no zemes
ne vāvere rickstiņus vāc
tik galviņa padusē klusā
ko mēģina izteikt šis stāsts

ground-dampened air accents dreary
   stillness
birds and squirrels silently perch
head dropped over breasts as if in
   slumber
what is this fateful tale

kā aizvijāmies tik tālu
dzīves garśās senći līdzi nāk
gadiem ciņās zem tumśās varas
nak dienas baltas, sengaidītas

how did we wind so far
ancestral tastes and smells signify
struggle under dark dominiated days
hope anticipated brightness and light

iedegas atmiņas tāsis un skaliņos
atnāk vectētiņś kūpinātāja dūmos
ieminot takas mācamies zemi
lidzdalīties tālākas gaitās

birch skin and pine twigs ignite
   memories
as I smoke food, grandfather visits
walk pedagogical paths of landscape
memories shared into tomorrow

Environmental educational leadership in the context of my scholarly research involves eco-poetics as focal practice, which is a convergence of landscape, translation of the poetic nature of stories, and time. I consider multiple theoretical layers of environmental education, language learning and Oral Tradition juxtaposed with Literary Tradition as outlined by Basso (1987), Cajete (1994), Cruikshank (1990b) Longboat (2006), Sheridan (1994), Sheridan and Longboat (2003). My mixed methodological approach includes (a) learning about ancestral stories from Elders that helped me better understand the landscapes of Northern Ontario, (b) the writing and translation of my poem "Lakeshore dreams" in Northern Ontario, (c) my translation of Imants Ziedonis' (1997) untitled poem as a beginning for developing a relationship with his work, and (d) a hermeneutic inquiry of ancestral stories in both oral and literary form. Interpretation of this work includes discussing the poem with my grandfather in relation to his youth in Latvia as well as an ethnographic study in which I engage in discussions about this investigation with friends and colleagues as well as my research supervisors Dennis Sumara and, subsequently, Joe Sheridan in the Faculty of Education at York University. The conversational aspects of Oral Tradition are an integral part of my understanding of these poems because the honor of having dialogues with Elders and Poets allows for an inclusion of questions regarding language and landscape. This chapter is a triangulation of (a) an analysis or close read of the poem, (b) an ethnographic study of eco-knowledge, and (c) an interpretation of eco-poetry that outlines why Indigenous knowledge is an essential aspect of environmental education and leadership.

ETHNOGRAPHIC LITERACIES AND PRACTICE

As I move between my translation of Ziedonis' untitled poem, the original poem as published in his Collected Works (1997), and a translation by Barry Callaghan (Ziedonis, 1987), I realize that there has been many years since I found a well read copy of his book *Flowers of Ice.* Leafing through the silver-covered book, I recall the cold winter evening of my first encounter with this work and the learning journey it inspires. Subsequent readings evoke further memories, framed around this initial encounter. While translating the poetry of Imants Ziedonis, I contemplate how oral and literary tradition become entwined in language and landscape learning. Moreover, I consider what an understanding of the relationship between Oral and Literary Tradition contribute to a discussion of leadership in environmental education. In order to explore these questions, I turn to Ziedonis as an exemplar of literary eco-poetics. Like much of his work written in the Soviet era, this untitled poem embodies a resonance of Latvian landscapes and echoes ecological epistemologies (ways of knowing) and ontologies (ways of being) of a particular place. His work serves as an example of literature that represents sustainable relationships with land that are commonplace for many who live in ancestral Latvian landscapes.

Engaging and returning to a particular nonurban landscape is a way that systems of public schooling could foster an awareness of the importance of the ecology of place. Eco-poetic work, for example, the interpretation of landscape learning, the crafting of a poem, and the reinterpretation of that poem in light of Indigenous stories could be a useful way of integrating environmental learning in systems of public education. Ecological leadership that fosters an interest in maintaining intergenerational knowledge through ancestral stories that embody a deep engagement with landscapes. This knowledge is kept alive through these practices because the retelling of these stories is a form of learning and entertainment that is available without the use of industrially created technologies like computers and televisions. Furthermore, these practices allow for a connection with Elders who bring with their stories the experience of lifetimes of learning. These intergenerational engagements and connections between families and land stretch back to the beginnings of human-time as they have been retold through generations as a way of passing on knowledge as well as entertaining generations of future listeners and orators.

Ziedonis' works are created and embedded in natural ecosystems. In taking a poem from its place of conceptualization and conception, it echoes a resonance of landscape (Basso, 1987; Cajete, 1994; Cruikshank, 1990b; Longboat, 2006; Sheridan, 1994; Sheridan & Longboat, 2003). Knowing the place a poem is conceived gives learners the opportunity to tap into the resonance of landscape from which it has been harvested. The Latvian language contains sounds of local landscapes. These sounds are sung in *tautas dziesmas* or "songs of the people," which illuminate the interconnectedness of land and life. The humming and singing of these songs as part of the process of investigating etymological references to Indigenous stories brings them to life. Ancestral understandings can be evoked through the use of an ancient language like Latvian, one of the oldest languages alive. It stands to reason that the oldest *tautas dziesmas* that have been passed down through Oral traditions contain very ancient information. Names and titles as well as ontologies and epistemologies form a living connection between orators, the sounds they translate, the language they use and the interpretations of listeners. The performance of ancestral and modern poetic forms brings them closer to the Latvian oral tradition. Reciting poetry, and thus engaging in the oral tradition, is important because it facilitates a dialogue among different generations. Engaging in the tradition of performance of ancestral stories helps to inspire dialogues among community members. Celebrations that correspond with particular times of the year are a way to remember important information as well as to develop a sense of community. Eco-poetic dialogues are essential for developing an understanding of place because they allow for a convergence of knowledge, experience, and understandings.

ECOLOGIES OF STORIES

Cross-cultural storytelling is an extremely difficult task. The term *story* in the English language brings with it a lengthy history. According to the Oxford English Dictionary (OED, 1989), during the thirteenth-century, *story* was defined as "a narrative, true or presumed to be true, relating to important events and celebrated persons of a more or less remote past; a historical relation or anecdote." Over the years this meaning shifted and currently use of the word *story* often brings with it an air of unbelievability, and evokes many derogatory connotations. The Latvian words *stasts*, which also evokes the word *pastastit*, *teika*, alluding to *pateikt* and *pasaka* all contain the idea of *telling* and *saying* within the word for different forms of stories. In the Latvian language, stories bring with them a retelling of an event. However, the original intention may not be exact depending on how long ago it was first told as outlined by Longboat (2006) Sheridan (2001) and Viks (2001) among others. Similarly, the term *folksong*, which Callaghan uses in his translation of Ziedonis (1987) brings with it connotations of "simple country folk" when etymologically retraced. Rather, when these traditional songs and stories are called forth and focused upon, it is evident they contain a metaphorical language illustrating ancestral beliefs and recollections about events that took place thousands and even hundreds of thousands of years ago as Brody (1988) and Viks (2004) among others contend. There are many forms of Latvian cultural stories, both sung and recited. Through time, however, due to dominating occupiers who suppressed and attempted to silence ancestral ontologies, epistemologies and teachings, the original meaning often becomes metaphorical. The original intention of these songs can only be understood through a physical engagement with particular landscapes. These landscapes contain information that is integral for evoking a deeper understanding of these stories. This engagement requires a movement between mental and physical connections with this world that traverses metaphorical and concrete planes of understanding.

Imants Ziedonis is a good example of a cultural storyteller. In Sean Kane's (1998) *Wisdom of the Mythtellers* he writes, "the storyteller is simply the one who speaks the myth on behalf of the listeners. The voice of the storyteller is the collective voice of the community" (p. 189). The meaning of his poem evolves as a reader focuses on particular stanzas, lines, and word combinations in the poem. Repeated engagements with similar versions of a particular story or event strengthen the relationship between the reader and the language of the text.

Engagement with language requires a process of interpretation. Plural meanings unfold as a reader spends time with the places poems are conceived. As I reread my translations of Ziedonis poem, I consider what is lost in processes of translation. I attempt to include everything that he describes, but my translation is also a response to the meanings he intends as I attempt to make the translation flow more poetically. Although I cannot even begin to match his rhyme scheme, a new flow of the poem develops.

As a cross-cultural storyteller, I realize the importance of the place the story is told. It is also important to provide listeners with a background as part of telling a story, as well as to respond to questions that arise through the process of storytelling. It is difficult to walk away from a story without some form of closure. However, the telling of a story is an opportunity to focus attention on a particular teaching or a lens to observe an occurrence. Eco-poetry introduces ideas that evolve through repeated dialogue with the story told by the writer. This dialogue with the text facilitates an internalization and understanding of some of the meanings a poem holds.

On one of my return visits to Ziedonis' untitled poem and my translation I am reminded of Eva Hoffman's (1989) *Lost in Translation*. She writes: "Eventually, the voices enter me; by assuming them, I gradually make them mine. I am being remade, fragment by fragment, like a patchwork quilt; there are more colors in the world than I ever knew." (p. 220). Rereading the poem merges previous understandings, current dialogues, as well as theoretical works of other authors. The meanings the reader evokes through the poem shift again. As Hoffman suggests, intended meanings are often *lost* through a mediation between different languages and ideas.

Information obtained from dictionaries alone is problematic because definitions are limited to short descriptions for the purpose of basic communication. Reading these definitions for the first time gives me limited access to the associations I gain through familiarization with the world of the poem. Although translations help me mediate between the two languages, neither type of dictionary (English-Latvian or Latvian-English) is specific enough to come to an etymologically satisfying understanding. Another difficulty I encounter in my translation is that many words have been omitted and lost between shifts from oral to literary memory. In addition, definitions do not provide an etymological synopsis of words and neglect connections with cultural and metaphorical messages, experiences and histories.

Writing this work in the solitude of Northern Ontario this fall, I realize how important my work of translation is for the maintenance of my Latvian language skills. Leadership in education requires me to turn to my grandfather for further insight. Developing my own interpretation to translate Ziedonis work leads me to ask others to also read and interpret this poem. Discussions that follow give me far more insight into the meanings Ziedonis' poem can evoke to his audience in Latvia than the dictionaries I employ for my task of translation. Reflecting on my experiences of living and being in Latvia, I realize how different the relationship with the poem is to those who read it in its place of origin. Discussing poetry with Elders brings me towards new understandings about how dependent we are on the land we live within.

TRANSLATING LITERARY AND ORAL TRADITION

In a recent discuss, Longboat stated:

> The most powerful relaying or transmission of those stories comes from people that have access not only to ancestral knowledge and realms of ancestral knowledge that exist in those ancient stories that they know, but put it in a context of their own personal life experience. So as they have experienced their own lives throughout their many years of existence in the world, that when they express those ancient stories within that kind of context and within the context of their own personal life experience it only serves to enrich the story that much more and makes it more meaningful and more alive and more vibrant so that it becomes more easy for us to understand it as opposed to it being a story of ancient long time ago that you know, the world was so different back then than it is now that when those people, Elders in particular, are able to take the essence and the principles and the ideas within that story and to put them into today's context makes it more meaningful and more vibrant and we remember those things easier so they

paint pictures for us in the way that they express it to us. They paint pictures for us by using their language and by illustrating those concepts within a picture so that it's easy then for us to remember what the picture actually looks like, so it's not only what they talk about but it's how they talk about it and how they construct it for us and how we remember and if we are given that picture over and over and over again we begin to see details that we haven't seen before and as our thinking and our life experience progresses those pictures become more vivid and more real and when we add those things and make them part of ourselves and incorporate those teachings and those ideas into our own understanding that creates a specific lifestyle and into our own lives then when we share them they become that much more richer and that much more vibrant to others that are listening... more than just information and knowledge it is the application and actualization of knowledge and experience that creates wisdom. (Longboat, personal communication, Oct. 11, 2005)

Mastering the art of writing eco-poetic work involves a dialogue between the work of developing connections between places, experiences, and the world of the poem. The process of writing eco-poetry makes it possible to use the technology of writing as a way to have a dialogue between self, other, text, and landscape. Writing the poem at the beginning of this chapter is at first a translation of the event from what happened. No words were said during the event. The text itself reflects mediation between experience, the English language and the Latvian language. The Latvian language was very important to my translation of the event because it was the first language through which I learned the landscape. However, my translation to the English language was essential for the purpose of this paper. Writing the poems, I realized that as I translated the poems I could not translate them to the level I wanted to. The stories that writing the Latvian poem Ezermala evoked could not be conveyed in a stanza to stanza translation. Mytho-poetic references could not be explained without writing pages upon pages of notes. As I turned to Latvian Elders, I realized as we discussed what I was trying to say that my direct translation did not convey the meaning I intended.

Moving words and phrases from the English language over a period of weeks and months made me realize how difficult it was to summarize rhetorical terms like, for example, *schemes*. Word order conveyed a different sense, as did the pattern of rhymes. As I tried to tell the story to Elders as it happened, when I went back over the poem in the English language, I had to find ways to express ideas that were very familiar to me in thoughts, but not readily available in the language I had chosen. When I did finally have what I thought would be an adequate description of the event, I realized that the way that I conveyed the story in the Latvian language could not be considered an accurate translation. This did not mean that either description was wrong. Rather, I was evoking the Oral Tradition of speaking the poem to realize what the images and meaning the words I had chosen helped me evoke.

Understanding landscapes that are not reconstructed by humans requires a length process of investigation of place. This investigation should not be limited to ecology, biology, and chemistry. Furthermore, understanding of place should include an understanding of traditional and ancestral stories because, when these stories are told, they represent a living dialogue of the sustainable relationship between human beings and the places that keep them alive. Objects and place are an integral aspect of the memory relationship. In *Re-Visioning the Earth*, Paul Devereaux (1996) discusses the powerful nature of visiting and remembering special places in nature that exist all over the planet. Eco-poetry is a way of making a metaphysical connection with nature. The different places in which I engage this poem become part of the process of interpretation. Refamiliarizing myself with the concept of thinking in the Latvian language in Latvian rural and pristine landscapes, I realize that the sounds that form words are embodied in those landscapes. Interviews with Indigenous scholars and environmental educators, as part of my research, help me understand that the oldest languages are filled with sounds of the bush, a view shared by some of the Indigenous informants who have helped me understand the deep relationship between language and landscape.

Louise Rosenblatt (1978) describes the importance of the interpreters experience in her transactional theory of reading. The reader brings a poem to life and is a cocreator of the poem. Although a great deal of the poem is lost through attempting to relate and translate thoughts, ideas and feelings exactly as they are, new associations and meanings can be discovered in this act of translation. Ideas are transformed, recreated, and reinterpreted through this cognitive act.

Rebecca Solnit (2000) describes a connection between movement and cognition. The interpretation of stories demands a (re)formulation of understandings in relation to a particular text as well as the places described in the poem. Sharing interpretations and stories can foster an awareness of how the reader understands themes and concepts that they embody. However, if the development of a deeper relationship with landscape and the language it enables the reader to evoke is to occur, the writer and the reader need to become familiar with that place. For eco-poetic work to have resonance with a particular place requires movement and interaction with that place.

POETRY AS ENVIRONMENTAL EDUCATION

Language given, created, or discovered within a particular place requires time and focus with that place. The landscape that people are in tune with has a capacity to affect the way people think. Poetic forms of writing have the capability to surprise and delight because they allow the imagination to summon learning through the spaces and gaps that poetry creates. Jonathan Culler (1997) writes: "poetry organizes the sound plane of language so as to make it something to reckon with" (p.28). Writing poetry is a way of organizing information. As the writer crafts and rewrites a poem, many interesting discoveries can be made. Asking what a poem means to someone else fosters a development of communication skills and is an integral part of modern identity formation. Eco-poetry is a technological tool that aids in the conceptualization and development of ideas regarding the importance of place. When students engage and reinterpret poetry in relation to Indigenous Knowledge it provides a space for growth of personal knowledge that relates with the places they live. Intending to share poetry with others, the writer must consider the intended meanings in relationship with the hidden meanings of the work. Poetry creates a space for a dialogue between the text and the world beyond classroom activities. According to Milner & Milner (2003), educational leaders should question what approach or school of thought will the reader employ: Moral/Philosophical, Historical/Biographical, Formalist, Rhetorical, Freudian, Archetypal, Feminist, Marxist, Deconstructionist, Reader Response, New Historical or a combination of these. Eco-poetics should be one of these if not, as David Orr (1992) would suggest, part of all of them. Personal experiences also influence how a poem is written or read. Reasons one has for reading and writing eco-poetically also make a substantial difference in how a relationship with a poem develops.

Eco-poetic interpretation is heavily influenced by experiences and attitude. Poetic writings are a method of collecting thoughts that emphasize the importance of ideas rather than the form they express. This philosophical work is always in flux because an understanding of poetry develops with time. Returning to a particular poem or other form of writing, associations with the words therein change. The experience of working with a poem is far different in a city like Toronto, than it is on the shore of a less populated lakeshore. Living in a place that has been remade or reconstructed by human hands and machines demands one to focus on human creation, far removed from thinking that evolves with the pristine state of nature that can be witnessed in Northern Ontario as well as other nonurban locations. Also, meanings that can be gleaned by the reader change over time due to personal experience. This is part of the reason it is so important for students to engage with landscapes beyond urban settings in order to consider the development of their identities in relation to the land that makes life possible.

Intergenerational knowledge is an essential aspect of Latvian Oral Tradition. Failure to continue to engage with nonurban landscapes is to lose a sense of identity that includes an understanding of Indigenous plant-life. This in turn leads to not understanding their inherent and medicinal values and, eventually, poor health and even death. The Latvian language is in tune with landscape and land because the sounds of language and landscape are the same. These sounds are passed on through generations of orators. Communication was once synonymous with *singing the landscape* as pointed out by Abram (1996), Basso (1996), Cajete (1994), Chatwin (1987), Cruikshank (1990a), Longboat (2006), Sheridan (2002), and Viks (2001).

Engaging with theories of interpretation challenges students to delve into the variety of perspectives eco-writers can develop. The wealth of perspectives that multilingual learners can contribute to the reading of a poem is an essential aspect of this meaning-making process. Making use of opportunities and time to explore ecological implications of what Lakoff & Johnson (1980) succinctly defined as *Metaphors We Live By*, the title of their book. Within a culture of consumerism, eco-poetic writing asks students to engage with a more sustainable way of living. Exploring ways of counteracting systems of short-term economic gains that are imposed on North American systems of education is essential.

The processes of exploring multiple ways of understanding a particular place can be developed through eco-poetic engagements. Gregory Cajete (1994) describes the unavailability of an exact translation of the word art in American Indian Languages. He describes the creation of art as "making or completing" (p. 40). Eco-writing is a way of making a connection with land upon which our lives depend. Paying particular attention to place changes how we look at ourselves. Writing about this attention is a way of enabling a change of attitude towards the sacredness of place.

> Writing is much more than an afterthought or an event of consolidation. It is, rather, an act of thought and reformulation, one that contributes profoundly to one's interpretations of one's experiences. That is, every act of writing (and, for that matter, every act of reading) contributes to the formation of one's identity. (Davis, Sumara, & Luce-Kapler, 2000, p. 224)

The creation of poetry is a way of translating personal experiences so that they can be shared with others. This process involves interpretation on the part of the poet because the process of writing involves the act of discernment. As I write, questions that guide my thinking include: What is important about this moment; What would others find interesting about this work; What else does this line or stanza mean? Language is more than a medium for socialization. Words represent out thoughts and ideas. However, they are also an integral part of processes of cognition that poetry inspires.

IMPLICATIONS FOR PEDAGOGY

Developing a relationship with eco-poetry requires a development of the ability to describe particular bioregions. Returning to the same works over extended periods of time creates deepening understandings about poems and the places in which they are created. Finding new vocabulary to express themselves during class discussions occurs when educators ask students to research words and use them in other writings. Daniel Nettle and Suzanne Romaine (2000) discuss the correlation between biodiversity and linguistic diversity in *Vanishing Voices: The*

Extinction of the World's Languages. As languages disappear, so too does our ability to understand the vastly differing landscapes of our world. Approximately 250 Aboriginal Languages in Australia have already disappeared. However, in *Jandamarra and the Bunuba Resistance*, Penderson & Woorunmurra (2000) suggest that this number is much larger. In light of the many challenges posed by a standardized curriculum that the governments of Canada, the United States and many other countries throughout the world are advocating, I question how educators can foster a desire for their students to develop an awareness of ancestral culture and traditions.

My research illustrates the wealth of learning that eco-poetry facilitates. The data for my research develops through my engagement, interpretation, and translation of language and place. My interpretation of eco-poetics and the research it leads me towards serves to illustrate the richness that etymological discoveries provide. Clearly, learning about the plurality of meaning that words hold contributes to the formation of one's identity. As Rosenblatt (1978) writes, the associations the reader evokes are dependent on personal experiences. Students need to respond to the texts and places we ask them to engage with in order to learn from interpretational practices that juxtapose developing relationships with place and eco-poetical works.

Educators have traditionally had a very solid grounding in theories of reading and writing. In the past, students were asked comprehensive questions that would demonstrate an understanding of the texts they read. Although this can be a part of an evaluative process, the relationship that can be developed between the student, language, and place is more important. Developing an understanding of the relationship of poetry and place helps learners to research experiences as well as a language because what these two activities should have in common is a return to particular events over an extended period of time. Focus on the creation of literary art; we learn what it means to be a writer, as well as a reader. This creative process enables educators to help students develop a meaningful relationship with not only the texts they ask their students to interpret, but also the places they live.

Writing eco-poetry helps students discover language to express their relationship between self, other, and place. Merging oral and literary traditions is a way of dwelling and engaging in a process of deepening understandings. Eco-writing asks writers to reflect on what is of importance to them as well as to find an area of ecological study that is of interest to themselves. Multiple-subject learning can be incorporated as a way of developing a relationship with a particular poem. For example, footnoting information from other areas of learning within the body of a poem provides a space where it is essential to communicate ideas effectively. As reflective educators, when we ask students to write poetically, we should also make it clear that writing is a work in progress. The interaction of language, place, and time evolves throughout the course of a lifetime. However, a dialogue with those who know the land as Indigenous Elders do can uncover the amazingly rich tapestry of a particular (local) place. Returning to poetry provides an opportunity to formulate and express ideas about places encountered.

Most of my time is spent immersed in the English language, however, to understand these poems, I travel through the Latvian language towards another space of mind. I wonder how a Latvian writer, like Ziedonis, would interpret my reading of his poem. Am I what Zygmunt Bauman (1998) refers to as a "tourist" even if I was to live in Latvia for an extended period of time, or more of a traveler? In his article "Tourists and Vagabonds," Bauman writes, "we are all on the move also in another, deeper sense, whether or not we take to the roads or leap through the channels, and whether we like doing it or detest it" (p. 78). This deeper sense of traveling signifies the notion of translating or living in a language other than what we hear in our day-to-day lives.

In speaking and thinking several languages, a dialogue occurs between language of place and mind. My reading and writing skills are more practiced in English than in Latvian. Meanings unfold as I communicate with relatives, friends, students, professors and colleagues, and my grandfather. Movement between the two languages becomes a part of this process of translation. The complex nature of the world makes it difficult to represent experiences in language because the meanings of words of either language represent are often untranslatable. Translations cannot be exact because they require mediation between stories, experiences, and places.

Most of our students are challenged to learn a second language within the Canadian system of schooling. It is important for teachers to help students develop a meaningful relationship with Oral and Literary tradition through providing opportunities to access stories they can relate to and learn through. Eco-poetic writing that is connected to a particular place that has not been *developed* or *destroyed* by people allows learners to focus on unseen realities. It helps them move beyond the arduous task of trying to communicate what they think the educator wants to hear, and to move towards being able to describe what they need to write about.

The work of translation moves across languages and cultures. Eco-poetic writing asks students to think about different associations readers and listeners can evoke. This form of poetic engagement also leads towards making connections with learning beyond classroom borders. Conversations about the poem with the author bring a relationship with the poem beyond literary tradition, which is an integral aspect of the oral tradition. Writing in order to expand ones understanding of an event is much different than writing a poem for the purpose of receiving a grade. Similarly, if the poet is writing for cathartic purposes, the text may be far different than one designed for the purpose of public performance. It is essential to engage with land that sustains us as part of a meaning-making process. Looking at Indigenous perspectives about landscapes is another useful way of fostering an awareness of ways of living that are sustainable.

To develop a deeper understanding of nature and to be in tune with it requires a lifelong interaction and engagement with what David Abram (1996) describes as the more-than-human world. The interpretation of these interactions and subsequent developments of understanding can be greatly expanded if done so through a relationship with Indigenous culture. The extensive depth of knowledge contained within ancient stories makes it essential to return to these stories throughout various ages and phases and stages of life.

References

Abram, D. (1996). *The spell of the sensuous: Perception in a more-than-human world.* New York: Pantheon Books.

Basso, K. (1987). Stalking with stories: Names, places, and moral narratives among the western apache. In D. Halpern (Ed.), *Nature: Nature, landscape and natural history* (pp. 95-116). San Francisco: North Point Press.

Basso, K. (1996). *Wisdom sits in places: Landscape and language among the western apache.* Alburquerque, New Mexico: University of New Mexico Press.

Bauman, Z. (1998). Tourists and vagabonds. In *Beyond globalization: The human consequences* (pp. 77-102). London: Cambridge.

Brody, H. (1988). *Maps and dreams:Indians and the British Columbia frontier.* Vancouver, BC: Douglas & McIntyre.

Cajete, G. (1994). *Look to the mountain: An ecology of indigenous education.* Skyland, NC: Kivaki Press.

Chatwin, B. (1987). *The Songlines.* New York: Penguin,

Cruikshank, J. (1990a). Getting words right: Perspectives on naming and places in Athapaskan oral history. *Arctic Anthropology, 27*(1), 52-65.

Cruikshank, J. (1990b). *Life lived like a story: Life stories of three yukon native elders.* Vancouver, BC: University of British Columbia Press.

Culler, J. (1997). *Literary theory: A very short introduction.* New York: Oxford University Press.

Davis, B., Sumara, D., & Luce-Kapler, R. (2000). *Engaging minds: Learning and teaching in a complex world.* Mahwah, NJ: Lawrence Erlbaum Associates.

Devereux, P. (1996). *Re-envisioning the earth: A guide to opening the healing channels between mind and nature.* New York: Simon & Schuster.

Hoffman, E. (1989). *Lost in translation.* Toronto: Penguin Books.

Kane, S. (1998). *Wisdom of the mythtellers.* Peterborough, ON: Broadview Press.

Lakoff, G., & Johnson, M. (1980). *Metaphors we live by.* Chicago: The University of Chicago Press.

Longboat, D. (2006). *Kawenoke the Haudenosaunee archipelago: The nature and necessity of biocultural restoration and revitalization.* Unpublished Ph.D., York University, Toronto, ON.

Milner, J., & Milner, L. (2003). *Bridging english* (3rd ed.). New Jersey, NY: Pearson Education, Inc.

Nettle, D., & Romaine, S. (2000). *Vanishing voices: The extinction of the worlds languages.* New York: Oxford University Press.

OED. (1989). *The Oxford English dictionary.* London: Oxford Press.

Orr, D. (1992). *Ecological Literacy: Education and the transition to a postmodern world.* Albany, NY: State University of New York Press.

Penderson, H., & Woorunmurra, B. (2000). *Jandamarra and the Bunuba resistance.* Western Australia: Bunuba Productions, Australian Print Group Pty Ltd.

Rosenblatt, L. (1978). *The reader, the text, the poem.* Carbondale, IL: Southern Illinois University Press.

Sheridan, J. (1994). *Alienation and integration: Environmental education in turtle island.* Unpublished Ph.D., University of Alberta.

Sheridan, J. (2001). Mythic ecology. *Canadian Journal of Environmental Education, 6,* 197-207.

Sheridan, J. (2002). My name is Walker. *Canadian Journal of Environmental Education, 7*(2), 193-206.

Sheridan, J., & Longboat, D. (2003). *Imagination and the ecology of the sacred.* Paper presented at the International Conference on Imagination and Education, Burnaby, BC.

Solnit, R. (2000). *Wanderlust: A history of walking.* New York: Penguin Books.

Viks, I. (2001). *Trejdevini latvijas brinumi.* Riga, LVA: Geizers 0.

Viks, I. (2004). *Trejdevini latvijas brinumi 2. Dala.* Riga, LVA: Jumava.

Ziedonis, I. (1987). *Flowers of ice* (B. Callaghan, Trans.). Toronto: Exile Editions.

Ziedonis, I. (1997). *Raksti: 7 sejums.* Riga, LVA: Nordic.

FOURTEEN

TEACHING TO THE LEARNING DEFICIENCIES OF THE PRIVILEGED

Karleen Pendleton Jiménez

THE LITERACIES OF "POVERTY"

In *The Culture of Education* (1996), Jerome Bruner describes how "the discovery of poverty" shook cognitive theorists from the assumption that learning existed outside of cultural influence (p. xiii). It was the "discovery of the impact of poverty, racism, and alienation on the mental life and growth of the child victim of these blights" that pushed educators to move beyond the idea of a prescribed model of learning for children irrespective of their socio-economic backgrounds (p. xiii). These "child victims" arrived at school with a lack of resources and cultural capital and were much more likely to be forced out of schools than their more economically privileged peers. He considers the idea that teachers need to broaden their own skills specifically for these youth. The youth were thought to experience "cultural deprivation" and the teachers would need to learn more in order to fill the gap to reach them (p. xiii). However, approaching students with the assumption that they possess *deficiencies* has not necessarily helped in making schools more hospitable places for marginalized children. Even with the best of intentions, research describing the cultural deficiencies of marginalized students, may conjure even bleaker images of the possibilities of their lives than they had originally constructed. In fact, Bruner ponders whether this model of research has brought schooling any closer to connecting with "children suffering the blight of poverty, discrimination, alienation" (p. xiv). While there is no end in sight to educational research guided by the *deficit model*, it has since been critiqued with research that recognizes the assets of marginalized students, such as multiple literacies and resilience. Presumably the assets of marginalized children, knowledge garnered through participation in nondominant families and communities, would not be possessed by their more privileged counterparts; marginalized children have knowledge that their more privileged counterparts do not have access to. On this assumption, I wish to turn the tables in this essay and consider what gaps in knowledge privileged students hold that traditional curricula are perhaps failing to address. And, how do these gaps in knowledge influence a privileged student's ability to learn? While it is still the utilization of a deficit model of research, I invoke it as both a critique to the system that created it and, possibly, as a useful pedagogical strategy for anti-oppression education.

In my experience of working with students from backgrounds of financial poverty, immigrants, visible minorities, language barriers, violence, drugs, and anything else you can think of that might fulfill a condition of poverty or at least a marginalization that would affect "the mental life and growth of the child" (Bruner, 1996, p. xiii), the teaching was easy.[1] If anything, I have found the students starved for education. They have often been eager to engage in classroom reading, writing, and discussion, and have been generally enthusiastic about the opportunity to connect with a teacher. What I have found to be far more difficult is to connect with students who have not experienced any of these supposed poverties, particularly in the teaching about social realities of inequity. For example, with maybe a few case studies, a little reading, and discussion, *poor* students learn and understand; how institutional oppression leads to the overrepresentation of certain racial groups in poor neighborhoods; how systemic homophobia contributes to increased levels of depression for LGBT (lesbian, gay, bisexual, transgender) people; or how hierarchies function in the university. However, *rich* people in the same classroom may never learn or understand these concepts. I have encountered resistance from the more privileged students when attempting to provide social and historical curricular content. At times, they simply refuse to believe information such as white men earn more money on average than any other social group; the history of colonization in Canada and the U.S. has shaped the current status of racial hierarchies; or women, as a social category, are more highly targeted for abuse and assault. Perhaps this data is not easy to accept emotionally (it might be felt that it implicates the student in systemic inequity, as will be discussed later), but I doubt you could locate any reputable research that disputes it. However, such proof does not necessarily hold influence over privileged students who cannot see these realities and refuse to internalize the data. This observation is supported by the work of Lisa Delpit (1995), who asserts that U.S. black students are much more likely to see and understand U.S. oppression than their white middle class counterparts (p. 24).

Perhaps teaching impoverished students about anti-oppression theory is not the same task as teaching them how to read and write. I have no doubt that white middle class students tend to perform better at these traditional skills. However, I have found that it is the very use of anti-oppression curricula that motivates these impoverished students to embrace reading and writing. Teachers who undertake such a curriculum should be prepared to accept what these students read and write: potentially harsh critiques of the system that is oppressing them that can include the school, classroom, and teacher (Brodkey, 1996). If marginalized students are given the opportunity to utilize their understanding of social oppression alongside the development of formal literacy skills, these students may achieve strength in both areas of knowledge; they could acquire both formal literacy skills and the ability to understand social power dynamics. However, their more privileged counterparts would be left reading and writing, but lacking any real tools to work through abusive power structures. The more privileged counterparts lack the literacies of poverty, and it is unclear what nature of curriculum might fill the gap.

Another important element in this discussion is the necessity of locating who might be considered privileged. There are numerous sociological stratification charts which rank access to power in terms of class, race, ethnicity, sex, gender, sexuality, geographical location, physical ability, and age. You can find where you sit on the chart and examine your own set of very real privileges and oppressions. It is essential to note that most people are a combination of both privileges and oppressions. Therefore, the *privileged* and *impoverished* that I make reference to throughout this chapter are roles that sometimes shift depending on context. However, I agree with Delpit (1995) when she asserts that while many individual differences between black and white populations exist, there is a need to explore a generalized dominant culture of power and its link to the white middle class. The recognition of a culture of power is crucial because it is otherwise impossible to understand why U.S. and Canadian education fails so many of its black students. For the purposes of this essay, I define the privileged as white, middle and upper class, heterosexual students in the U.S. and Canada.

What I am interested in are the following questions: How can privileged students learn about the ways in which social hierarchies currently privilege some through the damaging and diminishing of others? How can they learn about the individual choices that enact hurtful practices of hierarchy and systemic oppression? Finally, how can the learning of such content move from abstract understanding to social and political action?[2]

THE LEARNING GAPS OF THE STRONG

Gandhi is considered to be one of the greatest teachers in centuries for his pedagogy of nonviolent resistance (Kripalani, 1997, p.vii). However, he was stumped by a similar dilemma. He successfully taught nonviolence to Indians as a way of combating the British occupation, but when the British left, the violence didn't. He was criticized on this point,

> How can you account for the growing violence among your own people on the part of political parties for the furtherance of political ends? Is this the result of the thirty years of nonviolent practice for ending the British rule? Does your message of nonviolence still hold good for the world?

> ----------

> In reply I must confess my bankruptcy, not that of nonviolence. I have already said that the nonviolence that was offered during the past thirty years was that of the weak. Whether it is a good enough answer or not is for the others to judge. It must be further admitted that such nonviolence can have no play in altered circumstances. India has no experience of the nonviolence of the strong. It serves no purpose for me to continue to repeat that the nonviolence of the strong is the strongest force in the world. (Gandhi in Kripalani, p.47)

Substitute the terms Gandhi used with my own – positions of privilege as the strong, and positions of poverty as the weak, and the teaching of anti-oppression work as the teaching of non-violence – and Gandhi's confessed *bankruptcy* looks very much like my own *deficiency*. How do you teach people with power to see their own power and choose not to abuse it? If Gandhi couldn't figure it out, what do I think I can possibly accomplish in this chapter? Using pedagogy instead of violence to work with the privileged could fall into Gandhi's notion of using nonviolence against the strong. However, Gandhi's experience suggests that even if all of the current privileged people were literally pushed from the land, there would only be new strong people who would rise up and subsequently oppress. As Audre Lorde's famous quote confirms, "The master's tools will never dismantle the master's house"; an entirely new house would be required to establish new kinds of relations. The structure itself must change, not just the people supporting it

The obvious barrier to learning about social equity is the personal responsibility involved. Such learning constitutes what Deborah Britzman (1998) defines as "difficult knowledge":

> how can we grapple with the stakes of the learning when the learning is made from attempts at identification with what can only be called difficult knowledge? The term of learning acknowledges that studying the experiences and the traumatic residuals of genocide, ethnic hatred, aggression, and forms of state-sanctioned – and hence legal – social violence requires educators to think carefully about their own theories of learning and how the stuff of such difficult knowledge becomes pedagogical. (p. 117)

If you learn about the property of a chemical in a science activity, it would most likely have no impact on how you conduct yourself when you go home. But, there are high stakes in learning about privilege and oppression. It resembles Freire's (1971) description of "the danger of conscientizacão" or the "fear of freedom" which served as obstacles for students' learning (p. 19). However, in this case what is feared is more like the loss of freedom. This could include earning less money or having to pay more money for merchandise, doing more physical labor, waiting in line more or having less time in general, putting your body in physical danger for another person, putting your mind in emotional danger, putting your friendships at risk, or losing relationships. You might understand how your family's wealth today is directly connected to the history of colonization that built your nation. You might love your country less. These are all potential and probable effects of the learning. And what is to be gained? Compassion? Feeling good about not hurting other people? Feeling good about helping to create a society where people hurt other people less often? Are these rewards worth it? How can I teach in a way that will cause students to believe that these rewards *are* worth it? How do I answer the perennial questions that students inflict upon teachers: "Why do I have to learn this? Will I ever use it once I leave the classroom?"

The other tricky component to this learning is how conflicted our desires are. Even if one piece of the brain or body wants to learn about privilege and oppression, there are other pieces working at the same time to protect your money, workload, time, relationships, and so on. I believe that it is this type of contradiction which produces blind spots, gaps in our ability to see social dynamics. Because if they are seen, they might cause us to lose something else. They are gaps in our ability to learn concepts. No matter how smart, how progressive, or how worldly an individual might be, these gaps prevent learning. My question is, what is needed in the teaching to fill these gaps? And, just as importantly, what is needed to fill in these gaps on a long-term basis?

APPROACHES TO ANTI-OPPRESSION EDUCATION

However one chooses to teach about anti-oppression, the language used in the educational practices plays a significant role in the learning. As Sumara (2000) notes:

> Language . . . is not an innocent and transparent medium that might be used to represent objects, ideas, or actions. Rather, the webs of relations that are knitted into a language as it evolves contribute to habits of perception and interpretation . . . it exerts the most profound influence on what one can and cannot think. (p.200)

With this keen attention to the role of language in mind, I offer below a collection of possible approaches to the teaching of privileged students.

1. The Appropriation of Educational Psychology

I begin with a twist on a foundation of education; my idea is to build upon (or appropriate) the language of educational psychology. It seems that no matter how critiqued, how interrogated, how flawed the methods are exposed to be, students are seduced by educational psychology's promise of science, and reduce it whenever possible to tidy categories of normal (Gallagher, 2003). Jean Piaget and Erik Erikson, in their focus on the development of white privileged boys, constrain the rest of us: if we do not match the development description of the age, we are found to be "failures" (Gilligan, 1993, p. 9). The ubiquitous standardization of knowledge and tests rely on these founding concepts: (a) levels of knowledge should be learned at specified ages, and (b) Types of thinking coincide with stages of development. It is a beloved language in schools; it is the canon, however useful or harmful. I would like to access its power for anti-oppression education. I will build charts, for example:

Anti-homophobia Development

Stage 1 Obliviousness	– Has no idea why those two women walking down the street are holding hands, nor why one appears to be quite masculine, they're probably sisters
Stage 2 Aggressive Homophobe	– Laughs and points at the two women walking down the street – Shouts "Fuckin' dykes," and threatens them with a stick – Repressed homosexual desire
Stage 3 Egocentric/ Paranoid Homophobe	– Denial, e.g. thinks, "I don't care if you're gay but do you have to flaunt it?" as the two women walk by – Feels that same sex marriages diminish the value of heterosexual marriage
Stage 4 Liberal	– Smiles, pondering, "Isn't that sweet, there go those two nice girls from down the block who live with their cats" – Expresses pride in having a friend who is gay – Contributes to AIDS charities
Stage 5 Ally/Advocate	– Makes eye contact with women and nods in approval so that that they feel affirmed – Straight but not narrow – Develops and presents anti-homophobia curriculum – Marches as part of PFLAG at PRIDE – Maybe open to sexual experimentation

My chart in some sense mocks developmental theory, but in another sense it is an expression of my envy. Educational psychology is a privileged knowledge of schools and teachers. Perhaps the privileged teachers will listen to the privileged knowledge; perhaps it is the only medium that is heard.[3]

2. REVISITING SOCIAL "EQUALITY"

A foundational, and probably the least offensive, message of anti-oppression education is the goal of achieving equality for all. I question whether *equality* is the most effective language for anti-oppression pedagogy. While it sounds loving, and privileged students may be attracted to this warmth, we often unquestioningly assume that the objective of this learning is to create a condition of equality, or to eliminate power imbalances. Should we really strive to eliminate power differences as the term *equality* implies? But aren't power and hurtfulness two different things? I have to admit that I am not certain about this, but I do feel that it needs to be questioned. Should the goal really be to eliminate power or instead to eliminate abuse of power? In Gandhi's scenario, should the goal be to eliminate the strong or to teach the strong how to use their power without harming the weak? Is power itself bad? Would we even want to live in a world where power was nonexistent? Some feminists have believed that if they could eliminate power from sex, sex would be more pleasurable. It is unclear whether this happened. What is clear is that the abuse of power needed to be eliminated. What needed to be supplied was choice around how to invoke power. As Metis author Beatrice Culleton Mosionier (1999) notes:

> In our world society, there are dominant groups, followers, and loners, and always, there are those of us who are different. And that's natural. [But] we don't have to be bigots. We can give each other respect and dignity without losing anything at all. (p. 250)

There are other examples that address both issues of language and power. *Yellow Journalism* is described as journalism that hurts people's lives in the name of making money. Stories could be fabricated, and manipulated in any sense for financial rewards. The remedy is often imagined to be "objective" writing; objectivity is the aspiration of many journalists (and researchers). But every time anybody writes anything there is bias, regardless of attempts to be objective; therefore, why is this even presented as a goal? Its focus could blind writers to the very direction their bias is inadvertently leading them. Reflexive ethnographers, recognizing our inability to eliminate bias, urge researchers instead to confess their bias – alongside their findings – in order to develop stronger knowledge (Hammersley & Atkinson, 1995). In relation to power, could the use of power continue, but become more visible (Delpit, 1995), and be invoked with generosity rather than greed? What kinds of education could transform those with systemic power to acknowledge their positions and act on them with greater integrity? What language would invoke this sensibility: social responsibility, social generosity, social ecology?

In classroom practice, there is a popular phrase that exemplifies a language of equality: "Everyone is the same under the skin." While I believe it is offered with the best of intentions, there can be debilitating consequences for anti-racist pedagogy. For example, if a teacher candidate who is racist enters an education program, she or he will be taught that racism is unacceptable and that everyone is the same under their skin; moreover, the candidate will learn that the students under his or her care will need equal treatment regardless of skin color. That candidate has now gone from a person who hated or feared based on race to somebody who says that she or he doesn't notice a student's skin colour. Yet, this teacher is most likely still committing racist acts because neither position involves acknowledging and then interrogating the behavior nor the emotions attached to the racist impulse.

On the other hand, the concept that "everybody is racist in some way" is a more progressive position. It acknowledges that power and racism exist, and that there is a particular way that the individual is performing them. However, this might also let students off the hook – in thinking that they can commit the same oppressions as usual because everyone is doing it and nobody can really control it. Just as reflexive ethnographers do not let the existence of bias keep them from rigorous methods and the search for strong data, the acknowledgement of racism should not deter us in interrogating our thinking and seeking change. There are higher moral grounds (with better language) to search for.

3. THE USE OF THREAT AND THE POSSIBILITIES OF FEELING UPSET

In encouraging students to deal with oppression through recognition of their own role, I am not suggesting that the acknowledgement of one's own role in oppression is the only approach that should be used. The basic "prejudice is wrong, don't do it" message is still effective as a response to extreme acts. I do not think the better pedagogy is found in hyper-visible affirmations of power (such as commands), but I would not give up these tools in combating oppressive behavior. For example, laws which punish perpetrators of physical and verbal hate crimes or bashings are important. Even if the only thing learned by those committing these crimes is, "if I do it, I will suffer." As a visible lesbian, I certainly feel a little safer with people potentially being deterred by the threat. But how useful is the role of threat in anti-oppression education in the classroom?

Consider the following example. I used to have a friend who hated that I would go protest on the street. She felt that all that was needed to convince management/administration to change their ideas, policy, or behavior were negotiators willing to sit down at the table and discuss the issues. She saw our politics as radically different. I saw them as complementary. I do not believe that the institutions would sit at my table until they were sufficiently threatened by protesters. And I do not believe that the protesters could ultimately obtain what they were fighting for unless they have negotiators who can sit down at the table. And the truth of the matter is that she was better at sitting at the table and I was better at yelling on the street. The changes in the institution emerge with the combination of careful conversation alongside political threat. As teachers can we serve our privileged students as both calm negotiators and threatening protesters in order to persuade them to change their perceptions and use of power?

While threatening behavior seems antithetical to the teaching of social justice, there is support in brain science for the relevance of learning experiences that involve the kind of extreme emotions provoked through upsetting students (Davis, Sumara, & Luce-Kapler, 2000). There is a detailed discussion of the dynamics of the brain's biological capacity to learn. Here are a few facts presented that I want to consider for this chapter:

1) Learning is no longer seen as a process of taking things in but of adapting one's actions to ever-changing circumstances (p. 61).

2) Short-term (or working) memories are associated with temporary fluctuations in neuronal activities. In general, these patterns fade in a matter of minutes and do not much affect the structure of the neurons. Long-term memories,

in contrast are more stable patterns that are linked to actual changes in brain structure (p. 68).

3) "The same hormones that are associated with extreme emotions are also linked to memory development" (p. 70).

I draw from this research the notion that unless extreme emotions are evoked surrounding the learning of anti-oppression, students might not retain this information once they leave your classroom. The following example illustrates this point.

Patrick Solomon, the director of the Urban Diversity Teacher's Education Program at York University, noted that while they are still completing course-work, teacher candidates often respond that they are dedicated to a type of teaching which challenges current stereotypes and the abuses of power. However, later, when follow up research is conducted on graduated candidates now teaching in classrooms, their thinking can dramatically shift to meet the social norms of the school (Personal Communication, 1999). They are "adapting [their] actions to ever-changing circumstances" (Davis, Sumara, & Luce-Kapler, 2000). For the learning to stick across contexts, students must learn the material as a long-term memory, and this connotes the experience of extreme emotions.

It is debatable, however, whether extreme emotions are more likely to occur by feeling upset rather than experiencing joy, feeling fear rather than pride, or feeling anger rather than love. Or, could such extreme emotions be evoked in tandem? I do not think the experience of feeling upset is avoidable though if an educator includes genuine-lived conditions as part of the curriculum, such as the teaching of the devastation of colonization on the Indigenous peoples in the Americas. It is also unclear what the outcome of the learning for students will consist of, regardless of the best of pedagogical intentions. As Britzman (1998) warns in consideration of how an educator might approach the teaching of difficult knowledge,

> This exploration needs to do more than confront the difficulties of learning from another's painful encounter with victimization, aggression, and the desire to live on one's own terms. It also must be willing to risk approaching the internal conflicts which the learner brings to learning. Internal conflicts may be coarsened, denied, and defended against the time when the learning cannot make sense of violence, aggression,

or even the desire for what Melanie Klein calls the 'making of reparation'. (p. 117)

Britzman's argument raises the stakes on the learning risks involved in difficult knowledge. If an educator creates upsetting conditions for the learning of classism, the students might internalize how important an analysis of classism is in their future conduct, but they might also learn that they never want to think about these issues again because they found them too upsetting. They could ultimately close themselves to self-interrogation, rather than finding the opening that will allow insight and analysis to extend beyond the confines of the course.

Perhaps the most prominent example of anti-oppression education that evokes extreme emotions is the work of Jane Elliot (1999). She is the educator who began working with third grade white middle class students in the Midwest on issues of racism following the assassination of Martin Luther King Jr. She originally began teaching anti-oppression by separating students on the basis of eye colour (brown eyes or blue eyes), but continues her work internationally with both children and adults, addressing the racism that is most harmful in specific geographical regions (e.g. she recently worked with Aboriginal and white community members of Regina, Saskatchewan). Through the use of abrasive language, clear and unequal treatment, humiliation, and critical discussion, she provokes anger, resistance, tears, and long-term learning in her students; "The purpose of the exercise is to give white people an opportunity to find out how it feels to be something other than white" (Lester, 1999 as cited in Culleton Mosionier) Participants have noted that her pedagogy has successfully resulted in profound impact on their long-term learning. After watching her films, Culleton Mosionier (1999) found Elliot's work to be the only solution she has ever encountered in the task of "getting rid of racism" (p. 249). "[Jane Elliot] looked at racism from all angles; she'd seen its effects on all those involved; and she came up with a way to heal it" (p. 250). Indeed, even showing her films in my education courses resulted in the most talked about component of the term. I find that students can neither take their eyes away from Elliot's ruthless approach, nor cease in their grappling with what it means. Even if I had no other proof but my students' responses to Elliot's work, I would advocate the use of evoking strong emotions in anti-oppression education. As Culleton Mosionier describes, "Like many medicines, Jane Elliot's medicine can be hard to swallow, but from what I saw, her medicine is powerful and effective" (p. 250).

4. CALM AND DISLOCATION

While I have considered the functioning of the brain, the psychological risks of difficult knowledge, and witnessed the powerful results of Elliot's approach, in my gut I know I cannot evoke extreme emotions in my own students myself. I realize this is probably a jarring confession to follow the previous section. Nonetheless, my personality and style are warm and humorous, and it would upset *me* too much to provoke such strong feelings of hurt in my students. I cannot bring myself to do it. Perhaps the ethic of care embedded in the teaching profession (*in loco parentis*) prevents me; perhaps I just want to be liked too much by my students. At this point in my life I am more the "calm negotiator," having put aside my protester banners, at least during class hours. Do I then fail my marginalized students when I do not push for the extreme in my privileged students? Do my privileged teacher candidates depart my courses unchanged by the experience, obliviously contributing to the systemic oppression of their own future students? The potential of this layered failure haunts my teaching and is the reason for my writing this exploratory essay.

At present my compromise is delivering to students the upsetting work of other educators/authors: showing Jane Elliot's films, assigning the reading of novels such as *Push* by Sapphire (1997), *The Bluest Eye* by Toni Morrison (1994), *In Search of April Raintree* by Beatrice Culleton Mosionier (1999), *Bastard out of Carolina* by Dorothy Allison (1993), *As Nature Made Him* by John Colapinto (2001), and *Londonstani* by Gautam Malkani (2006). The only novels I assign in my classes are devastating reads in the impact of social oppression on individual lives (to accompany socio-cultural theory articles). I imagine that nothing less will touch people. Ultimately, many of my students do experience hurt, feel anger, resist, fight shame, and cry, as a result of my curriculum, but I use the language of others to get there and allow them the privacy of the dark while I show the films or their own rooms where they read.

And I do not know if dislocating the extreme emotions to these outside sources takes away from the genuine learning of those within the classroom (though we do engage in many critical discussions). As Freire warns us, avoiding the context, dialogue and relations of the immediate classroom could render the information abstract and lifeless (Freire, 1971). Perhaps my approach is not enough, and what is needed for profound learning in the privileged is the skill of dealing with the elephant in the specific room. In other words, maybe in the teaching of social justice, the variable is the elephant, not the location. Maybe it should be about how to teach about difficult issues, regardless of the issue, rather than how to teach about a specific issue (e.g. opening a discussion about the racist implications of which students in the classroom are afforded the most time to talk, rather than a discussion about the impact of racism on migrant workers worldwide). Maybe it includes both being made upset through confrontation and also the relationships established through the sharing the experience of being upset.

CONCLUSION

This chapter is only an opening into thinking about the anti-oppression pedagogy of the privileged. There are many more strategies and examples that could be examined and implemented. Essential to the tools I have already offered, and any more I might come up with, would be the audience's belief that this work is necessary. To invest in this, you must believe that something is wrong with the way things are, and that it is okay to try to change people's politics. To mess with them. This might seem like a dogmatic approach to education, but consider the objectives of Bruner's conceptualization of education:

> The construction of curricula proceeds in a world where changing social, cultural, and political conditions continually alter the surroundings and the goals of schools and their students. (Bruner, 1963, pp. 8-9)

In this sense, my writing is not radical at all. No matter what the politics are, writers of pedagogical theory are invested in creating experiences of learning which aid students in their ability to live and contribute to a better functioning society. I believe that people should learn about anti-oppression pedagogy because it will help them to live in, and contribute to, a less hurtful culture.

NOTES

[1] I have worked with Mexican American University students and high school aged LGBT (lesbian, gay, bisexual, transgender) students in the San Diego, California area, transitional students in a pre-university program, and preservice education students in Toronto and Peterborough, Ontario

[2] These questions do not emerge from the desire to offer privileged students even more resources than their less privileged counterparts, but a belief that changing an oppressive status quo could benefit from privileged people working beside, rather than against, their less privileged counterparts.

[3] For an account of how privileged teachers have difficulty *hearing* knowledge that is not produced by privileged theorists see (Delpit, 1995, pp. 191-192).

References

Allison, D. (1993). *Bastard out of Carolina*. New York: Plume.

Britzman, D. (1998). *Lost subjects, contested objects: Toward a psychoanalytic inquiry of learning*. Albany, NY: State University of New York Press.

Brodkey, L. (1996). *Writing permitted in designated areas only*. Minneapolis, MN: The University of Minnesota Press.

Bruner, J. S. (1963). *The process of education*. Cambridge, MA: Harvard University Press.

Bruner, J. S. (1996). *The culture of education*. Cambridge, MA: Harvard University Press.

Colapinto, J. (2001). *As nature made him: The boy who was raised as a girl*. New York: Harper Perennial.

Culleton Mosionier, B. (1999). *In search of April Raintree* (Critical ed.). (C. Suzack, Ed.). Winnipeg, MB: Portage & Main Press.

Davis, B., Sumara, D., & Luce-Kapler, R. (Eds.). (2000). *Engaging minds: Learning and teaching in a complex world*. Mahwah, NJ: LEA, inc.

Delpit, L. (1995). *Other people's children: Cultural conflict in the classroom*. New York: The New Press.

Freire, P. (1971). *Pedagogy of the oppressed*. New York: Continuum.

Gallagher, S. (Ed.). (2003). *Education psychology: Disrupting the dominant discourse*. New York: Peter Lang.

Gandhi, Mahatma (1997) *All Men Are Brothers: Autobiographical reflections*. (Krishna Kripalani, Ed.). New York: Continuum.

Gilligan, C. (1993). *In a different voice: Psychological theory and women's development*. Cambridge, MA: Harvard University Press.

Hammersley, M., & Atkinson P. (1995). *Ethnography: Principles in practice* (2nd ed.). New York: Routledge.

Malkani, G. (2006). *Londonstani*. New York: Penguin.

Morrison, T. (1994). *The bluest eye*. New York: Plume.

Sapphire (1996). *Push*. New York: Vintage.

BIOGRAPHIES

C. A. Bowers is the author of nineteen books that examine the cultural roots of the ecological crises, including the role that public schools and universities play in furthering the crises. His most recent books include, *The False Promises of Constructivist Theories of Learning: A Global and Ecological Critique* (Peter Lang, 2006), as well as three online books that focus on the ecological importance of the world's diverse cultural commons, how to engage students in an understanding of the local cultural commons and the processes of enclosure, and historical studies of the conceptual roots of different forms of enclosure. Chet may be reached at http://cabowers.net/

Ken Brien, Ed.D. (University of Alberta), is an Assistant Professor in the Faculty of Education at the University of New Brunswick. He teaches undergraduate and graduate courses in the areas of School Law, Administrative Theory, and School Administration. His research interests include legal, policy, and governance issues in educational administration. He is currently involved in research associated with educational reform and professional learning communities. He previously worked as a high school teacher and administrator in Northern Ontario, including service as a vice-principal. Ken can be reached at kbrien1@unb.ca

Yvette Daniel, PhD (York University) is Assistant Professor at the Faculty of Education, University of Windsor. She teaches pre-service and graduate level courses. Her research interests are in the area of educational leadership and policy, theories of educational administration, teacher education development, and issues of urban education and teaching for social justice. She has just completed one pilot study on the complexities of new teacher induction, and another on school discipline policy and practice in Ontario. She is currently involved in developing an urban education partnership with the local school community. Yvette may be reached at ydaniel@uwindsor.ca

Tatiana Gounko, PhD (University of Alberta) is an Assistant Professor in the School of Education and Professional Learning at Trent University in Peterborough, Ontario (Canada). She teaches courses in Educational Law, Ethics and Professional Conduct, and Sociocultural Perspectives on Human Development. She earned her undergraduate degree in English and Literature from Yakutsk State University (Russia) and her M.Sc. (Educational Administration and Supervision) from the University of Nebraska-Omaha (USA). Prior to starting her PhD program in Canada, Tatiana worked as an English lecturer in the Faculty of Foreign Languages at Yakutsk State University. Her research interests are in higher educational reform and the role of international organizations in shaping education policies in post-Soviet Russia and around the world. Tatiana may be reached at tatianagounko@trentu.ca

André P. Grace is a professor who works in educational policy studies and inclusive education at the University of Alberta in Edmonton. He sits on the Sexual Orientation and Gender Identity Sub-Committee of the Diversity, Equity, and Human Rights Committee with the Alberta Teachers' Association. He has a primary research interest in issues impacting the personal safety and professional security of lesbian, gay, bisexual, transidentified, and other sexual-minority teachers. He is currently conducting a national study entitled *Attending to Sex, Sexual, and Gender Differences in Inclusive Education: Perspectives, Needs, Challenges, Risks, Liabilities, and Possibilities across Educational Interest Groups*. The Social Sciences and Humanities Research Council of Canada is funding this research. André may be reached at andre.grace@ualberta.ca

Luigi Iannacci, PhD is an Assistant Professor in the School of Education and Professional Learning at Trent University in Peterborough, Ontario. He teaches courses that focus on language and literacy as well as special needs learners. He has also taught mainstream and special education in a range of elementary grades in Ontario. His research interests include first and second languages and literacy acquisition, critical multiculturalism, and critical narrative research methodology. Luigi can be reached at luigiiannacci@trentu.ca

Karleen Pendleton Jiménez, PhD (York University) is a writer and Assistant Professor in the School of Education and Professional Learning at Trent University. She is the author of short stories, personal essays, and a children's book titled, *Are You a Boy or a Girl?* (Two Lives Publishing, 2004). Her recent scholarly work can be found in the following collections: learning, teaching and community, and Chicana/Latina feminist pedagogies and epistemologies for everyday life. Her research and teaching interests include critical pedagogy, Latina Canadian studies, anti-homophobia education, and the teaching of writing. Karleen can be reached at kpendletonjimenez@trentu.ca

Andrejs Kulnieks is a PhD Candidate in the Faculty of Graduate Studies in Education at York University. He has worked as a teacher at the primary, junior, and secondary levels for the Toronto District School Board, as well as a teaching assistant, writing tutor and course director at York University. He has published articles in *The Canadian Journal of Environmental Education*, the *Journal of the Canadian Association for Curriculum Studies*, as well as *Educational Studies: A Journal of the American Educational Studies Association* in the areas of literacy, curriculum theorizing, and environmental education. He is a singer, song-writer, and bass player and is currently finishing a poetry manuscript that merges landscape photography and travel writing. Andrejs can be reached at andrejs_kulnieks@edu.yorku.ca.

Carmen Pickering is a researcher with the Canadian Teachers' Federation. Her professional focus and research interests include workers' and teachers' rights and benefits and she has many years experience as an advocate for labour and proponent of sound industrial relations. Carmen's work gives her responsibility for a range of issues related to teacher welfare, collective bargaining, and relevant legislation and policy. Her writing has been published in legal resources for the education community including *Education & Law Journal* and *CAPSLE Comments*, a publication of the Canadian Association for the Practical Study of Law in Education. Carmen may be reached at cpick@ctf-fce.ca

William F. Pinar teaches curriculum theory at the University of British Columbia, where he holds a Canada Research Chair and directs the Centre for the Study of the Internationalization of Curriculum Studies. He is the author, most recently, of *The New Synoptic Text and other essays: Curriculum Development after the Reconceptualization* (Peter Lang, 2006). William may be reached at william.pinar@ubc.ca

William Smale, PhD (University of Alberta) is an Associate Professor in the School of Education and Professional Learning at Trent University in Peterborough, Ontario (Canada). He teaches undergraduate courses in Educational Law, Ethics and Professional Conduct, and graduate courses in Research Methods and School Law. His research interests include educational administration, early school leaving, deviance, early childhood interventions, mentorship, and higher education in developing countries. William may be reached at williamsmale@trentu.ca

Darren Stanley is an Assistant Professor in the Faculty of Education at the University of Windsor in Windsor, Ontario. He teaches undergraduate and graduate courses in the area of Mathematics Education. He has published in the areas of curriculum, complexity and mathematics in the *Journal of Curriculum Theorizing* (JCT), *Complicity: An International Journal of Education and Complexity*, and *For the Learning of Mathematics* (FLM). As part of his responsibilities in the faculty, and as an emerging educational leader, he currently serves as Editor for the faculty's own journal: *Journal of Teaching and Learning*. He can be reached at dstanley@uwindsor.ca.

Kelly Young, PhD (York University) is an Associate Professor in the School of Education and Professional Learning at Trent University in Peterborough, Ontario (Canada) where she teaches courses in English Language Arts Curriculum Methods and Classroom Management. She has published articles in *Language and Literacy: A Canadian Educational E-Journal*, the *Journal of Curriculum Theorizing* (JCT), the *EcoJustice Review: Educating for the Commons.* (EJR), and the *Journal of the Canadian Association for Curriculum Studies* (JCACS) in the areas of literacy, curriculum theorizing, and eco-justuce environmental education. Her poetry and fiction have been featured in *Provoked by Art: Theorizing Arts-informed Inquiry* (Backalong Books, 2004) and *Breath: Writing Herself into History* (Palabras Press, 2006). Kelly can be reached at kellyyoung@trentu.ca